THE TURQUOISE BRICK RO

> "
> FOLLOW THE YELLOW BRICK ROAD.
> FOLLOW THE YELLOW BRICK ROAD.
>
> FOLLOW, FOLLOW, FOLLOW, FOLLOW,
>
> WE'RE OFF TO SEE THE WIZARD,
> THE WONDERFUL WIZARD OF OZ.
>
> YOU'LL FIND HE IS A WHIZ OF A WIZ!
> IF EVER A WIZ THERE WAS!...
> "

THE WONDERFUL WIZARD OF OZ [P-1]

Yellow brick road: denoting a course of action or series of events viewed as a path to a particular (especially positive or desired) outcome or goal (*The Oxford English Dictionary*). This bright, golden road is a fitting modern representation of the much older, spiritual philosophy known in Buddhism and Kabbalah as The Golden Path.

To some, this path illustrates the progression of all beings from egoism to enlightenment. This is more closely related to the stories in this book than you might think.

We invite you to join us on a journey along the yellow brick road, which turns turquoise and eventually becomes part of something bigger.

The creators of this book were fuelled by heaps of root vegetables, bitter greens, potatoes, mushrooms, onions, ginger and herbs, organically grown by Riverford farmers.
They also enjoyed lots of pickled goodies from their friends at the Three Pools Permaculture Farm, often with a few more glasses than expected of biodynamic red wine from Vintage Roots.

Thanks to Wikipedia for being such a genius research tool – a great way to get some initial background information. We honoured your support (Donation of £100: CNTCT-42819105).

The machines were powered by 100% renewable energy from Good Energy. Our printer Sure Print Services South East Ltd were chosen due to their green credentials (ISO 14001, World Land Trust member, IPIA member).

We love books and have decided to print even in digital times. We have tried to keep our climate impact as low as possible. Where we could not avoid causing emissions (directly or indirectly), we have calculated our carbon footprint and offset it through Gold Standard, creating sustainable development benefits for communities around the world. Thank you to the Ethical Consumer team for helping us select the best offsetting solution.

This book is printed on FSC certified paper, sourced from SFI and/or FSC certified mills. In addition, we lend our ongoing financial support to the Woodland Trust and My Trees. All the financial matters around the book are handled by our responsible and ethical bank Triodos; like us committed to create better future.

For every ten books that we sell directly, we donate one copy to a learning institution in a socially deprived area, or to a thought leader or community enterprise with a social cause.

www.riverford.co.uk

www.threepools.co.uk

www.vintageroots.co.uk

www.goodenergy.co.uk

www.sure-services.com

www.woodlandtrust.org.uk

www.mytrees.world

www.goldstandard.org/take-action/offset-your-emissions

www.ethicalconsumer.org

www.triodos.co.uk

THANK YOUS

To the supportive love of my life, Kerstin, for her constant brainstorming, editing, rigorous feedback, and mindful patience. No way would I have done this without her (Darling, the next book is ours).

To my daughter Thalia for inspiring me to write this book. Even though I came across the framework as a grown adult, it has helped me tremendously to gain a better understanding of life. I wonder what my experiences would have been if I'd had this insight at the age of 13 – show me!

To my mum for fighting and staying alive to see this book come together. For ensuring I could stay in Louisenlund and showing me how strong women can be. I will always be a part of you and you of me. I wouldn't be where I am now without your love and sacrifices.

To my father for taking me backpacking at an early age, opening my eyes to human and nature's beauties, realities and oddities. Also, for ensuring I have a home from where I can write these lines in peace and quiet. I owe you so much.

To Silver for showing me what 6th level working culture looks like and thus opening up a whole new world of management, communication and leadership to me. After many poor role models, you opened my eyes to what empowering leadership looks like, made a coach of me and changed my life for the better.

To Craig for being such an intuitive and solution-oriented visual artist. You brought the levels to life, produced brilliant designs, and are just a very kind person who happens to be excellent at what you do.

To Jon for helping me along the way and introducing me to Craig, Emma for her initial feedback on my writing, Alison for her structural input and, combining forces with Andrew, for designing the journey. To Mathew & Emma, Sarah & Anderson, Thalia for helping me with the title. To Sandra & Dick for sharing their experiences and for their kind support, Sabine and Rachel for their input on psychosynthesis, and Siobhan for her specific feedback on Buddhism.

To Nabil, Nick & Pascal for sharing their insight into a world I know so little about, Jens and Marc for being such splendid role models, naturally. To the ladies of She Leads Change for doing what they do in the way they do it. To Rene, Hartmut and Nicola for helping me paint the world yellow, and to Hartmut and Christopher for ensuring I stay true to the Turquoise layer. To Said for being such a genuinely kind and supportive person. To historian Rolf for providing historical insights.

To Valentina for the hardcore editing and being such a positive force, to Séverine for the proofreading, and Craig for bringing the words to life.

To Cathrin and Hanno at HS-Pforzheim for helping with the referencing and plagiarism, Iris at Kirkland & Ellis for the legal support, and Nathalie at MDX for the online plagiarism checking.

Last but not least, to our dog Chocolate for ensuring I regularly go out to Regent's Park to get some fresh air. And again to my darling Kerstin for helping me every step of the way.

To Clare W. Graves whose curiosity, dedication and academic rigour have helped to create one of the most meaningful roadmaps for humankind.

To Union College, a private liberal arts college in Schenectady, New York, for supporting and financing this kind of research. You have served humankind more than you possibly will be aware of.

To Jostein Gaarder for writing *Sophie's World* and helping me understand that it is easier to relate complex topics through stories. To strategyzers, Alexander Osterwalder and Yves Pigneur, for showing me that I can actually enjoy reading a business book whilst sitting on a beach on Ko Chang.

To Don Beck, Christopher Cowan, Natasha Todorovic, Bill Lee and others for capturing the knowledge, adding practical colours to the levels, and making the value system more applicable through Spiral Dynamics®.

To Ken Wilber and Integral Community for putting so much passion into integrating the framework with endless other models and schools of thought. It is also helpful to have some insight into second-tier thinking. Let's hope humankind reaches this dimension as a collective.

FOREWORD

The last thing I ever wanted to do was write a book. It sounds exciting but involves a lot of administrative work. People who know me recognise that I am more of a creative and spontaneous character. I enjoy being a free spirit, not crawling through pages of small print to find out what I can and cannot do, so no attractive book deal for me as a first-time author.

Suddenly, plotting, writing, publishing and marketing a wordy fruit of labour turns into a costly, time-consuming and risky venture. After all, I might just be as ignorant and naïve as so many artists with their work. Maybe I will have to use unsold copies as wedges for the rest of my life. Who knows?

I generally love co-creating but can also hardly see anything through just by myself. I am such an extrovert that I need to bounce ideas off others. If I ever write another book, it will be as a collective. As you can see from the previous section, many people were involved in the actual process but I wanted to write this one on my own to see it through as soon as possible. Being self-employed means I miss the convenience of a regular pay check and enjoy pushing things through.

I wanted to get this book out there for two main reasons.

Firstly, I believe the framework that Clare W. Graves developed during his time at Union College is mission critical for the continuation of our human development. Sometime soon, we will need an orchestrated approach to get us out of the current ecological and social mess. I see Graves' roadmap as instrumental for this. I really fear that we are running out of time and our ignorance is killing our habitat, the very basis of our evolution.

Secondly, this book is meant to be a fun read and to make the original work more accessible. Thanks to Craig, it is also visually appealing. I was introduced to the framework in 2005, bought two books but found them so dense and theoretical that I shelved them. Then in 2008 I had to familiarise myself with the model to work with a particular client. It was so valuable, I was shocked I had never heard of it before. From then on, it helped me make sense of past events, to understand in what ways history keeps repeating itself, and how common trial and error is, in the business world especially.

This book merely aims to introduce all kinds of people to Graves' fantastic work. It still puzzles me how few have heard of it and I am on a personal mission to change this. I strongly believe that this shared insight will help us become more self-aware, develop more understanding and tolerance, consequently gaining greater awareness of what we need to change to save the planet and redeem our species. We can achieve so much more.

Clare W. Graves deserves the recognition and continuation of his work. More and more people are building on his initial research though there is a lot of unhealthy tension, which I have personally experienced. It is time to put our differences aside as 'Gravesians', remind ourselves that we have more in common than separates us, and illuminate a shared way forward. If we cannot do this, as passionate professionals with such insight, what hope is there for the world?

Graves' framework acts like a map, enabling us to understand where we are, to recognise the universal development paths and our individual role in our destiny. Let's all venture off onto the turquoise brick road!

THE STORIES

CLARE W. GRAVES, HIS LEGACY AND OUR FUTURE

"

I AM NOT SAYING IN THIS CONCEPTION OF ADULT BEHAVIOUR THAT ONE STYLE OF BEING, ONE FORM OF HUMAN EXISTENCE IS INEVITABLE AND IN ALL CIRCUMSTANCES SUPERIOR TO OR BETTER THAN ANOTHER FORM OF HUMAN EXISTENCE, ANOTHER STYLE OF BEING. WHAT I AM SAYING IS THAT WHEN ONE FORM OF BEING IS MORE CONGRUENT WITH THE REALITIES OF EXISTENCE, THEN IT IS THE BETTER FORM OF LIVING FOR THOSE REALITIES. AND WHAT I AM SAYING IS THAT WHEN ONE FORM OF EXISTENCE CEASES TO BE FUNCTIONAL FOR THE REALITIES OF EXISTENCE THEN SOME OTHER FORM, EITHER HIGHER OR LOWER IN THE HIERARCHY, IS THE BETTER FORM OF LIVING. I DO SUGGEST, HOWEVER, AND THIS I DEEPLY BELIEVE IS SO, THAT FOR THE OVERALL WELFARE OF TOTAL MAN'S EXISTENCE IN THIS WORLD, OVER THE LONG RUN OF TIME, HIGHER LEVELS ARE BETTER THAN LOWER LEVELS AND THAT THE PRIME GOOD OF ANY SOCIETY'S GOVERNING FIGURES SHOULD BE TO PROMOTE HUMAN MOVEMENT UP THE LEVELS OF HUMAN EXISTENCE. [P-2]

"

0.1 WHAT IS THE GRAVES VALUE SYSTEM?

The Graves Value System (GVS) is a two-tiered system developed by Clare W. Graves, a professor of psychology, who described eight levels that he believed epitomises human development to date. Each level represents a specific worldview based on certain values, beliefs and behaviours, and a place where the people who uphold that view feel at home. Tier 1 consists of six levels: A, B, C, D, E, F. Tier 2 comprises currently of two identified levels: G and H. Humankind has not yet advanced beyond the first eight levels.

It is a bio-psycho-social framework in that the values in each level influence mindsets in terms of consciousness and what is good or bad, right or wrong. Interestingly, through activation of previously unused parts, the brain seems pre-designed to cope with all the upcoming levels.

> ## " IT IS ABOUT THE LEVELS OF HUMAN EXISTENCE, THOSE EVER-EMERGENT, EVER-SPIRALLING PSYCHOLOGICAL WAY STATIONS ALL HUMANS GO THROUGH "
>
> ### THE NEVER-ENDING QUEST [C-1, P. 38]

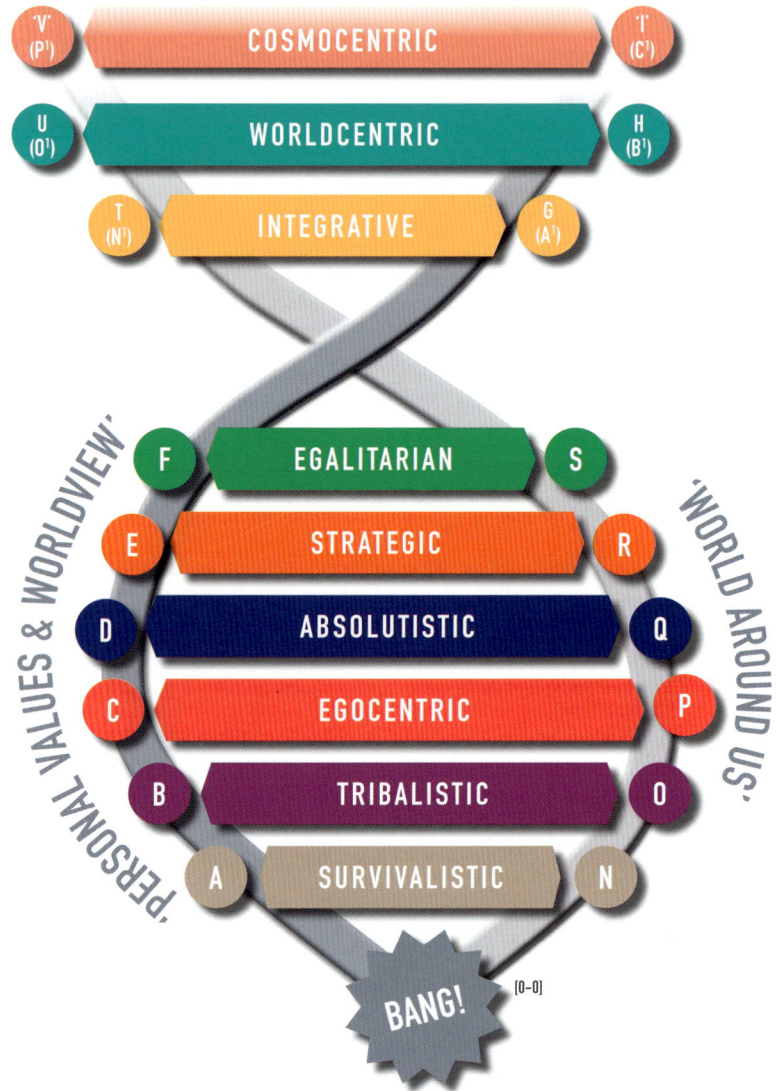

As individuals move through the levels, they learn that specific values and ways of living that were once appropriate no longer are, due to changed circumstances. The model implies that human nature is not static and people need to adapt their values and mindset in order to develop. As people progress or regress, they swing between individualistic values of self-expression [A, C, E, G] and communal or collective values of self-sacrifice [B, D, F, H].

In *The Never-Ending Quest* [C-1], written by Christopher Cowan and Natasha Todorovic, Clare W. Graves stated, "it is about mastering existential problems and how to progress in life. Our coping tactics are dependent on individual development and evolving societies and organisations." [C-1, p. 136] Furthermore, he explains people's nature is not set in stone, rather it is ever emergent. An open-ended model sets Graves' approach apart from that of many of his contemporaries who aimed for a final state. Evolution will hopefully progress and this model considers the ongoing development of human life and consciousness.

In a 1967 article, Canadian journalist Nicholas Steed dubbed the works of Clare W. Graves as 'the theory that explains everything'. Graves did indeed succeed in developing a complex and comprehensive theory construction that is valuable and useful in many areas of human existence, through his inclusion of biology, psychology, sociology and systems thinking as vital co-elements. The genius of his work is that it is incredibly complex and sophisticated, yet still easily applicable to individuals and groups,

including management cultures. He identified nine levels of maturity and described eight, four of which are most relevant to today's Western life, being the levels at which more than 80% of Western businesses operate. [3-6]

One of the beauties of the GVS is that it provides an overview of different aspects of life and how they evolve. It helps us understand people, groups, organisations, markets, societies, and their behaviours. It can be applied at the macro level, to political developments and trends, and at the micro level, to interpersonal interactions. It is a great framework to identify similarities, differences, and patterns, as well as understand what fits or not in a particular context.

The GVS is based on "25 years of naturalistic observation, research and contemplation", including over 1000 empirical studies, and might prove to be one of humankind's greatest mission-critical achievements [C-1, p. 405]. Graves did not want to explain everything or provide all the answers to life's ongoing questions. He sought to provide a framework that pulls together a broad range of approaches to human nature and brings them into focus.

The result is a system that enables us to grasp life's complexities and to have much more informed discussions.

As a consequence, the GVS helps to cross-reference and integrate disciplines as broad as psychology, sociology, biology, neuroscience, education, anthropology, history, and systems thinking. Graves urged people to rise above established disciplinary boundaries.

His understanding of human development is based on the idea that there is a natural interplay between an individual and their surrounding environment. If personality is to an individual what culture is to a group, then human progression or regression along the levels is based on the relationship between personality and culture.

I believe a framework like this is needed today more than ever. We live in an increasingly **v**olatile, **u**ncertain, **c**omplex and **a**mbiguous (VUCA) world. The GVS framework can act as a guide and clarifies the confusing, controversial and opposing aspects of human behaviour and the worlds we live in.

A	I SURVIVE	N	SURVIVAL
B	WE'RE SAFE	O	TRIBALISTIC
C	I CONTROL	P	EGOCENTRIC
D	WE'RE SAVED	Q	ABSOLUTISTIC
E	I IMPROVE	R	STRATEGIC
F	WE RELATE	S	HUMANISTIC
G [A1]	I INTEGRATE	T [N1]	SYSTEMIC
H [B1]	WE INTUITIVELY EXPERIENCE	U [O1]	HOLISTIC

THE GVS CAN BE APPLIED TO BOTH PERSONAL AND PROFESSIONAL CONTEXTS

The better known work directly based on the GVS are Spiral Dynamics and Integral Theory. To date, we have only come across a few people who have built directly on Graves' original work.

These are all great starting points and, in chapter 10.4, you can read more about the now growing number of people building on work derived from Graves' initial achievements.

- Don Beck and Christopher Cowan, two scholars of Professor Graves, who based their own philosophy, Spiral Dynamics, on the GVS and introduced a practical colour scheme; [0-1]

- Ken Wilber built his integral work [0-2] on the back of the GVS and continues to integrate the levels to a wide range of models and principles. Furthermore, he is a pioneer in exploring Graves' tier 2. Sadly, his AQAL model uses different colours for some of the levels;

- Hartmut Wiehle, Kerstin van Eckert and I have created the Pathfinder [0-3], a combination of the GVS and the McKinsey 7S Framework, to assess and design systemic change within organisations;

- Payback, a Pathfinder client, combined the GVS with Dank Pink's take on motivation (Purpose, Mastery, Autonomy) to engage their employees more effectively and target specific candidates more easily; [0-4]

- And most likely some more with whom we never crossed paths...

0.2 WHAT IS THE FRAMEWORK GOOD FOR?

The GVS framework is a map that ensures we are all on the same page and can share insights as we navigate human development[0-5]. The model focuses on values that motivate individuals and groups, or that they strive for.

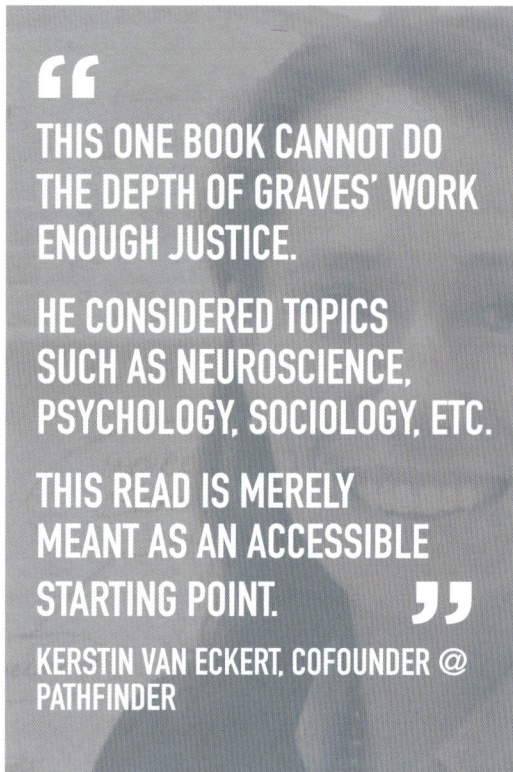

> **THIS ONE BOOK CANNOT DO THE DEPTH OF GRAVES' WORK ENOUGH JUSTICE.**
>
> **HE CONSIDERED TOPICS SUCH AS NEUROSCIENCE, PSYCHOLOGY, SOCIOLOGY, ETC.**
>
> **THIS READ IS MERELY MEANT AS AN ACCESSIBLE STARTING POINT.**
>
> **KERSTIN VAN ECKERT, COFOUNDER @ PATHFINDER**

1. It aptly explains the value of diversity, providing a base from which to develop the necessary levels of tolerance, understanding and appreciation for a more harmonious world [0-6];

2. provides a common ground for people from all walks of life to come together and have more informed discussions, by offering a language and colourful logic [0-7] that can accelerate the exchange of ideas and decisions;

3. helps to avoid potential areas of misunderstanding and conflict;

4. explains the development stages that all people go through as they progress;

5. provides a series of questions that reveal what values motivate individuals [0-8];

6. defines the toolkit needed to thrive in a volatile, uncertain, complex, ambiguous (VUCA) world;

7. makes existing development models more accessible while also stress-testing them;

8. can withstand the test of time through its open approach;

9. provides a common foundation for different disciplines, such as neuroscience, psychology, and business,[0-9] and a shared reference map.

0.3 WHAT IS THE FRAMEWORK NOT MEANT FOR?

While Graves' analysis of human development, and of the stages of change and transformation[0-10] required to reach enlightenment, was truly profound and sophisticated, the framework he developed was not intended to provide a definitive bible for life. Bearing this in mind, we should not expect the GVS to:

1. define people and systems themselves;

2. capture and explain the psychological depth of individual human beings;

3. be perfectly accurate, because life is neither simple nor monochromatic, but rather colourful with all of its complexities; or

4. provide answers to questions about life and the universe.

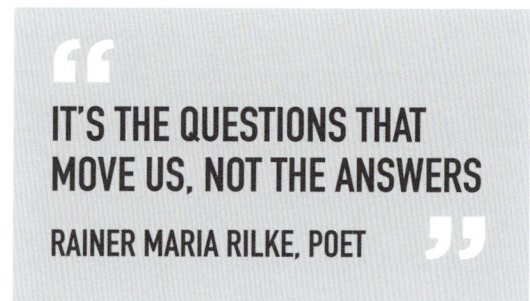

> **IT'S THE QUESTIONS THAT MOVE US, NOT THE ANSWERS**
>
> **RAINER MARIA RILKE, POET**

0.4 WHAT ARE THE ESSENTIAL PRINCIPLES?

To avoid misunderstandings, here are some specific axioms to provide clearer guidance on Graves' model:

1. The GVS defines eight universal development stages that apply to all of humanity; [0-11]

2. Clare W. Graves coded the levels with letters (e.g. A-N, B-O as shown in the diagram on p. 10). Each level has been assigned a colour by the creators of Spiral Dynamics to make it even simpler to follow; [0-1]

3. Each level is a simplification or stereotype based on general archetypes from Graves' research. So, no individual, organisation or society will ever fully match a particular level;

4. The framework is non-judgemental – all levels are of equal value in this world; none is better than another;

5. There is no need for change if one is at ease within a certain level;

6. Skipping one or more levels is not possible (I have tried), because every level provides attributes and skills to build on;

7. As people and societies grow, value systems become more complex; [0-12]

8. Every level, and its matching colour, displays different constructive and destructive attributes corresponding to positive and negative behaviours that respectively strengthen and weaken our societies and institutions; [C-1]

9. The framework can be applied to all contexts – individuals, teams and other groups[0-13], companies, competitors [0-14], markets[0-15] and societies;

10. In Tier 1 (the first six levels), an individual, company or society will be drawn to their level of gravity, meaning where they feel most comfortable and identify with the respective values. Here, every level believes there is one best way – their way;

11. Tier 2 recognises that all values are relevant at different times, as every situation is unique and contextual. All paths are possible, so one should decide according to the situation at hand;

12. The system is usually stronger than the individual.

0.5   WHAT CAN YOU EXPECT TO GET OUT OF THIS BOOK?

WANT TO GAIN CLARITY ON WHERE YOU ARE MOST AT PEACE?

Life is about finding happiness in harmony with our environment, and that happiness is directly linked to being in alignment with our own values. Life becomes much easier once you figure out who you really are, including what you want and don't want in life. Then you can start to be true to yourself. As Aristotle said, 'Knowing yourself is the beginning of all wisdom.' The more authentic you are, the more you can live your life. Unsurprisingly, the GVS is a values-based framework that helps you navigate your own value system in relation to other systems around you. **This book will help you find your place in the world based on your values.**

WANT TO FIGURE OUT YOUR CURRENT AND IDEAL LEVELS OF DEVELOPMENT?

Change is inevitable. There are only temporary states of being, because everything, including our environment and circumstances, is in a constant state of flux. We grow from infants to toddlers, then children, teenagers, adults, and if we are lucky, we reach old age. We all progress through clear physiological and mental stages that can be viewed through psychology, gerontology, psychiatry, and social work[0-16]. It is very useful to understand where you are at any given point in time in order to be mindful and enjoy being at the level where you feel most comfortable. It is also important to know which aspects of yourself you need to change, and when it is most appropriate to do so. After all, changes are one of the most important aspects of life. Transitioning periods from one stage to another are often difficult to manage, but understanding what is happening in the process can make things easier. **This book aims to help you navigate personal change more deftly.**

WANT TO FIND OUT THE APPROPRIATE LEVEL OF BUSINESS FOR YOUR ORGANISATION?

Businesses need to change over time, just as people do. For example, a ten-person startup that scales to fifty over the course of two years needs to adapt significantly to deal with the increasing number of employees and resulting complexities[0-17]. Besides the obvious changes inherent in that shift, such as budgets to account for additional costs and growing operations, values-based mindsets and working styles need to be adapted too. Not all of the factors that have led to the success of the business to date will necessarily lead to its future growth. **This book will help you understand the importance of change for businesses, and how to manage it.**

> " A FASCINATING INSIGHT INTO THE UNDERSTANDING OF CULTURE AND VALUE SYSTEMS, AND SUBSEQUENTLY, OF OUR WHOLE EXISTENCE "
>
> CRAIG CORNOCK,
> FOUNDER, CORNOCK DESIGN

WANT MORE CLARITY ABOUT WHAT IS HAPPENING IN YOUR PROFESSIONAL WORLD AND WHY?

As organisations adapt with the times, differentiating between change and transformation is a helpful skill to learn. Change entails one or a set of adaptations within any of the development levels. A company running a LEAN programme to eradicate unnecessary work procedures, or one implementing a CRM software to increase customer engagement, are examples of change. Transformation, on the other hand, is a more significant shift of behaviours and practices, which results in advancing to the next level; it impacts nearly every aspect of the way people work, both within and without the business. For example, an efficiency-driven corporation embarking on a digital transformation needs to understand that providing new technology alone is not sufficient; instead, that technology will enable a larger, necessary cultural shift to happen. In this case, the company moves from being guided by efficiency, cost reduction and predictability, to looking at customer orientation, market opportunities and cost-benefit thinking. Here the implementation of a CRM solution is one part of an orchestrated change initiative.

The same logic applies to individuals and societies. Worldviews at each level of the GVS framework are fundamentally different, as you will see when you read about PharmaCorp and PerformVenture in subsequent chapters. **This book will clarify the difference between change and transformation, and help you understand the steps entailed to achieve both.**

WANT TO LEARN HOW BEST TO APPLY DIFFERENT MANAGEMENT TOOLS?

There are many books and voices claiming to know the right approach to business. This has created a lot of confusion in the professional sphere. In my view, there is no single right approach. Which tool or set of tools to use depends on the type of business, the level it is currently operating at, and the level it is trying to progress to. There are many great modern management practices, such as project management, design thinking, agile development, teal organisations, systems thinking/leadership, permaculture, and circular principles. These approaches have all been borne out of mindsets from specific development stages and, therefore, embody the values of their respective levels. As the proverb goes, it is 'horses for courses'. Understanding the level that each toolkit falls under can help to apply the right tools to a particular business. **This book helps you to determine which are the most appropriate management approaches, values and tools for different businesses.**

WANT TO PROACTIVELY IDENTIFY TRENDS AND FUTURE-PROOF YOURSELF, YOUR BUSINESS, OR YOUR COUNTRY?

Twenty-first century management has evolved into a more human-centred, collaborative approach. New operating models have been devised to manage people in organisations. Markets and societies are also on the same development path, with new approaches being tested to advance them. Bhutan's Gross National Happiness Index [0-18] and Finland's trial run with the Universal Basic Income [0-19] are good examples of this. Insight into the GVS can help figure out what is happening next and where to go from there. It is also great for understanding historical developments.

This book puts modern management practices into context by making sense of SEMCO Style, Google's re:Work, Holacracy, Sociocracy 3.0, Teal Organisations, Responsive.org, and by explaining their cultural relevance [6-12].

INTERESTED IN EXPLORING OTHER GRAVES-RELATED MODELS?

In this book, you will read stories about individuals, companies, markets and societies typical of their particular development level. It is a lively foray into Graves' research and findings. The initial leap was done by the creators of Spiral Dynamics. Since then, many others have also built on his work. **This book will help you to understand the logic underpinning work done by Spiral Dynamics®, Ken Wilber's integral work, GPi's Pathfinder, 9Levels, and 3LM's Holistic Management, among others.**

THIS BOOK OFFERS DIFFERENT VALUE TO DIFFERENT PEOPLE:

Lively, colourful stories about the families, communities and world around you

Purely personal advantages, such as how to win faster

A logic that is easy to integrate with others while helping to make sense of the world around you

A path to help the planet, with better understanding and appreciation of the growth stages required to get people and societies to live more sustainably

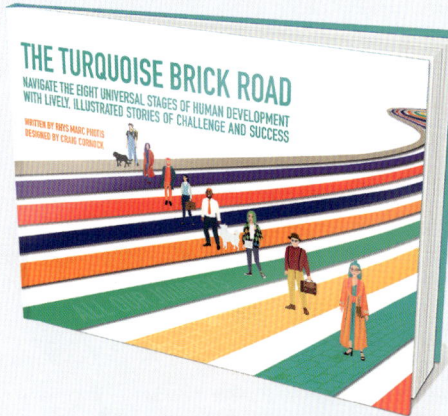

THE TURQUOISE BRICK ROAD
NAVIGATE THE EIGHT UNIVERSAL STAGES OF HUMAN DEVELOPMENT WITH LIVELY, ILLUSTRATED STORIES OF CHALLENGE AND SUCCESS

WRITTEN BY RHYS MARC PHOTIS
DESIGNED BY CRAIG CORMACK

Shared insight that helps to match people, businesses and societies

A guide to understanding people better, which in turn helps to live and work in a happier, more balanced and purpose-driven manner

A method with which to predict trends and development patterns, providing a clear competitive advantage

0.6   WHY DID I WRITE THIS BOOK?

FUTURE-PROOFING MYSELF AND MY BUSINESS

We live in a world where we are too often disconnected or disassociated from one another: politicians from the public they serve, executives from their employees, people from the producers of what they consume, and so on. Furthermore, this world is becoming overly complex and confusing. Mission-critical challenges like politics, climate change, and the leadership crisis, create much distorted noise that causes us to miss opportunities to come together [0-20]. **The challenges of the 21st century can only be tackled in one way: together! The GVS framework helps create a shared understanding, awareness and way forward.**

AN INSIGHTFUL AND VISIONARY LEGACY

One of my main reasons for writing this book was to honour Clare W. Graves–a hard-working visionary who deserves greater acknowledgement. Many other geniuses, like Socrates, Vincent van Gogh, Nikola Tesla, and Dr Subhash Mukhopadhyay, only received the level of appreciation they deserved long after they passed away; much more valuable insight has potentially been lost forever. I believe that what Graves developed is truly groundbreaking and can help us stay true to ourselves–unlike what I did in my youth. Looking back at my career path, I understand when and how I progressed. However, many changes were unclear and stressful at the time. I wish I'd had the clarity then that I have now. **Graves gave me a greater appreciation for and insight into who I am as an individual, who we are as a society, and where we are heading.**

A PERSONAL ROADMAP: UNDERSTANDING AND APPRECIATING PAST, PRESENT AND FUTURE

I always struggled with the concept of generations, that is how and if previous folk had tougher lives, or whether subsequent ones truly progressed. Is any generation actually more advanced than the previous one? Should it be? These questions become a very personal matter when you grow up with two entrepreneurial and very successful grandfathers, as I did. Success doesn't necessarily mean harmony, however. In fact, it can often mean the opposite. So I frequently wondered if there was some kind of logic to explain our evolutionary stages. **The GVS helped me make sense of generations and the development stages of individuals, companies, markets, and societies.**

A PROFESSIONAL ROADMAP: CLARITY ON WHERE YOU ARE AND THE BEST PATH AHEAD

Professionally, the development stages of my career seemed clear to me [O-21]. Let's be fair, most of us start off guided by our parents and then try to figure out our lives as we go along. In the beginning, it is all about doing – getting things done, learning and exploring. I was too busy to look at the bigger picture when I was young. Had I known about the universal roadmap that Graves designed, I would have made much better career choices. **The GVS levels provided and still provides me with a broad but clear professional roadmap and underlying logic.**

A CULTURAL MAP TO BETTER NAVIGATE THE GLOBE

Living in different countries and travelling internationally helped me to figure out that people all over the world have more similarities than differences. Certain values, for example, are shared by seemingly very different countries. Germany and Japan score highly on reliability and order, Canada and New Zealand on environmental consciousness and inclusivity. I started to do a lot of cross-cultural work to help teams from different countries understand each other better and work together more effectively and smoothly. **Like a geographical map, Graves' values-based cultural map helps me to navigate global life.**

UNDERSTANDING AND LEARNING FROM PAST EXPERIENCES

Throughout my life, I had moments when I thought the outcome of my work should have been more positive than it was. I witnessed and got caught up in tension and conflicts, sometimes without even understanding why. I know we can only live life going forward and understand it in hindsight, but the latter is only possible with additional insight or the benefit of a bird's-eye view [O-22]. **The GVS levels helped me make sense of many past experiences and, in so doing, put my mind at ease. Now I know why...!**

BE HAPPIER BY SPENDING MORE TIME WITH PEOPLE WHO SUIT YOU, INCLUDING YOURSELF

I believe that knowing yourself is the first step to a happier life, in harmony with the people and world around you. The second step is to figure out other people's level of awareness and authenticity, and if these come from a healthy, constructive place or not. Being aware of the GVS evolving levels helps me stay true to myself and shield myself from people who do not add value to my life. **The GVS makes it easier to live with yourself and others.**

SHARING IS CARING: WE ARE ALL IN THIS WORLD TOGETHER

I want to bring the GVS to life. Graves was an academic, so I wanted to write a book in which stories bring to life the framework created by his genius. This is meant to be an easy read. Working with the visual artist Craig Cornock showed me how well someone can understand the logic of the GVS with visual representation, even without briefings or prior knowledge of it. **Insight into the GVS changed my life for the better and I want to share this in a lively and colourful way with as many people as possible.**

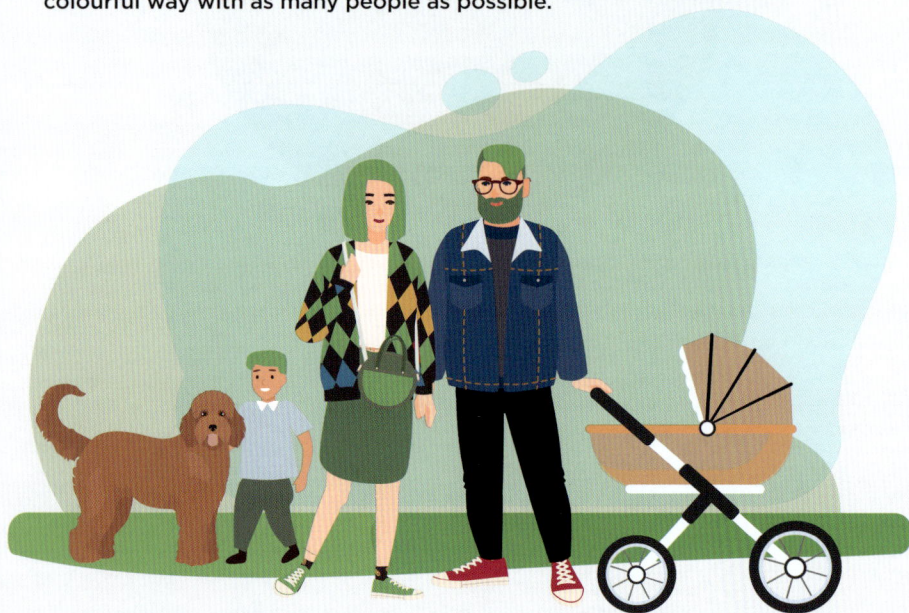

AUTHOR'S COMMENT:

Ironically, this is not the book I had planned to write. The initial story was about a young professional who explores the world and, in so doing, understands that people, companies, markets, and societies operate at eight different universal levels. Next, she gains insight into the seven essential parts of a business, and how they relate to and depend on one another. By sheer curiosity, she combines the two logics to better understand what businesses look like at these different levels, and how they differ. This is also where she comes across sixth level agile development and imagines what it would look like as a business operating logic.

At this point, faith enters the picture and she inherits a struggling 80-person company. She sees this both as a challenge and an opportunity to transform the company into an agile one. She rises to the challenge. With a clear picture in mind, she starts by understanding the seven parts of the organisation, at which level each one is, and develops a plan on how to align, coordinate and grow each of the seven areas to a sixth level of maturity. Her personal journey, as well as that of her key players and the ups and downs they face, help explain how we are all part of this world and how companies need to grow if they want to transform and stay in business.

That was the original plan. For now, this book explores the eight levels that would have been covered in the first chapter of my original book. I am still interested in writing that book, but will only do so if I find 1–2 people to co-create it with. Are you interested?

0.7   WHAT HAS CHANGE GOT TO DO WITH THIS?

Shifting between the GVS levels entails change. The levels provide a practical map for progression, regression, transformation and how to differentiate between these. Each of the eight levels Graves described comes with a specific value set and viewpoint that people hold. For example, being a successful food trader in India requires a different value set and practices to making it in the well-established Bank of Finland.

Limitations of one level provide opportunities to grow. Change often happens regardless of effort or pushback, but true growth is optional and requires intention [0-23]. This means holding on to some values that are dear to us, letting go of others, and embracing new ones. Spiritually, in many ways, it is a reincarnation and, in technical terms, it is like installing a new operating system [0-24].

The GVS can provide insight into the past and a possible glimpse into future development stages, should you choose to progress. Libraries are full of volumes about change, and yet people are naturally resistant to it. Books like *Who Moved My Cheese* [0-25] and the *Our Iceberg is Melting* [0-26] address this topic through stories, whilst *Immunity to Change* [0-27] takes a more research-based approach. The latter makes reference to a recent study showing that, when doctors tell heart patients they will die if they don't change their habits, only one in seven (~14%) will follow through successfully.

"Desire and motivation aren't enough: even when it's literally a matter of life or death, the ability to change remains maddeningly elusive. Apparently, it is our individual beliefs, along with the collective mindsets in organisations and societies that combine to create a natural but powerful immunity to change." [0-27, p.18]

Graves identified that people relied on ways of existence that have worked for them so far. If you are fine with what got you here, why change a winning formula?

For example, people from Graves' 2nd tribal level would say "one shall live according to the ways of one's elders."[C-1, p. 219] We can always find reasons to avoid change if we look hard enough [0-28]. A large-scale, but fitting example is today's climate discussion. It illustrates well the resistance of billions of people, and humankind as a whole, to changing our behaviours in favour of the planet, our own habitat, even though the growing number and intensity of signs make the need for change very clear indeed.

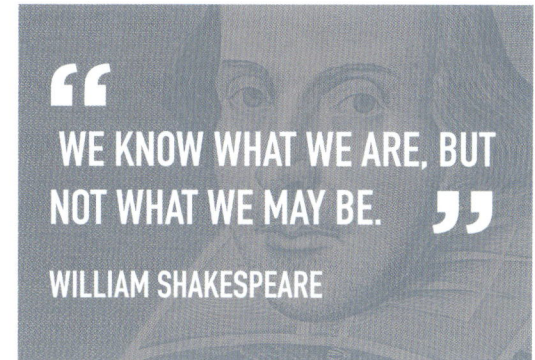

> ❝ WE KNOW WHAT WE ARE, BUT NOT WHAT WE MAY BE. ❞
>
> WILLIAM SHAKESPEARE

WE HAVE PROGRESSED ALREADY

You will have already progressed along various levels by the time you read this book – from an instinctive infant [Level 1], to a trusting toddler [Level 2], to an egocentric child [Level 3], and hopefully by the time you go to school you will have learned to become organised and obey authority [Level 4]. Accepting the 4th level and progressing beyond it is optional.

We all have within us a natural code to progress. The seedlings we start off as, and still are in many ways, are designed to grow with the capability to reach any of the levels. As pointed out by Graves and others, progressing requires a constant interplay between inner drive and external feedback; life is a continuous back and forth. Disciplines such as psychology, psychosynthesis [0-29], and Neuro-Linguistic Programming (NLP) indicate powerful forces at play and are worth exploring if you are interested in the science of change.

CHANGE TO ADAPT

When our situation changes, or the world around us, we are often well advised to adapt. In general, we can more easily revert to a previous level because we have lived through it, even though we are rarely aware of it.

Let me give you an example:
A startup entrepreneur (3rd level) helps to grow a business and finds herself in a 100-person scaleup a few years later. It might seem like a success story, but does this make her truly happy? Her business has progressed to the next level (4th), but has she grown with it or just adapted? If she still wants to work on several different tasks and not according to a specific role description, processes or procedures, it is healthier to (re)turn to a startup (back to 3rd level) to have a more unstructured workplace that suits her better.

Here is another example:

A seasoned entrepreneur enjoys running his boutique consultancy and taking calculated risks (5th level). He is also about to become a father for the first time. Suddenly, an unexpected epidemic forces his business into administration and brings his professional existence to a halt. In such a situation, it is understandable that this father-to-be should seek a full-time job with regular working hours and a reliable pay check at the end of the month (4th level). Sometimes life happens and we don't have any alternative but to adapt, for the time being. At times like this, we need to play along and accept the rules of the game.

Regressing and progressing usually happens from one level to the next. Jumping multiple levels might not be a good idea because experience and insight gained in one level provide the basis for growth in the next.

POSSIBLY, NO FURTHER CHANGE NEEDED

In today's world, many individuals do not need to develop further. Our DNA, upbringing, and the world around us influence and can even dictate what we feel is a suitable level.

Let me provide an analogy:
If you were born a son of a successful entrepreneur (e.g. in the real estate industry), you will naturally live through the first two levels. You then enter the 3rd level, where your ego develops. Your role model is your father, who is a hard-working, powerful property billionaire. At some point, you go to school, but you understand early on that you don't need to play by the rules like most others. Money and power will get you out of many difficult situations. The idea of needing good grades to get a good start to your professional career doesn't apply to you, because at some point you will inherit half a billion dollars, invest it into an already exponentially growing property market, become a TV star and even, later, president of your country. Millions of people admire you and more still will bend over to please you, simply because they know of your powerful place in the world. Of course, you would believe that the respective 3rd level values (e.g. capitalism, power, money, winning at all costs) are what is most important in the world. Why wouldn't you?

With the GVS in mind, we can understand why this person is convinced that everyone should value these things too. He never needed to grow beyond the 3rd level, because his value set brought him to such a powerful position.

This is an extreme example. Generally speaking, there is no need to change if you are truly content with where you are, with yourself and the world around you. However, the world is becoming more dynamic and unpredictable, just when we thought we had seen it all. The latest coronavirus pandemic is a good example of how unpredictable life can be. It can't hurt to be prepared and have a map to navigate these turbulent times.

AUTHOR'S COMMENT:

In a business context, if we change our ways of working but remain within one level, this is referred to as change. For example, implementing a new ERP software like SAP or executing a Six Sigma programme.

Complete progression from one level to another is not just a change but a transformation—for example, moving from a ten-person startup to an organisation with 60 employees, or going from an efficiency-driven company selling products to a customer-oriented consulting firm selling solutions.

Both change and transformation are essential to life, and it is only the transitioning periods that prove to be frustrating and unsettling at times. This has to do with uncertainty, which, in turn, is what most people instinctively refute as a survival mechanism.

However, self-directed change is usually for the better and we are well advised to take matters in our own hands. Essentially, we must change or we will be changed.

> **FOR A SEED TO ACHIEVE ITS GREATEST EXPRESSION, IT MUST COME COMPLETELY UNDONE.**
>
> **THE SHELL CRACKS, ITS INSIDES COME OUT AND EVERYTHING CHANGES.**
>
> **FOR SOMEONE WHO DOESN'T UNDERSTAND GROWTH, IT WOULD LOOK LIKE COMPLETE DESTRUCTION.**

CYNTHIA OCCELLI, AUTHOR, MOTHER & BUSINESS WOMAN WITH A LAW DEGREE

0.8   IN WHAT WAY ARE VALUES AN ESSENTIAL PART OF THE GVS?

People who like the idea of lifelong learning and understand that the only constant in life is change will remain anchored if they know themselves well. Knowing – and sticking by – your values is an important aspect of this. It can guide decision-making in challenging times.

As mentioned earlier, understanding your values is helpful. Values need to be nurtured in order to come to life, and there are three main stages to consider.

Firstly, do you have enough self-awareness to know which **values** you hold dearly? Can you name them? For example, I value family.

Secondly, important values are part of our **beliefs**, because they explain why something is important to someone. Asking others why a value is important to them can help gain more clarity. For example 'Why is family so important to you?' 'Family is a value to me because it provides me with a sense of belonging, safety and continuity.'

Thirdly, values and beliefs directly influence our **behaviours**, which can be witnessed and observed. That is why actions speak louder than words. For example, the fact that I go home at 5 p.m. on Fridays, spend every Christmas with my family, and consult them before making big life decisions are behaviours that support my value and belief in family.

I believe it is important to understand what motivates people in life. Therefore, every level in this book lists what drives the respective characters. This is in reference to Dan Pink's book *Drive* [0-4]. He postulates that human motivation is largely intrinsic, and that the aspects of motivation can break down into three main drivers:

Purpose: To seek meaning at work; it is the highest form of motivation

Mastery: To get better at something; a skill or characteristic

Autonomy: To have a healthy level of influence on how, when, where, and with whom we work.

He argues against old models of motivation driven by rewards and fear of punishment, especially those dominated by extrinsic factors such as money.

Pink's persuasive theory on what motivates people – at home, school, or work – is backed by four decades of solid scientific research on human motivation, and highlights an extreme mismatch between the human capital practices that are still in use today and those that really work.

Value: A noun like 'punctuality', 'health', 'honesty', or 'personal freedom'...

Belief: Why do I believe in this value? I believe in punctuality because I respect my and other people's time, and don't want to waste it.

Behaviour: An action that is visible and can be measured. "I set a calendar entry for every event. I always plan ahead, arrive well before the agreed time to also be mentally ready when the meeting starts. In the last six months, I was only late once and that was out of my hands."

Value: Politeness

Belief: We all live relatively close together, so being respectful and considerate of other people benefits everyone.

Behaviour: Often saying "Thank you," "Please," and "Sorry" (for example, even saying "sorry" if someone steps on your foot). Queuing properly.

Value preferences can change over time. This is true for individuals as well as organisations and societies. These changing value preferences are reflected in the GVS.

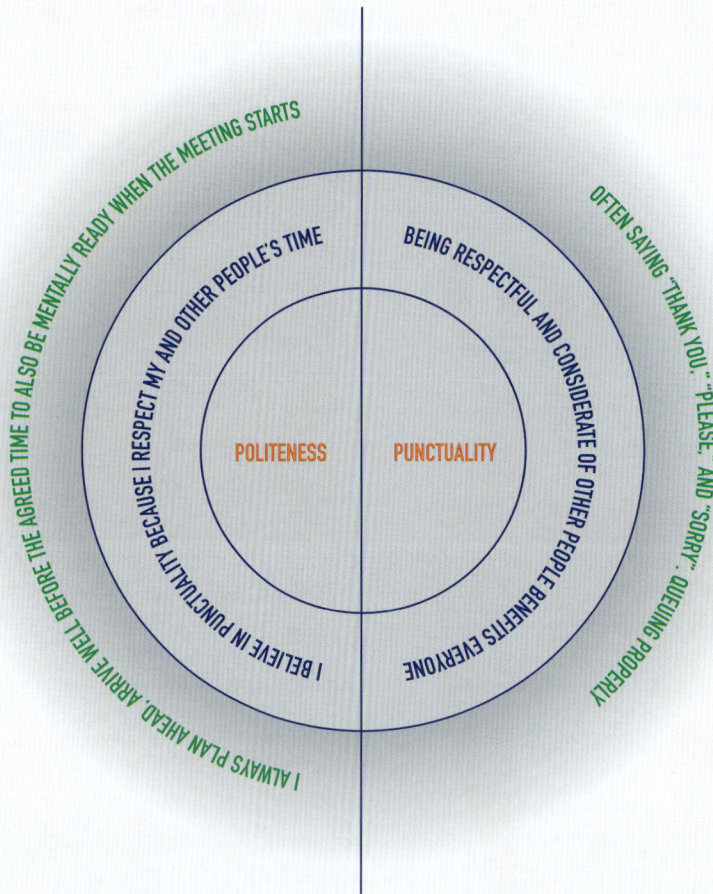

I focused on four of the eight levels for demonstration, because that is the level at which the majority of people in this world operate.

Values vary on each level. Each of the columns below reflects its own level of motivation:

3rd LEVEL INDIVIDUALISTIC	4th LEVEL GROUP-ORIENTED	5th LEVEL INDIVIDUALISTIC	6th LEVEL GROUP-ORIENTED
Strength	Stability	Competition	Self-determination
Determination	Clarity	Performance	Creativity
Honour	Sense of duty	Measurable results	
Compassion			
Courage	Reliability	Status	Consensus
Adventurism	Loyalty	Accountability	Empathy

At some levels we are more focused on ourselves (levels: 3, 5), while we engage more with people on others (levels: 4, 6). Life's pendulum swings back and forth as we progress, and so do our values. We might feel drawn to the values of a specific level, but we most likely hold values from all levels. Life is colourful and so are we as individuals.

This can lead to dilemmas when we hold two or more conflicting values. This is usually a situation where there is no right decision to make. There are no right or wrong values; how can one value be better than another?

Many movies, in fact, most Bollywood movies, make use of such an engaging technique. Shall I choose tradition or true love?

All this makes up who we are and defines our perspective on life. The world we see reflects our own values, beliefs and state of mind.

0.9 HOW TO ENSURE CONTINUOUS GROWTH?

The values from the previous chapter's example are the healthy, constructive ones and make up one side of the coin. Each level – like most people – also has a negative, destructive side. Each of the eight stories coming up in the chapters ahead illustrate this by sharing the experience of a different protagonist who is stereotypical of that level. One side of the coin has healthy values and virtues that the character holds dear.

Each protagonist has a person in their life or knows of a place that is at the same level, but unpleasant to them. For example, people who lead by fear are manipulative and lack transparency. Values like force, greed or bureaucracy fit on the other, darker side of the coin.

AUTHOR'S COMMENT:
I am still at the beginning of exploring these universal growth values and drivers, as are the people around me. We are in the process of gaining more insight.

Universal growth values are fascinating but quickly become complicated and vague. In addition, every level equips you with values that are equally necessary for a healthy development. For example, a sense of belonging (2nd level), self-confidence (3rd level), discipline (4th level), and so on. These and other values provide a healthy grounding, a bit like a tree that needs roots, a trunk, branches to grow leaves.

There is a 3rd side of a coin: some **growth values** reside on the edge, and are a bit different in the way that they are more universal. To ensure continuous growth all the way, it behoves us to also focus on the following values and bring them to life:

- SELF-AWARENESS
- CURIOSITY
- GROWTH MINDSET
- TRANSPARENCY
- PERSONAL ACCOUNTABILITY

- MINDFULNESS
- GENEROSITY
- HUMOUR
- TOLERANCE
- NATURE

If you are interested in this topic and in co-creating, please feel free to get in touch.

Wherever you are in life, if you stay true to these values, you are likely to progress to your desired extent in line with the levels.

> **COOPERATION AND CONFLICT ARE TWO SIDES OF THE SAME COIN; BOTH ARISE OUT OF MAN'S RELATIONSHIP WITH HIS FELLOWS. THE LARGER THE GROUP, THE GREATER THE POSSIBILITY OF DEVELOPMENT THROUGH COOPERATION, AND THE GREATER THE POSSIBILITY OF CONFLICT.**
>
> **JULIUS NYERERE, TANZANIAN POLITICIAN**

0.10   HOW TO USE THIS BOOK?

The forthcoming eight stories paint a picture of a stereotypical protagonist working in a typical organisation and living in a society representative of their particular development stage.

The book attempts a balancing act: on the one hand it tells the stories, on the other hand, it is meant as a reference book so you can return to the chapters at a later point.

The eight individual stories/chapters all follow the same logic:

SUMMARY

GENERAL LIFE

-    Values

-    Strengths + weaknesses

TYPICAL INDIVIDUALS

-    Family life, sports, heroes, movies, cars, and personal interests

-    Professional purpose, mastery, autonomy

-    Examples of the unhealthy, destructive side of this level

-    A known concept that naturally fits into the level and helps to illustrate this type of manifestation

LEADERSHIP

TEAMS

PLANNING & STEERING

ORGANISATIONS

-    Typical business tools

MARKETS

LIMITATIONS AND GROWTH (TO NEXT LEVEL)

PESTEL

AUTHOR'S COMMENT:
The first two levels are not as clearly structured as listed above. They are naturally a bit different, because business practices and some other aspects haven't yet manifested themselves so clearly.

For a better understanding of the framework, turn to section 10.1 before continuing.

You will most likely relate to some levels more than others. That is reflective of life and also what you gravitate towards at the moment. More than anything, I hope you enjoy the read.

STORY BOOK

REFERENCE BOOK

AMON   BO   CONAN   DOC   ELI   FLORENCE   G   HORTENSE

BRISHNA   CHARLIE   DEVINA   EBONY
MACHIAVELLI   FEENA   GIDEON   HALA

FOOD, DRINK
WARMTH
SAFETY

Survival Mode

PERSONAL SUCCESS
DETERMINATION
POWER

Ego & Fear

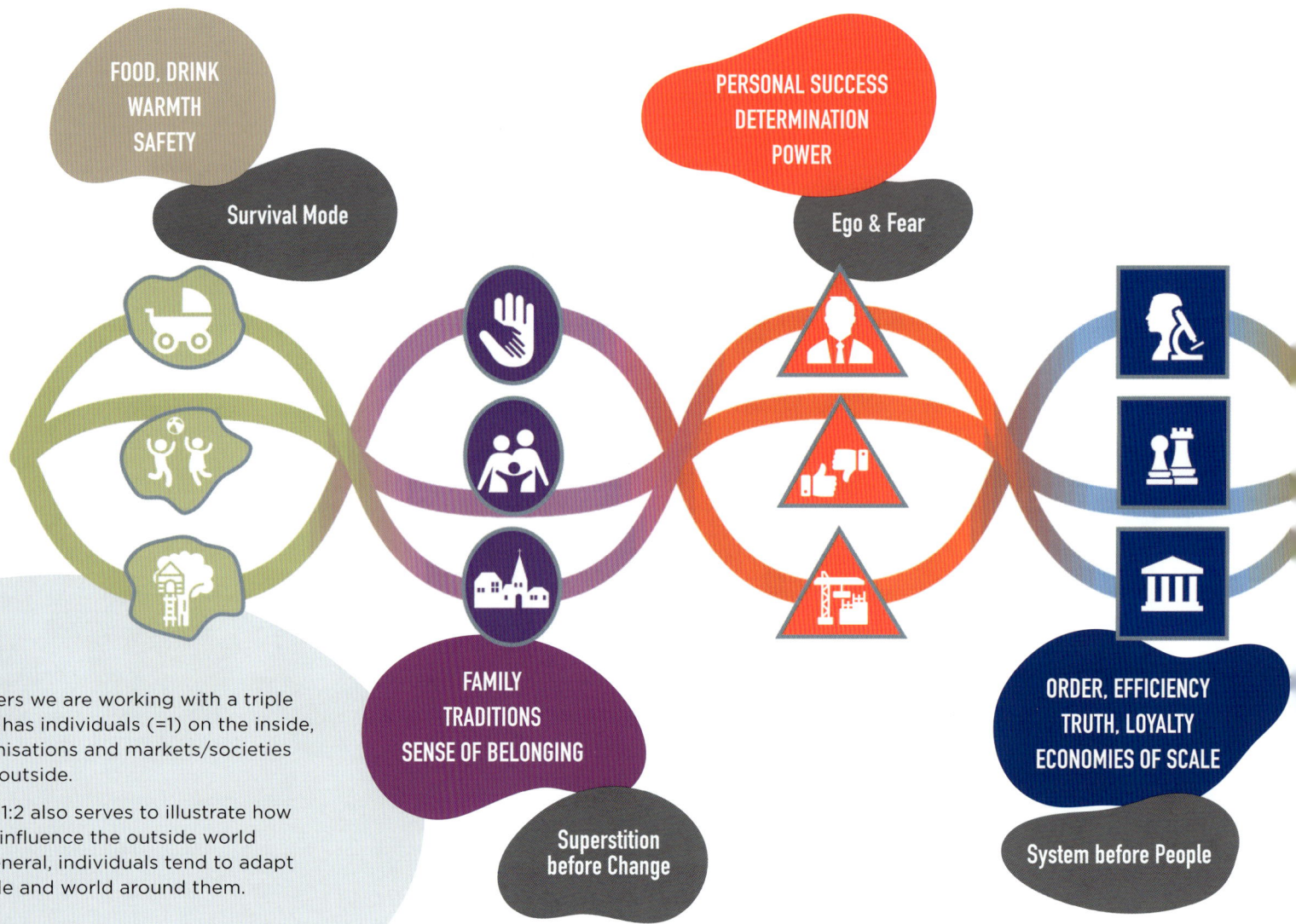

As pathfinders we are working with a triple helix, which has individuals (=1) on the inside, teams/organisations and markets/societies (=2) on the outside.

The ratio of 1:2 also serves to illustrate how much more influence the outside world exerts. In general, individuals tend to adapt to the people and world around them.

FAMILY
TRADITIONS
SENSE OF BELONGING

Superstition
before Change

ORDER, EFFICIENCY
TRUTH, LOYALTY
ECONOMIES OF SCALE

System before People

ORDER, EFFICIENCY
TRUTH, LOYALTY
ECONOMIES OF SCALE

Targets before People

PERSONAL AUTONOMY
SYSTEMS-THINKING
INTEGRATION OF
KNOWLEDGE

Self-centredness
before Worldly Action

SELF-DETERMINATION
SHARED
RESPONSIBILITIES
ADAPTATION

Conformity before
Individuality

COLLECTIVE INTUITION
GLOBAL HEALING
HOLISM

Spiritual Consciousness
before Earthly Action

1st STAGE

BEIGE: EXISTENCE & SURVIVAL

"

THEY ARE SIMPLY ADULT HUMAN BEINGS WHO HAVE TAKEN ON THE FORM OF EXISTENCE THAT HAS THE GREATEST SURVIVAL VALUE FOR THEM IN THEIR WORLD; BUT THEY ARE ALSO ONES WHO ARE ARRESTED AT THIS LEVEL BECAUSE CERTAIN SOCIETIES WILL NOT DO WHAT IS NECESSARY TO OVERCOME THE REASON FOR THE ARRESTMENT. [C – 1, P. 207]

"

AMON'S EXISTENCE

Amon is desperately trying to keep up with Amaroq. He hopes Amaroq knows where she is going. The distance between them and the village mob is increasing by the second. Still, Amon is wondering what will happen if they catch up with him? Why are they doing this at all? Would Amaroq defend him?

No need to test this out. He is running frantically for the rocks that lead up to the rift. The gap is difficult to spot when you don't know what you are looking for, which makes it the best possible hiding place. It is far from perfect being a dead end, but Amon cannot think of any other way out.

He can no longer hear them chasing but that does not mean they're not there. As Amon reaches the first rock, he sees Amaroq looking down from above, waggling her tail. Is it all just a game to her? Maybe it is best if she doesn't know that they could hurt her. How can she forgive humans after what they have done to her?

They both make it to the little cave underneath the larger opening. He takes Amaroq in his arms and suddenly feels safe and whole. It is good to have a best friend once again, especially one so attentive and agile. Amaroq is pitch black and a typical mutt. Figuring out her combined breeds is just too difficult. Not that Amon would know anyway because owning a pet dog is rather unusual where he comes from. One thing he knows for sure is that she is 'a lot of dog' –

strong and brave, loyal and social at the same time, like a wolf. That is why Amon named her Amaroq, the Inuit word for wolf.

After a few hours, Amon sees the reflection of the sunlight turning reddish, and he knows it will be dark soon. He hopes the mob has gone but, to make sure, Amon lets Amaroq venture out first. She would quickly sniff them out and lead them astray. He is right; they are nowhere to be seen.

The walk back to his cave is magical at this time of day. Amon loves the nature in this area. There are so many different greens and an abundance of life. The amount and diversity of the wildlife is astounding. He didn't even know lizards could live under water. After settling here for just over two years, he knows the territory quite well. Prominent landmarks make it relatively easy to navigate – rocky hills to the north and east, various lakes, ponds, rivers and streams crossing the meadows and forests. As they approach a wide river running past a rocky hilltop into a lake, Amon knows it is safer to remain on the south-west side of it. However, he sometimes gets carried away in the lush nature and goes astray, but Amaroq soon points him in the right direction. It is time to get back to the cave to shelter and hide away. Today, they will not make it back before nightfall, so it makes sense to stop and gather some food. Foraging is a good option in this part of the world, which always has something to offer. Besides, these two have learned to hunt together and, with the

number of rabbits around, opportunities are plentiful. The light is fading and it is time to start looking. Falling asleep on an empty stomach is not easy, as Amon knows all too well.

It has happened so often on his way here. Amon comes from a very dry place, far away, where people had to group together to survive. As a shepherd, he was always looking for water and pasture, whereas here greenery is everywhere, and he loves it.

In his previous life, he married his childhood sweetheart, Amaunet. Two years his senior, she was like a goddess to him, as early as in primary school. Imagine how happy he was when he finally won her over. Everything felt just right. Yet, not long after, it all went up in flames.

He now understands the underlying dynamics but still cannot grasp the level of destruction, pain and hopelessness. What is the purpose of causing such harm? A few weeks after the manmade thunder started, it rained fire and, suddenly, the life he once knew was no more. Amaunet was visiting her parents at the time. Amon lost his kindred soul in one of the first air raids and ended up fleeing with thousand others. They marched for weeks trying to stay alive. The physical pain was a great distraction after having lost the love of his life.

They all ended up in a camp. He had heard of these places but first thought he was in a city, such was the scale of the camp. Out of over 100,000 refugees, half were children, many of whom suffered from chronic malnutrition and did not go to school. [1-1] Amon spent more years there than he can remember. It is a strange life trying to get by every day while having to watch your back. Life becomes a blur. The day he attended the 21st birthday party of a friend who, like countless others, was born in the camp, Amon decided to leave. He had learned that about three million people live like this and close to 30,000 flee their homes daily through persecution and crises. [1-2] He wasn't going to stay there forever and, what, raise a family?

During his time at the camp, Amon was lucky enough to make friends with some of the international volunteers who told him about the so called world order – what was going on politically – and also provided him with some interesting reading material. He came to understand that his situation was the result of something much bigger, which was not going to end any time soon. He learned that, before World War II, politicians generally avoided wars, as they had to be financed through taxes, which would affect their popularity and jeopardise their re-election. Amon was told all of this changed during World War II when the largest economy in the world started to finance the war simply by printing money. [1-3] For the Federal Reserve – which is partly private and managing twelve privately owned Federal Reserve Banks – this was very lucrative. Including the word federal in a title does give it a semblance of integrity. [1-4]

Over time, Amon started to recognise the vicious cycle. A presidential candidate seeking election needs a few millions to run their campaign. Therefore, they obtain sponsorship from people and businesses. As this is legal, donations are tax deductible. After election of the candidate, it is payback time.

Should public opinion turn against the president at any point, they will play the nationalist card and foster our instinctive sense of belonging – them and us. A tried and tested approach is to invade a far-away country, which also secures contracts in the millions and billions to drive the war machine. Printing as much money as necessary ensures that payments can be covered. Then, of course, the war-torn infrastructure that has just been obliterated needs rebuilding. As the president and their team control the invaded country, they decide which corporations can divide it up and reconstruct it. This is a ready-made list of supporters for the next campaign.

Once Amon fully understood these dynamics, he lost all hope of ever returning home. Was it still his home? How could it be if everything and everyone he knew was gone?

Amon was determined to leave at all costs. A series of calculated and fortunate actions and events helped him move out of the camp. He didn't know where he was heading, he just wanted to get away and kept going. His experience as a shepherd came in handy. He had always enjoyed the wild and, the day he came across Amaroq, he knew he had found his new place in the world. A stray dog in a bad shape, she was very scared of him in the beginning, but he took good care of her and they became inseparable.

Amaroq never leaves his side. She is a great guard dog and they comfort each other. They have even figured out how to hunt wild rabbits together. Amaroq crouches in the high grass while Amon walks towards her in a big circle and makes a lot of noise. They are quite successful and Amon usually grills some of the lean meat while Amaroq devours the rest.

They occasionally need essentials like lighters, tools or bandages. In those cases, Amon visits Purpleton, the nearby village, and works as a day labourer to make some money. He likes helping Bo, the local shop owner, because she is fair. She clearly states what she wants and how to do it – Amon appreciates that level of clarity. She is good with plants and Amon enjoys helping out at her new garden centre. Bo also gave him a foraging pocket guide and a forager's calendar, both of which have helped him greatly.

Helping out people in neighbouring Lilaton was a contrasting experience. That place has a strange vibe altogether and Amon still regrets ever having ventured there. One day, he cut himself badly and needed some help. The locals called Brishna over to treat him, a big woman with a very serious look. She told him that her local ancestry goes back hundreds of years and that nothing happens here without her say-so. She made it clear that her job was to protect their way of life from any external threat. Amon got the message. As payment for her assistance, she asked Amon to help remove boulders in the fields. That experience felt very unfair for they left him the largest ones and insisted he worked on during the breaks.

It was at that time that a few of the Lilaton teenagers became aware of Amon; those youngsters who sometimes gathered in a gang and tried to chase him. Amon had never met or spoken to them so did not understand why they would throw stones at him. He did learn his lesson though and stayed well clear of those villagers.

Amon truly values his freedom. After years in a crowded camp, he loves being in nature again. In fact, he feels like he is part of it. He and his companion live such immersed lives that the feeling of separation has disappeared. He feels firmly rooted in the ground, he breathes the oxygen from the trees,[1-5] swims in the lakes, catches a fish when he is lucky and feeds the remains to the bugs. The little green bugs he uses to bait fish; everything seems to work in cycles here.

It is so natural and he experiences life in the moment. Just like the river, these two go with the flow. There is no place for ego in such an engaged life. Amon feels he has become one with himself on the inside. Most days, he achieves equilibrium with the outside world and, at that point, there is complete oneness. In the camp, he had read in a copy of the National Geographic about the Tasaday tribe in the highland rainforest of the Philippines, who live or lived as he does today. It sometimes feels like he is featuring in the two movies he liked when he was young, *The Gods Must Be Crazy* and *The Quest for Fire*.

Maybe he is more human now than most others on this planet. After all, the word human derives from the Latin *humanus*, an adjectival form of homo. The generic name homo is a learned 18th-century derivation from Latin *homo*, man or earthly being. [1-6] Amon is not convinced about *homo sapiens* though, *sapiens* stemming from Latin for wise. He has not seen enough evidence of this yet, on the contrary.

He wonders what life has in store for him.

> **THERE ARE NO GODS IN THE UNIVERSE, NO NATIONS, NO MONEY, NO HUMAN RIGHTS, NO LAWS AND NO JUSTICE OUTSIDE THE COMMON IMAGINATION OF HUMAN BEINGS.**
>
> **YUVAL NOAH HARARI, AUTHOR OF SAPIENS**

2nd STAGE
PURPLE: DOWN-TO-EARTH

THE 2ND (PURPLE) STAGE REPRESENTS A PHASE OF FEELING SAFE BY BEING PART OF A GROUP WHILST AT THE SAME TIME LOOKING FOR DIFFERENTIATION AS OUR NATURAL AWARENESS OF SELF DEVELOPS. WE ALL PLAY DIFFERENT ROLES IN FAMILIES, TRIBES AND SOCIAL GROUPS. PEOPLE ENJOY A SENSE OF BELONGING AND LIFE IS EASIER WHEN JOYS AND CHALLENGES ARE SHARED. INDIVIDUALS AT THIS LEVEL THINK IN TERMS OF RITUALS, SUPERSTITION, AND STEREOTYPES, WITHOUT NECESSARILY KNOWING "WHY THINGS ARE THE WAY THEY ARE." [C-1, P.217]

THEY ENJOY BEING PART OF A LARGER FAMILY, ARE SET IN THEIR WAYS AND KNOW HOW EVERYTHING WORKS AROUND THEM. THEIR FOREBEARS LIVED LIKE THIS AND THERE IS NO NEED TO ROCK THE BOAT. AT THIS STAGE IN LIFE, IT IS VITAL TO KNOW YOUR LOCAL AREA, TO HAVE A STRONG SENSE OF BELONGING, AND TO TRUST THE PEOPLE AROUND YOU.

WORKING AS A TEAM FEELS VERY NATURAL – TYPICAL BUSINESSES COMPRISE MAINLY TRADITIONAL FAMILY SMES. PEOPLE LOOK OUT FOR EACH OTHER AND IT IS NOT UNUSUAL FOR MANAGEMENT TO HELP OUT EMPLOYEES IN NEED. COMPANY OWNERS RECOGNISE THAT THEIR FIRM IS AN IMPORTANT PART OF THE SOCIAL FABRIC. BESIDE THE WORKPLACE, COLLEAGUES MIX THROUGH FREQUENTING THE SAME SPORTS CLUBS OR SOCIAL CIRCLES.

HERE, MOST MARKETS TEND TO BE RURAL AND HAVE BEEN OPERATING THE WAY THEY DO FOR MANY GENERATIONS. CONNECTIONS ARE ENDLESS AND EVERYTHING HAS A NATURAL FLOW. ONCE THEY HAVE SECURED THEIR PLACE WITHIN THE SOCIAL INFRASTRUCTURE, BUSINESSES FIND IT EASY TO NAVIGATE THE MARKETS, WHICH ARE USUALLY QUITE STABLE.

"

THE CURRENT EXISTENCE PROVES THAT HOW WE HAVE DONE THINGS IN THE PAST WORKED WELL AND SO WE NEED TO CONTINUE IN THE SAME WAY AS OUR FOREFATHERS. [C-1, 218]

"

BO'S PURPLETON

At this point we get to meet Bo who lives with her large family in the countryside. She has lived there all her life, and knows the world and people around her. Her family and ancestors seem to have always lived in Purpleton, which sits on a peninsula with a mystical history. Purpleton had great ambitions of becoming a town but never really achieved its full economic potential.

The village is one of three at the northern, most remote part of Purpleshire, which is a wild and picturesque part of the world. Houses in the villages look very traditional and were built with cob, a mixture of clay, sand and straw. Cob is a breathable material that regulates temperature and stores heat during the day, which affords houses a lovely, cosy ambience into the evening. Twisted oak beams are another local building material of choice which, when the special Purpleshire sunlight is right, allows the houses to seamlessly blend with their natural environment.

Four of the villages are quite connected, with people often visiting each other. The smallest two, Wantabe and Lilaton, are the odd ones out.

Wantabe is more traditional than most - some villagers even protested against the laying of new internet cables. At least Wantabees get involved in most social events. The one that really stands out is Lilaton with its 230 inhabitants who seem to think they don't need the outside world. Their forward-looking young people leave and the traditionalists stay, and often marry, within the village.

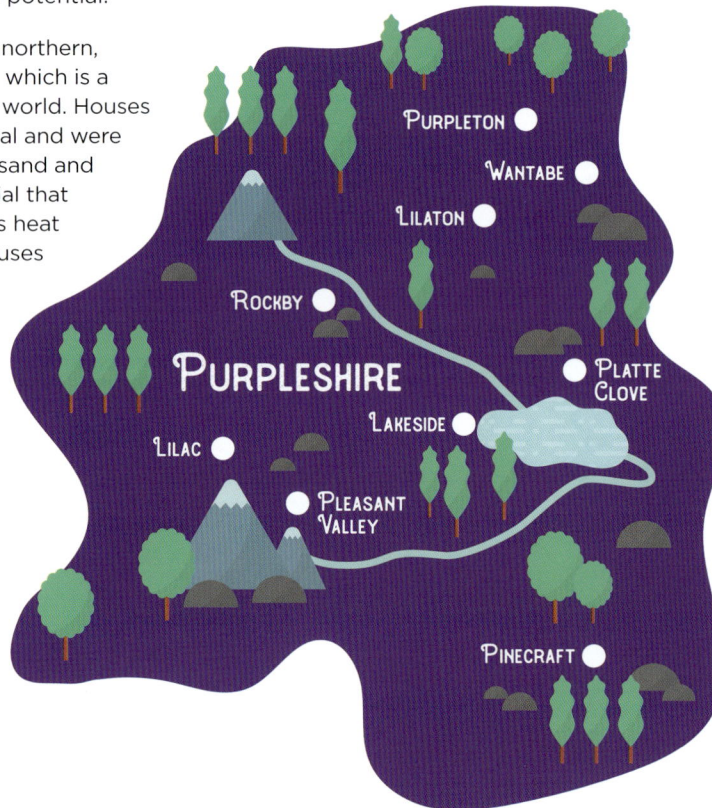

PURPLETON

WANTABE

LILATON

ROCKBY

PURPLESHIRE

PLATTE CLOVE

LAKESIDE

LILAC

PLEASANT VALLEY

PINECRAFT

All in all, it is a beautiful but remote part of the world where many things are still done as in the good old days. Bo sometimes wonders when that actually was. The surrounding national park makes the area very green and, at times, it seems that Purpleshire exists within a time zone of its own.

Bo knows everyone nearby and all seem to be connected somehow, or have a few familiar stories to tell. She also spends a lot of time walking her dog Bilbo in the woods where she played as a child. It is a great place for foraging. She sometimes imagines fairies coming out once she has left the woods. Spending time there helped her figure out what is important to her:

SENSE OF BELONGING

INTIMACY

TRUST

TRADITIONS

FAMILY & FRIENDSHIPS

RITUALS

FILIAL PIETY

RESPECT

HOSPITALITY

On the one hand she sees that local life has a lot of positive aspects:

- BEING PART OF A FAMILY, TRIBE, TEAM AND LOCAL COMMUNITY;

- BEING ABLE TO DEPEND ON RELATIONSHIPS (GIVE AND TAKE);

- PEOPLE LOOKING OUT FOR AND AFTER ONE ANOTHER;

- LIVING IN HARMONY WITH THE SURROUNDING WORLD.

On the other hand she is quite modern and sometimes referred to as a rebel. It is not that she wants to be critical but she would like to see some negatives addressed:

- STICKING TO TRADITIONS EVEN WHEN THEY CONTRADICT THEMSELVES, BECAUSE THEY ARE BASED ON OUTDATED BELIEFS OR DON'T CONSIDER CHANGES AND NEW FINDINGS;

- IGNORING OUTSIDERS AND WHAT IS BEING LEARNED FURTHER AFIELD;

- STUBBORNLY STICKING TO TABOOS.

Adhering to customs handed down from past generations helps us better understand our purple roots. Traditions usually reinforce values such as freedom, faith, integrity, personal responsibility, a strong work ethic, and a supporting group. With this in mind, Wantabe and Lilaton are two good examples of unhealthy 2nd (Purple) stage developments. As the world around us changes, it is important to look at traditions in light of new insight. An unhealthy system develops when traditional customs unnecessarily disadvantage individuals, when leaders use them to serve their own power and interests, or when people are treated differently. This usually goes hand in hand with a limited level of learning, growth and openness to others. Lack of transparency is used for personal gain, individuals are ousted for challenging the elder's thinking.

FACT:

Today, witch doctors in Africa still hunt people affected by albinism (a skin condition) to use their body parts in potions supposed to bring good luck and wealth. Victims are kidnapped and then dismembered by hired killers. The UN estimates that, in Tanzania alone, around 80 people with albinism have been murdered since 2000.

Outdated beliefs have no limits, as is evident with superstitions involving killing animals in large numbers. This has usually something to do with health, luck, some incurable disease, or even impotency at times. If the tiger has become endangered, it is not just down to the fur trade but also because some of its parts are used in folk medicine.

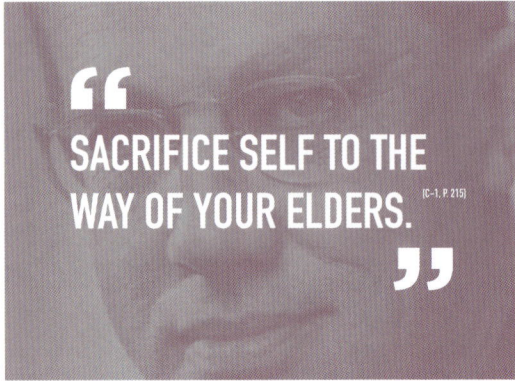

> ## " SACRIFICE SELF TO THE WAY OF YOUR ELDERS. " [C-1, P. 215]

> *Home is where love resides, memories are created, friends always belong and laughter never ends.*

INDIVIDUALS

Bo loves everyone in the house and stables. She has three kids and is particularly fond of her youngest daughter Alys (15th century spelling of Alice). Alys has just turned two, is officially a toddler and seems to have entered a different level of awareness in the way she is more actively engaging with the world around her.

Bo knows that her story and that of her children begin in their house. She does her best to continue the tradition of providing a loving and caring home. The spirit of their home is nicely captured in the slogan above the front door, which one of her ancestors must have engraved there in the good old days:

She believes that humans need to love and be loved. For example, she loves her sister-in-law for dedicating so much time to looking after the indigenous wildlife. As a result, she has a magical garden full of native plants and buzzing life. She also loves her husband James whom she has known since nursery - the one with the old oak tree. They are best friends but still have a healthy romantic appetite for each other.

Purpleton is also known for all its social activities and groups, small and large. There are various sports clubs, religious groups, professional organisations, co-working spaces and even online communities. People also play a sport similar to shin kicking (a traditional game with stones), but only played in this part of the world. Purpleton is one of five villages that come together for a tournament every year. Lilaton refuses to join in.

Purpleton has won so many years in a row that it seems to have become somewhat of a tradition. Some say it has to do with Purpleton's team always turning up with the largest number of supporters and the energy of their forefathers.

The inhabitants from neighbouring Wantabe intend to put an end to this in the upcoming tournament. Rumour has it that they have put time and money into regaining some of the ancient techniques and tricks. They have always been a bit odd in that they believe in the higher powers of nature, spirits and the influence of their ancestors. Mary, from next door, says they still perform rites to honour superhuman powers and appease them with sacrifices. Bo has her doubts about these ancient practices though she may well consider them if Wantabe were to reach the top of the leader-board.

Bo runs a small shop that she took over from her father. She expanded it by adding garden products, but otherwise left it much the same. It was a fairly easy transition once her father let go properly. He then started helping the local priest and now seems busier than ever.

Bo is motivated as follows:

PURPOSE	MASTERY	AUTONOMY
Upholding family traditions Sense of belonging	Learning from the elders Honing one's skills over time Becoming one of the elders	Working with people we like A natural work-life balance

AUTHOR'S COMMENT:

Like Bo and Alys we all have 2nd level purple roots. It is healthy to consider where you are from and who your family and friends are.

I have 'purple' foods in the cupboard in case I have a bad day. For some it might be macaroni and cheese, for others a comforting soup, and for me it is fried potatoes, with chilly pickle and two eggs on top.

Something else of a purple nature that I am considering is joining a local choir, because a bit of healthy purple has never harmed anybody.

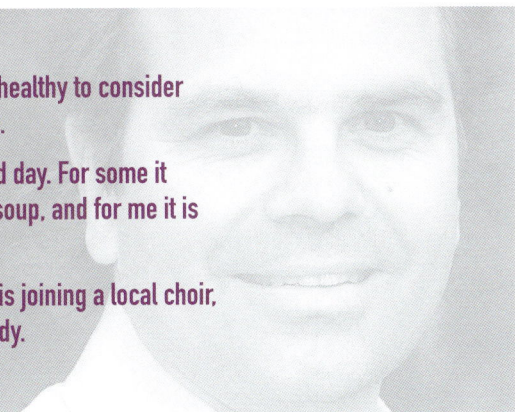

> **"**
> THE MODEL IS THE 'FRIENDLY PARENT' WHO WORKS ALONGSIDE, SHELTERS THE PERSON, MAKES THE WORK FUN AND PLEASANT, AND, ABOVE ALL, RESPECTS AND OBSERVES THE TABOOS. [C-1, P. 220]
> **"**

LEADERSHIP

Bo's idea of leadership is defined by her sense of responsibility for her six employees. They don't mind that Bo sets the rules, quite the opposite. They feel well looked after and comfortable. Bo feels proud taking care of others although she doesn't like being referred to as the 'matriarch'. Ultimately, they know she is looking out for them.

Bo read a lot about Confucius when she was young. She always loved his Golden Rule – 'Do not do to others what you do not want done to yourself.' [2-1] She tries to follow Confucianism's five virtues, which, in many ways, define her leadership style and principles [2-2]:

1 BENEVOLENCE IN TERMS OF SYMPATHY FOR OTHERS

REN is regarded as the most important of the virtues, and some effort is made to define it, with the Golden Rule being only one attempt. We are all in this world together. We all have lives to live, ups and downs, and bills to pay. When Catherine, one of the employees, was in financial difficulties during her divorce, the shop helped out with a loan.

2 MANNERS, RITUALS, POLITENESS AND FEELINGS OF RESPECT

LI is also given a lot of consideration and refers both to outward actions and inner feelings of respect. The concept embraces not only etiquette but also customs, rituals and conventions of all kinds. When things go pear-shaped, like last week when two of the shelves broke and lots of glass jars came crashing down, Bo didn't freak out, but instead kept her cool. There was no need to blame James for overloading the shelves as he'd already understood that he'd made a mistake.

3 DUTY, HONESTY AND FEELING REMORSE AFTER DOING SOMETHING WRONG

YI is based upon the idea of reciprocity. *Yi* can be translated as righteousness, though it may simply mean what is ethically best to do in a certain situation. The term contrasts with action done out of self-interest. While pursuing one's own self-interest is not necessarily bad, one would be a better, more righteous person if one's life was based upon following a path designed to enhance the greater good. Thus an outcome of *yi* is doing the right thing for the right reason. As a leader you take on a responsible role. Everyone looks at the leader for guidance. As the eldest child, Bo accepted early on that she would be exposed to all kinds of things in her role. Working at the local shop means you get to hear all the gossip in the town. However, she knows there are always two sides to a story and that engaging in pettiness or jealousy is not what a leader should do.

4 KNOWLEDGE AND WISDOM TO DIFFERENTIATE BETWEEN RIGHT AND WRONG

CHI is about sincerity, a level of objectivity and the cultivation of knowledge. Virtuous action towards others begins with virtuous and sincere thought, which begins with knowledge. A virtuous disposition without knowledge is susceptible to corruption, and virtuous action without sincerity is not true righteousness. Cultivating knowledge and sincerity is also important for one's own sake; Bo loves learning for the sake of learning and righteousness for the sake of righteousness. The world changes and we need to progress.

5 LOYALTY, GOOD FAITH AND FILIAL PIETY

XIN is about playing your part. Furthermore, it is a virtue of respect for one's parents and ancestors, and of the hierarchies within society: father–son, elder–junior and male–female.

Confucians stress that a person's worth is determined by public actions. The concept of *xin* defines a set of social relationships and clearly describes how people are supposed to behave towards one another. Loyalty in Confucian terms takes five forms:

- subject to ruler
- son to father
- younger brother to older brother
- wife to husband (woman to man)
- younger person to older person.

Under the concept of *xin*, the superior person receives respect and obedience from the subordinate person but is by no means a dictator. In our story, Bo is supposed to reciprocate with love, goodwill, support and affection towards the subordinate person.

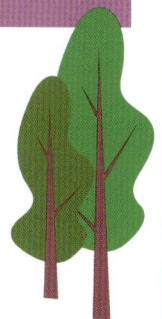

The teachings of Confucius focus largely on the respect of one's parents, elders, and ancestors. The main goal of Confucianism is bettering individuals and society. Its primary objectives are to educate people to be self-motivated and self-controlled, in the belief that everyone should be responsible for creating a harmonious society. Bo believes people in Purpleshire would benefit from Confucian wisdom, but China is too far away for most people to relate to its culture and beliefs, and there is no use trying to educate people who are just not interested in learning.

The business runs smoothly and Bo's father and her sister Matilda are always there when extra help is needed or when Bo wants to spend time with Alys.

Bo involves Matilda in day-to-day matters with regard to the shop and they usually figure out the best way forward together.

People trust Bo, because they know she has a kind heart, makes business-savvy decisions and acts in everyone's interest. Expanding the shop meant she could bring on two new full-time employees – one of them being cousin Mary - and also add value to the community.

Sometimes tensions and conflict arise, but the employees usually sort out their differences behind closed doors. Bo steps in if needed, but that hardly happens as everyone knows their place.

> ## "
> THE GOOD MANAGER MUST ACCEPT THE INDIVIDUAL'S STYLE OF LIFE AND ACCOMMODATE TO IT. [C-1, P. 221]
> "

TEAMS

The shop in Purpleton is a typical example of a 2nd (Purple) stage business. It has been family-owned and run for generations and will hopefully continue being part of the social fabric in generations to come.

The most important Purple ambition is to ensure the survival of what has been built. In the team it is not so much about individuals, rather the collective and that everyone is looked after.

The organically grown order within this system ensures that everyone has a role with specific tasks, some of which are so specific they can only be carried out by certain people. Men in the shop do more of the physical work and women more of the

service and decorations. These are classic roles and the way it has always been done. There is no need to talk about equality.

All of the employees look up to Bo. As mentioned, they always accept her decisions even if they disagree at times. Everyone enjoys their work and mornings there feel like family time. One can understand their pride for working in one of the oldest commercial establishments in Purpleshire, because so many people depend on it.

On the 2nd (Purple) stage, the focus is clearly on the group. If the business environment changes, the team faces challenges together. If an outside threat comes up, like when Starbucks was looking to open a garden café, the entire community comes together to fight it off.

In remote regions like the Amazon, people still live in 2nd (Purple) stage tribes, but 3rd (Red) stage capitalism and 4th (Blue) stage industrial 'progress' are forcing healthy Purple communities to change.

However, it is part of our human DNA and upbringing to want to be part of a group. It is something humans have been doing for over 40,000 years, as reflected in traditions, festivals and rituals across the globe.

PLANNING AND STEERING

We all seek some kind of stability, something a company can provide. In Bo's case she has grown into the natural order of the business, like so many generations before her.

Generally, Bo feels very comfortable in her role and accepts the duties that come with it. She truly enjoys being needed even though it means putting her own needs on the back burner from time to time. As a mother she is used to that.

The bigger questions relating to the future of the business will always be discussed by the family, usually over Sunday lunch when everyone comes together. Many relatives have an interest in the business so a healthy level of consensus is needed.

ORGANISATIONS

More otfen than not, Purple organisations don't seek to grow but to keep the status quo. Bo's store, like most Purple businesses, has fewer than 15 employees. It is your typical home-grown micro to small enterprise.

Their usual customers comprise of individuals and other small companies. The shop is very much part of the local community and offers a lot of local fare from farm produce to art work to packs of shins.

Employees are a vital part of the company but everyone knows Bo is the boss and she can be fierce. The wellbeing and security of employees is as important to her as ensuring continuation of the business.

They all understand the need to adhere to economic realities.

The company actively supports its members whenever possible. For example, it isn't unusual for 2nd (Purple) stage businesses to provide loans or some other help when employees are struggling. People are aware of each other's life circumstances. In return, they are very dedicated to the business and often put their personal interests back.

> ## "
> IT IS ABOUT PEOPLE AND THEIR DEPENDENCE ON ONE ANOTHER. EVERYONE PLAYS A ROLE IN THE COMMUNITY AND THAT IS ALSO REFLECTED IN BUSINESS.
> "
>
> HARTMUT WIEHLE
> MD @ VALUES 4 CHANGE

AUTHOR'S COMMENT:
There are still some Purple pockets in Africa, South America and Asia, often found in rural communities where everyone knows each other and people are connected in more than one way. For example, Alex used to be married to the pub owner, whose father works in the same shop as Louis, a friend her father met when they both started volunteering in the local wildlife support group before she was born. The group meets in the pub once every two weeks and most of the food comes from the shop.

There is still a lot of healthy Purple out there. However, we have seen unhealthy developments with aggressive tribes forming recently, for example on the back of football clubs, nationalistic groups turning hostile or, for that matter, any group of people seeing outsiders as a threat without reason.

How many feuds are still raging today for which no one recalls the origin or cause? We all share 2nd (Purple) stage and thus have more that unites than separates us. Let's keep an open mind and an open heart.

MARKETS

There are no more 2nd (Purple) stage countries left in the world. 3rd (Red) stage capitalism and/or 4th level (Blue) politics have made sure of that.

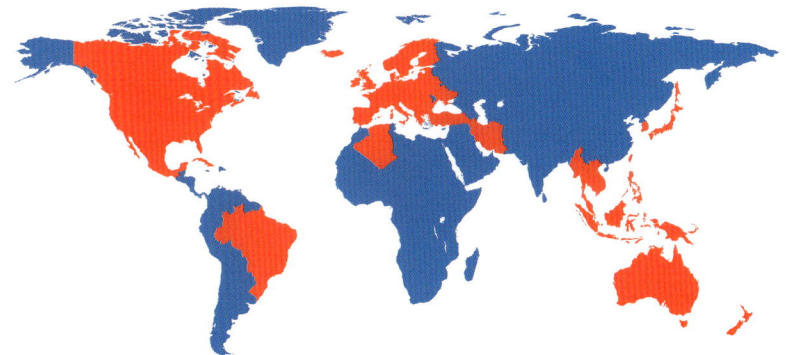

> ## "
> ## THE EGOCENTRIC EXISTENTIAL STATE EMERGES FROM LIVING IN THE TRIBALISTIC WAY WHERE YOU ARE HEMMED IN BY TOTEMS AND TABOOS. [C-1, P236] "

LIMITATIONS AND GROWTH INTO NEXT LEVELS

The 1st (Beige) stage is all about survival. The 2nd (Purple) stage already provides some stability, as long as you are a valued member of the group. However, it is very easy for us humans to become too comfortable. Everything can be kept the way it has always been, no matter what. After all, two universal human characteristics are that:

- **we are reluctant to change and**

- **we are likely to abuse power if it serves us (e.g. to avoid change).**

So it is natural that elders in tribal hierarchies should come up with stories, anecdotes and possibly superstitions to justify their actions or the lack of them. Such techniques can be used to avoid changes. Ultimately, who can argue with traditions that are centuries old? People are easily worried when traditional practices are being questioned.

Open questions can create so much fear that people might even turn against those who challenge the status-quo and its practices.

There are other reasons why 2nd level Purple systems reach their limits. They grow too large and need another form of governance. This might also have to do with running out of land or territory.

At the same time you have 3rd level (Purple) characters, like your typical youngsters, who are full of energy, want to explore, test boundaries and turn the 2nd level Purple world on its head. Something has to give and people will need to move on.

The characteristics of 2nd (Purple) stage markets look as follows:

"OUR COMMUNITY IS OUR MARKET."

POLITICAL

- Bigger matters are managed by the elders
- Groups of elders manage the different social topics
- Parents or elders look after younger ones (Paternalistic and maternalistic leadership)

ECONOMIC

- Many small enterprises
- People depend on each other
- People still exchange goods (vs money)

SOCIAL

- People are generally comfortable and focus on local matters
- Community is important and people look out for each other
- Filial piety (care for one's parents)

TECHNOLOGICAL

- Slow innovation; mainly driven by individuals and business
- Generates lots of data (but doesn't make 'bigger' sense of it)
- Credit cards are not widely accepted
- Too much tech advancement might be looked at suspiciously

ENVIRONMENTAL

- Not fully aware because one is part of the local ecosystem
- People live locally and look after their environment

LEGAL

- Officially – in today's world there might be 4th (Blue) stage laws because every bit of land is under some national jurisdiction. However, laws might be managed more locally. For example, when a local policeman knows people and will try to solve problems directly
- No police; the parties involved sort it out (elder might step in as judge)
- Many interpersonal topics are sorted out directly between the parties

3rd STAGE
RED: I WANT TO BREAK FREE

BE IT MODERN CONQUERORS DRIVEN BY PERSONAL GAIN, POWER
OR INDEPENDENCE - SOMETIMES AT ANY COST - OR PEOPLE
SEEKING A CHANGING AND STIMULATING WORK ENVIRONMENT,
SOME MIGHT VIEW LIFE AS CHAOTIC.

AT THIS LEVEL, INDIVIDUALS ARE SELF-MOTIVATED AND ONLY
COLLABORATE IF THERE IS A PERSONAL INTEREST/BENEFIT.
THIS COULD BE RAPID GROWTH, BALANCING INDIVIDUAL NEEDS
AGAINST PERFORMANCE, OR OPERATING IN MARKETS WITH
GROWTH POTENTIAL.

TYPICAL GROWTH MARKETS INCLUDE BRAZIL, RUSSIA, VIETNAM,
PARAGUAY OR THE PHILIPPINES, WHERE EVERYTHING IS
POSSIBLE. WITH AN ENDLESS RANGE OF TECH DEVELOPING AT
AN UNPRECEDENTED SPEED, MANY INDUSTRIES FIT INTO THIS
ZONE OF INFINITE POSSIBILITIES – THINK FINTECH, BLOCKCHAIN,
ARTIFICIAL INTELLIGENCE (AI), VIRTUAL REALITY (VR), ETC.

"

WHEN READINESS FOR CHANGE OCCURS, IT TRIGGERS MAN'S INSIGHT INTO HIS EXISTENCE AS AN INDIVIDUAL BEING — AS BEING SEPARATE AND DISTINCT FROM OTHER BEINGS. NOW HE IS NOT ONE-WITH-ALL, FOR HE IS ALONE, ALONE STRUGGLING FOR HIS SURVIVAL AGAINST THE 'DRACONIC' FORCES OF THE UNIVERSE. [C-1, P. 223] "

CONAN'S ARENA

Meet Conan, just back in the city after a weekend in Lilaton with his family. It's always nice to visit Purpleshire. The forests and meadows are so lush at this time of year, great for a hike or deep reflection. It must be one of the most idyllic places on earth. After years away, Conan still knows most people there. They all actively support each other, whether that is needed or not. To Conan going there is a bit like time-travelling, because nothing seems to change. It brings him back to fond childhood memories of being at one with the world.

However, Conan is always happy to be back in the city. It's buzzing and full of opportunities. He lives in Glamden, a very sought-after part of town that is as colourful as life itself. He rents out a small flat in one of the trendiest streets. Glamden is known for its music scene, art galleries and prestigious restaurants. Many places are so popular that there are long queues – the price to pay for having famous people in your area. A few ventures open up, give it their all, but do not make it. On the plus side, it's vibrant and there's always a new venue to discover. When Conan's friend visited the other day, he googled evening events in Glamden on that Friday night and got over 300 hits; there's no boredom in a place like this. He's spoilt for choice.

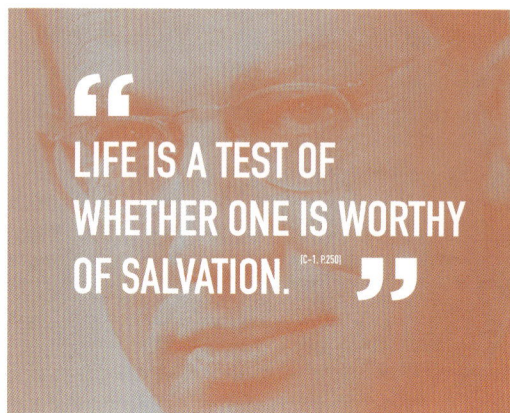

> **" LIFE IS A TEST OF WHETHER ONE IS WORTHY OF SALVATION. "** (C-1, P.250)

This is not only true of his personal life but also extends to his business. Conan founded a FinTech startup with a friend a few years back. It's been a roller coaster and the company constantly seems to have to adapt and change. The city is brilliant for this, with so many networking events and new people to meet. For example, Conan and his co-founder had problems with the product-customer fit in the beginning. There was no money to bring in a consultant and, clouded by bias for their own clever creations, they often fell into the trap of not being able to come up with other practical ideas for the startup. Luckily, they went to a business event one evening, shared their challenges with a few people over drinks and nibbles and, by the early hours, they had a solution.

Now that they're beginning to create traction, they're looking into further events and professional help to master the product-market fit. Nothing like this could ever happen in Lilaton.

Another advantage to the city is the abundance of pretty women. As you can imagine, a district like this attracts the right kind of desirable goddesses. Not that this is currently Conan's concern - he's found a gorgeous match of his own. Cleo is everything a man could dream of: she has a sexy figure, knows how to dress and always makes sure she looks good. Conan loves that she makes heads turn; just the kind of woman he wants at his side. That his girl sings in a band starting to make a name for itself is the icing on the cake. This means less queuing and a growing number of VIP tickets on offer. Bring on the good life!

Conan still has enough helpful Purple in him to avoid losing sight of who he is. Living a cool life isn't always easy, but he's clear about what motivates him. Conan is a firm believer in the power of self - self love, self esteem, self confidence, self knowledge and self realisation - and leveraging his drive to achieve his goals. After attending a recent self-development workshop, he stuck his core drivers (values) on the fridge:

A HEALTHY EGO

STRENGTH

DETERMINATION

POWER

COURAGE

HONOUR

Conan sees a lot of positive aspects in his 3rd (Red) life, and they certainly outweigh the negatives:

- **TRYING OUT NEW IDEAS;**

- **CHALLENGING THE STATUS QUO AND TAKING INITIATIVE;**

- **BEING DETERMINED TO FIND ONE'S WAY;**

- **LOOKING AFTER ONESELF;**

- **SPACE FOR RISK TAKING.**

He also knows there are things that aren't so good and that he's sad to see developing in his younger brother Charlie:

- **MANIPULATING PEOPLE OR SITUATIONS TO GET ONE'S WAY;**

- **NOT GIVING OTHERS THE TIME OR SPACE TO EXPRESS THEMSELVES;**

- **CONSTANTLY TRYING OUT NEW THINGS;**

- **LEADING WITH FEAR;**

- **BEING ERRATIC AND UNPREDICTABLE.**

Big cities attract a lot of folk who want to make it in the world. Life there is more diverse, happens at a faster pace and offers more opportunities. Conan remembers the quote he read in a bar on the day he arrived:

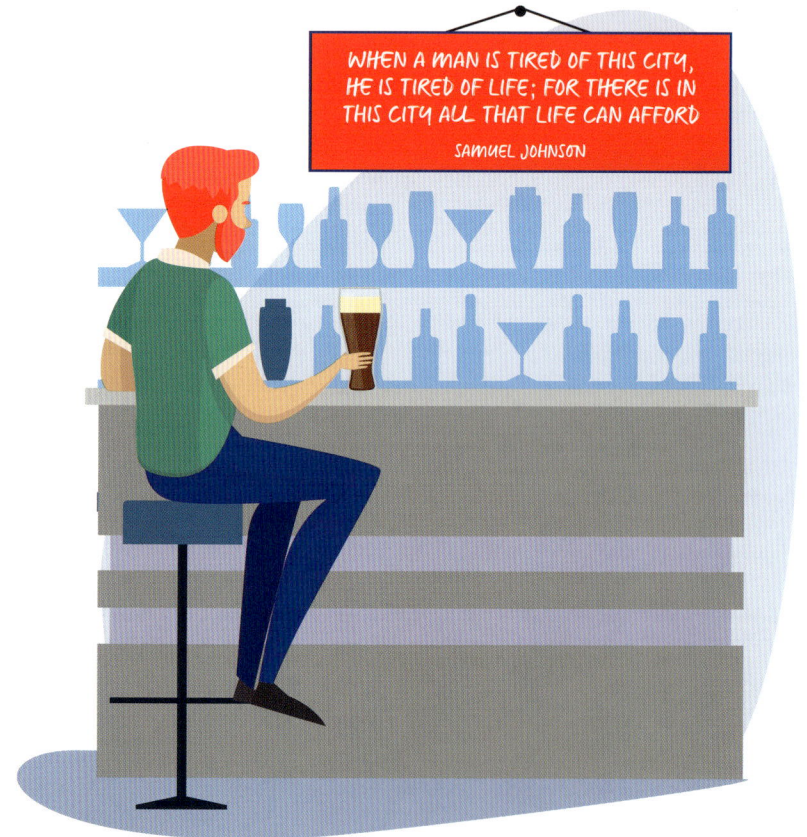

> WHEN A MAN IS TIRED OF THIS CITY, HE IS TIRED OF LIFE; FOR THERE IS IN THIS CITY ALL THAT LIFE CAN AFFORD
>
> SAMUEL JOHNSON

INDIVIDUALS

This vibrant metropolis reflects what Conan expected from life after Lilaton.

But it isn't all better in the city. He has a small flat, about the size of his bedroom back 'home', yet people are impressed when they hear his address. He hardly invites friends anyway. It's not that he doesn't want to, but it is tiny, especially with someone of his frame.

Six feet tall and built like an athlete, Conan may not be as handsome as actor Joe Keery, but he looks more of a man, with his natural charisma and striking appearance. The latter represents a clear advantage if you love extreme sports and winning.

Conan lives for challenging himself and stretching boundaries. He started off with BMX racing when he was young, then Thai boxing followed when he visited Thailand as a child. While his parents were busy doing missionary work, he had lots of time and really got into the national sport, which also helped him channel his energy.

Over the years he tried out all kinds of extreme activities - free solo climbing in the Dolomites, ice climbing on the Matanuska Glacier, and even volcano surfing on Mount Yasur in Vanuatu. Despite the protective gear such as jump suits and goggles, there is a very real danger of getting badly cut, breathing in poisonous gases, or being burnt by splattering molten lava. Conan loves challenging his fears.

One of his childhood heroes was the daredevil Evel Knievel. Nowadays, he follows other adventurers, all of whom push the boundaries of what is perceived as being possible – think Alex Honnold, Will Gadd and the like.

However, all these activities require time and travelling to faraway places, which is hardly conceivable when you run a serious startup business. Conan's main sport is therefore Thai boxing, which he can practise in the city. It is fast, ferocious and as tough as it gets. When Conan started off, Thai boxing consisted mainly of kicks, knee strikes, clinches and simple punching techniques. The range of traditional Muay Thai (Chok) punches was limited. But things have changed and, with his stature, Conan can combine Muay Thai with western boxing styles to his advantage. [3-1].

It isn't always fun and can be painful – he recently hurt himself badly. It happened while practising his spinning back fist, an advanced punching technique and quite a stagy move. Conan stepped right with his left leg, then lifted his right leg and span around on his left with the right arm fully extended. When he realised that he was about to hit his sparring partner with the back of his hand and knuckles, he put all his strength into the rotation, but then slipped and managed to pull some ligaments in his hip. Conan loves this punch; its movements and motions are unlike any other and his opponent would have come crashing down if he'd made contact.

Even when watching films with Cleo he's into action-packed adventures. They both enjoy superhero movies and their all-time favourites are Indiana Jones, Peter Quill (*Guardians of the Galaxy*) and Jordan Belfort (*The Wolf of Wall Street*).

So many things to do, so little time. Conan spends most of his waking hours in the shared workspace driving his startup forward. He'd tried working at a corporate bank in the beginning, but he soon felt like a zombie, stuck in a humongous machine full of bureaucratic cogwheels; it wasn't for him. So he co-founded an innovative startup to revolutionise the world of retail banking and personal finance – the one he'd just come from. It was time to shake things up and tear down the establishment. No legacy systems, outdated mindsets or restrictions, just the cloud, fresh thinking, radical ideas and blockchain-based services.

Conan is driven by action, independence, power and making things happen. He is motivated as follows:

PURPOSE
Personal success
Winning
Seizing opportunities

MASTERY
Gaining results
Continuous drive
Rising to challenges

AUTONOMY
Personal freedom
Space to conquer
Setting high targets

He believes in his capacity to take on an entire industry and come out victorious. And why not? The world's most famous inventors are household names. Years from now, he wants to be mentioned in the same sentence as Steve Jobs, Elon Musk and Jack Dorsey. As the Nike slogan goes, 'Just do it'.

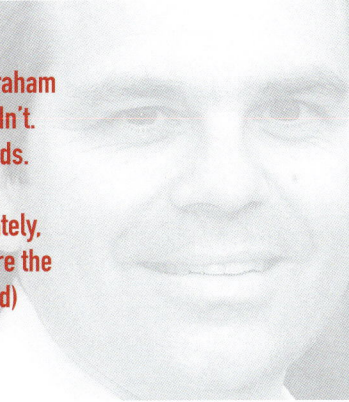

BROTHERS IN ARMS

Conan started dreaming big when he was young. He would spend days with his brother Charlie following the great explorers: Alexander the Great, Xuanzang, Ibn Battuta and Marco Polo. He and Charlie shared a lot of great times. They still agree on many things today; for example, that men aren't equal, we all make our own luck, capitalism is good, no need to feel guilty if you're at the top, and that there are three kinds of people:

1. Strong, far-seeing and chosen

2. Motivated, but short-sighted

3. Inherently weak and lazy who need guidance. [C-1, p.233]

BROTHERS APART

The two brothers left Lilaton around the same year, but since then their lives have gone off into very different directions. Charlie is in and out of jobs. He doesn't seem to understand that building a venture takes time and effort, and he keeps blaming others for his misfortunes. There's always some financial scheme that he asks Conan to invest into. Charlie only appears when he wants something. Cleo nicknamed him 'Wiifm', which is short for 'What's in it for me?'

They had a big falling out over the way Charlie treated and used some people. He took advantage of individuals within Conan's circle, which caused lots of problems. Conan tried to confront his brother, but he would bend the truth to his convenience and was so erratic there was no reasoning with him. Charlie is even braver and more daring than Conan. It's as if he lacked fear or guilt. The other difference is that there's often some level of aggression, impulsiveness, unpredictability and dominance. Someone always seems to get hurt and yet Charlie expects to be admired. But it's more a case of him admiring himself.

Conan has learnt about the 'Icarus paradox' which shows that originality, self-drive and confidence can bring about enormous success, while ignorance and pride can generate disaster. [3-2] This ancient wisdom applies just as well to modern culture, especially to the actions of large corporations – consider CEO Ken Lay at Enron. A number of recent "studies on corporate decline point to the fact that organizations tend to get trapped in their previous success patterns and lose their flexibility to change and adapt (the so-called "success breeds failure" phenomenon)." [3-3] Conan believes business has seen more than its fair share of overweening pride and he wouldn't add to that.

All this led to the two brothers drifting apart. Conan often thought about why they'd become so different. It might be that he always seeks to learn and develop himself, whereas brother 'Mr Me & Now' expects immediate rewards without putting in the work.

A few years ago, Conan attended a course on self-awareness that helped him identify what values matter to him, why he believes in them and how to translate these into behaviours. He learnt that values are what we hold dear and strive for. They directly influence our behaviours and decisions. Being clear about important values makes Conan's life easier. Realising that his startup is currently more of a priority than his family in many ways makes it a breeze to decide whether to catch up with work at the weekend or go back to Lilaton. Obviously the world isn't black and white, but his values help him to prioritise his life without feeling guilty.

When our values connect with the world as we see it, they shape our belief system, our attitudes or part of our mindset. This is about how we believe things should be and what's important.

Here are 2 excerpts from his course notes:

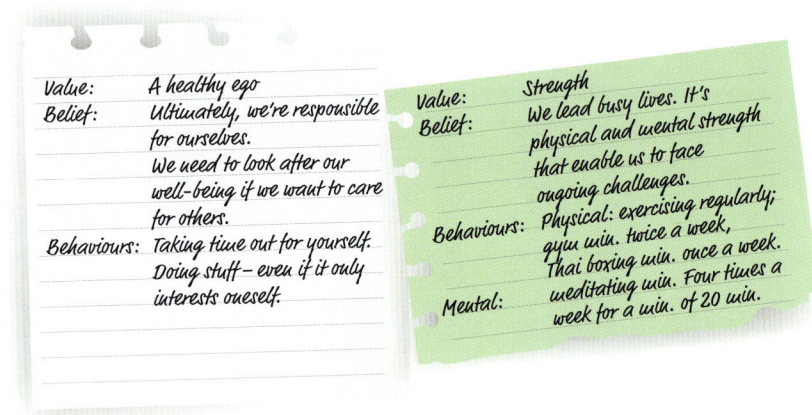

Value:	A healthy ego
Belief:	Ultimately, we're responsible for ourselves. We need to look after our well-being if we want to care for others.
Behaviours:	Taking time out for yourself. Doing stuff – even if it only interests oneself.

Value:	Strength
Belief:	We lead busy lives. It's physical and mental strength that enable us to face ongoing challenges.
Behaviours:	Physical: exercising regularly; gym min. twice a week, Thai boxing min. once a week.
Mental:	meditating min. Four times a week for a min. of 20 min.

Conan noticed how his values had evolved over time through social and personal changes. For example, as a young man adventurism was more appealing than health, but health has now become one of his top five priorities, perhaps due to recent events. He gained in clarity and awareness thanks to these exercises. Being able to link a situation with a value does accelerate decision-making.

To stay grounded, Conan also encourages people to give him feedback to help him understand how he comes across. This has enhanced his self-awareness and allows him to learn and to adjust his behaviour when needed.

LEADERSHIP

Conan gets a lot of respect from his teammates. His co-founder is in charge of software development while Conan and his two teams look after everything else. Every day is different. Running a startup means life throws stuff at you and sometimes you just have to wing it. Conan is a formidable salesman and adept at handling emergencies. He always likens the emotional roller coaster of a startup to being pregnant, because one minute everything is great and the next you can be down and frustrated.

Everybody respects Conan for who he is and what he wants to achieve. He has a clear hierarchical structure in his head. His leadership style could be classified as opportunistic, self-oriented, energetic, ambitious and driven. He has endless energy, is quick at developing ideas further, demonstrates a high level of enthusiasm and is fantastic at responding to new client needs. Conan is direct and sometimes labelled as authoritarian, which he doesn't think is a bad thing when people need direction and jobs have to get done. It does help that he can express what's important to him and how that relates to his actions. It seems his guys can figure out what is mission critical and get on with it. He is very authentic, and this being the most crucial aspect of leadership goes a long way.

While Conan enjoys being in charge and deciding what he will work on, it also makes life so much more exciting not knowing what's around the corner. Bring it on!

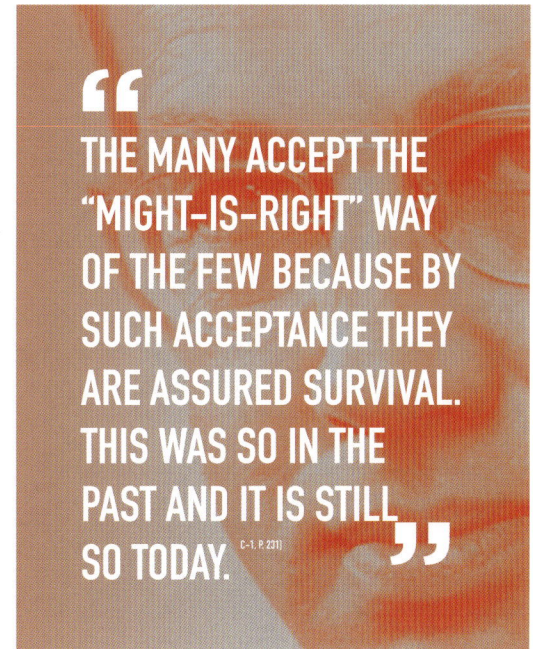

> " THE MANY ACCEPT THE "MIGHT–IS–RIGHT" WAY OF THE FEW BECAUSE BY SUCH ACCEPTANCE THEY ARE ASSURED SURVIVAL. THIS WAS SO IN THE PAST AND IT IS STILL SO TODAY. (C–1, P. 231) "

TEAMS

As Homer once said "Too many kings can ruin an army."

Everybody knows who's in charge and the two founders try hard not to step onto each other's toes. Neither of them is interested in power plays as they haven't brought the business to an esteemed level yet.

Team members have a rough idea of their responsibilities although one can never be sure. A lot of the work is unpredictable, work areas change and morph into one another. Also, everything happens so fast sometimes. Conan has a Nike poster hanging above his chair – for whatever reason, a bigger chair than anybody else's. The poster reads, 'Just do it' in large letters, a slogan that Conan regularly declares as applying to their company too. He likes to keep them on their toes, no rest for the wicked, but there is method in the madness. Operating in a competitive environment encourages people to outperform each other, to achieve more. The winners get more attention and consequently more (important) responsibilities.

Team members are busy most of the time. Nobody wants to be seen as having nothing to do. There's often something to figure out and if not, you'll look for work or ask colleagues if they need help. Even worse is making mistakes that show up in the open. Who's to blame and shame?

The office usually has a buzz to it and an incredible atmosphere. Conan refers to 'his' people as the 'red gang' and they're a force to be reckoned with, especially when they hit the bar for after-work drinks. Work hard, play hard.

PLANNING AND STEERING

There is little planning. The business is much too unpredictable and needs to be able to react quickly.

The objective is to grow the customer base and develop a model with regular turnover. Cashflow is king and an Excel spreadsheet covers the basics. The two founders have a strong gut feel about where they want to go.

They're clearly in charge and will steer people heading in the wrong direction or when a task requires attention.

> " I KNOW NOT WHAT THE FUTURE HOLDS, BUT I KNOW WHO HOLDS THE FUTURE. "
>
> HOMER, GREEK AUTHOR

> " A RED ORGANISATION IS OFTEN LIKE A SPEEDBOAT – AGILE, FAST AND IN IT TO WIN IT. "
>
> KEVIN MONSERRAT, FOUNDER @ CONSILIENCE VENTURES

ORGANISATIONS

As with Bo's venture back in Purpleshire, there are few written rules or guidelines. Conan's objective is to prove its business model and make everyone involved rich and powerful.

Graves once said "Life is a jungle – one god-damned great big jungle. It is survival of the fittest and that is all." [C-1, P.228]

Team members are all in it for one or more of the following reasons:

- Some want to make a difference. They're driven by the idea that they can be part of a revolution in banking; 'tearing down the wall.' You should see their Pink Floyd poster with bank names covered with darts.

- Others consider this cutting-edge technology and its application as a great opportunity to develop their skill set. They'll be highly sought after in only a few months, no matter what.

- A few have a stake in the business and want to see it fly, purely for financial reasons.

So, like the two founders, they're all in it for themselves although they share the same goals: reaching unchartered waters, monetary rewards and glory. It feels similar to being conquerors again.

AUTHOR'S COMMENT:
The ethos of capitalism is firmly rooted in this level. Free capitalism affords commercial freedom, consumer choice and economic growth. It is relentless, limitless, driven by greed and has an insatiable appetite. Its main objectives are survival, profit and power. There's no consideration of people's wellbeing, nature or the planet. For example, many of today's standardised food production practices are harmful to people and the planet, but they increase efficiency or profit margins.

It is too often a win–lose attitude.

MARKETS

Conan has always been fascinated by the US and how an entire continent was conquered by people with entrepreneurial spirit and hunger for the unknown. America has developed further in a lot of ways since then, but, when it comes to business, the entrepreneurial can-do attitude remains. Conan sees the American dream and a healthy appetite for risk as two characteristics deeply rooted in US history; cultural aspects that still shine through today. For example, US investors are much more willing to back risky startups than fully fledged business plans. This attitude coupled with a market of three hundred million consumers is a powerful combination.

Conan would be intrigued to find out what it's like setting up a company in a Red country. Maybe he will one day, you never know!

However, there's no need to venture abroad. There are plenty of industries here still in their early days – renewable energy, cybersecurity, biotechnology, AI and VR to name just a few. Conan could have started in any of those, but it was FinTech that he chose as he'd had first-hand experience with the financial industry's outdated ways of working.

LIMITATIONS AND GROWTH INTO NEXT LEVELS

The 1st (Beige) stage is all about maximising safety in the state of being. The 2nd (Purple) stage provides not only a sense of belonging, but also a caring community. The 3rd (Red) stage breaks out of the traditional mould – it's the young and restless, like Conan, looking for new shores.

Charlie's experience, however, proves that you cannot always pursue your own interests alone. We can all tell when people take liberties and overstep the mark. We then get wary and push back. As with capitalism, the ego can have an endless hunger but there have to be limits somewhere. "A bit of discipline has never harmed anyone" as Doc keeps telling Conan (you'll meet her in the next chapter).

Furthermore, as in any setup, having too many red chiefs will eventually cause confusion; 'too many cooks...' Conan knows that his startup will have to

become an 'organisation' when it grows beyond 30 people. The two founders won't be able to directly manage such large numbers. Logically, functions and team leaders will need to be created and the startup will turn into a scaleup.

There will always be some who take advantage of capitalism (a truly Red concept) for their personal benefit. If there are no boundaries, they'll exploit the hell out of whatever they can. Consequently, rules, standards and limits have to be introduced moving to the next level; everything has its limits.

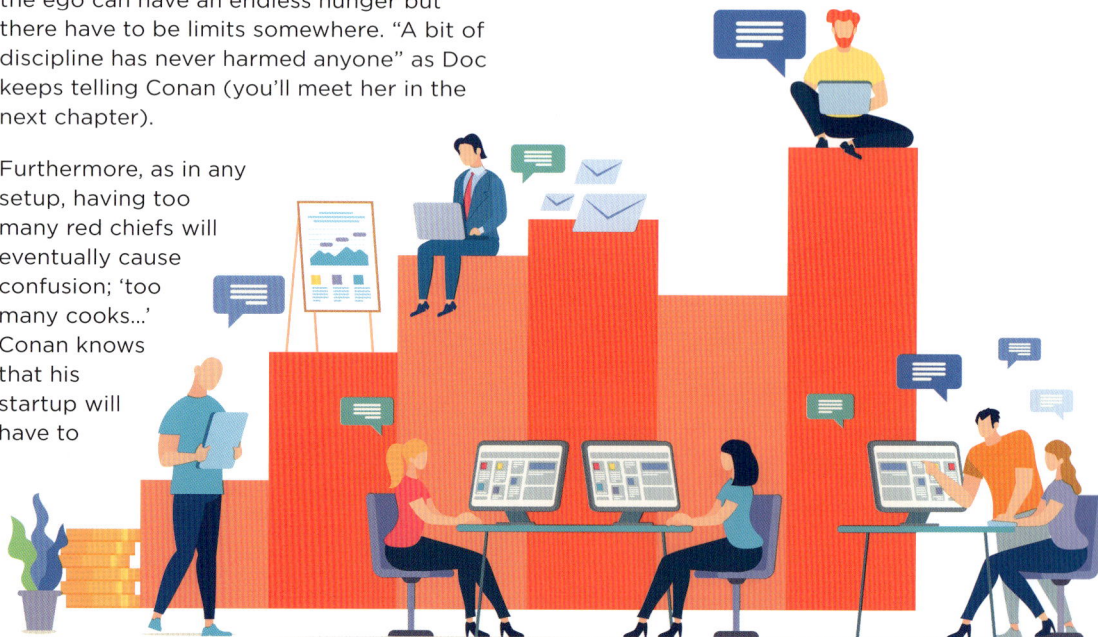

The characteristics of 3rd (Red) stage markets are as follows:

'MARKETS ARE PURE GROWTH OPPORTUNITIES'

POLITICAL

- Power-driven; possible 'dictatorships'
- Money talks
- Corruption is possible

ECONOMIC

- Growing fast and unpredictably
- Hardly any entry barriers
- Possible to shape opportunities

SOCIAL

- Social inequality; often a small core of wealthy people
- Individualistic culture; many 'work to live'
- Success matters; 'Greed is good'
- Hard work = long hours; well-being often overlooked

TECHNOLOGICAL

- Developing / exploring new opportunities
- Lack of standards and fast pace of change
- Unpredictable

ENVIRONMENTAL

- Exploitative 'nature'
- Nature not protected
- Natural resources are there for the taking

LEGAL

- 'Flexible'
- Not many rules
- The stronger person is right

4th STAGE

BLUE: STABILITY AND ORDER

THIS LEVEL SUITS GROUP-ORIENTED, LOYAL PEOPLE WHO SEE THEMSELVES AS PART OF A WIDER CLUSTER, WHO LOOK FOR CLARITY, STABILITY AND A FORMALISED WAY OF MAINTAINING THEIR AND SOCIETY'S WAY OF LIFE.

FORMAL RULES AND GUIDELINES GOVERN WAYS OF WORKING, PEOPLE ARE LOYAL TO EACH OTHER, WORK WITHIN THEIR REMIT AND KEEP IT ALL WELL BALANCED.

A POPULAR LEVEL WITH LARGER ORGANISATIONS, ITS CLEAR HIERARCHIES, ROLE DESCRIPTIONS AND DOCUMENTED WORKFLOWS. PROCESS AND COMPLIANCE ARE ESSENTIAL. TYPICAL EXAMPLES INCLUDE J.P. MORGAN CHASE, BANK OF AMERICA / CHINA, SHELL, AXA, MUNICH RE, ETC.

YOU'LL FIND IT IN COUNTRIES LIKE THE UK, JAPAN, FRANCE OR GERMANY – MATURE, HIGHLY REGULATED MARKETS WITH LOW GROWTH RATES AND LARGE NUMBERS OF INSTITUTIONS. IT'S LIKELY TO BE A DEMOCRACY AND TO HAVE MARKETS MIXING POLITICS WITH GOVERNANCE, SUCH AS THE FINANCIAL, INSURANCE AND UTILITIES SECTORS.

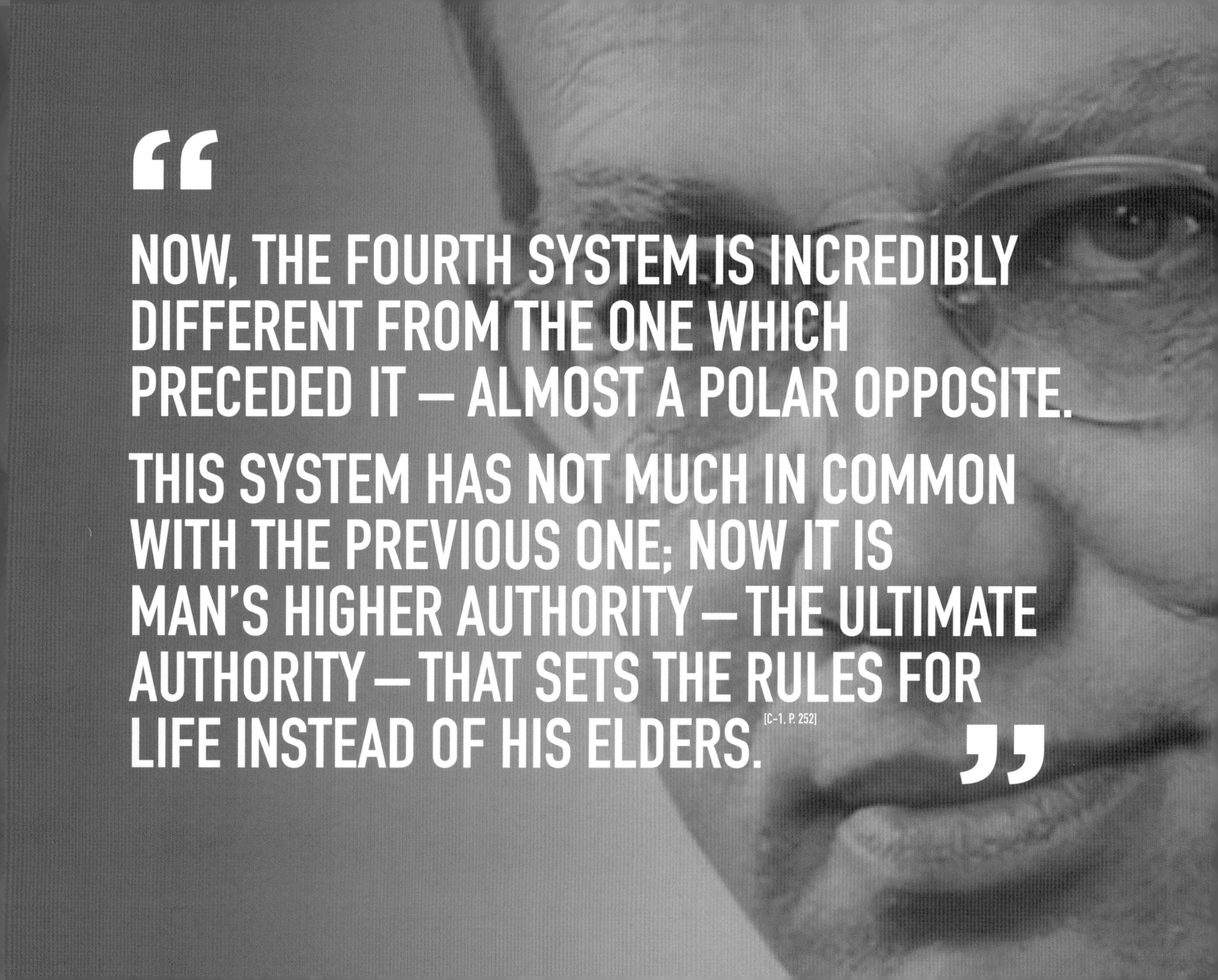

"

NOW, THE FOURTH SYSTEM IS INCREDIBLY DIFFERENT FROM THE ONE WHICH PRECEDED IT — ALMOST A POLAR OPPOSITE.

THIS SYSTEM HAS NOT MUCH IN COMMON WITH THE PREVIOUS ONE; NOW IT IS MAN'S HIGHER AUTHORITY — THE ULTIMATE AUTHORITY — THAT SETS THE RULES FOR LIFE INSTEAD OF HIS ELDERS. [C-1, P. 252]

"

DOC'S ENVIRONMENT

Here we are, at the Research Campus (the RC) on the south side of the university grounds. The view couldn't be more different from what we've seen so far. Purpleshire is all wild and natural – even houses don't have straight lines. Glamden is more structured, but still chaotic in that a lot goes on – traffic, noise, lights, people everywhere. It's a typical urban jungle. The RC, on the other hand, is relatively new and looks very different – all roads and paths are logically arranged, with clear lines, colour coding and signposting everywhere.

This is where we get to meet Dr Delta Descartes. She doesn't like her first name so everyone calls her Doc. Her parents were both scientists; her dad was an expert in genetics. In scientific notation, delta signifies change, and being the fourth letter of the Greek alphabet, it also means 'born fourth'. At this point, you've guessed that she's the fourth child.

Anyway, Doc is just pulling into her designated parking slot with her electric storm blue Toyota Prius Gen 3. It isn't her first Prius and she has got used to the model. She's impressed that Toyota has improved fuel economy by 10% with each successive generation. With rising fuel prices, this is a plus for Doc. Today's Prius is also a dependable vehicle and features among the most reliable cars rated every year.

Doc uses it mainly for her 15.5-km commute from her home in Qualorder Residential Park, a new contemporary development set in the suburbs of the nearest town and boasting a range of three and four-bedroom dwellings. She loves the 110 sqm residence that she shares with her husband Dan and their ten year-old daughter Camilla. Dan is also happy with their house, because he managed to secure a 25-year mortgage at a very reasonable fixed rate. That should come as no surprise as he's an accountant for one of the big national accountancy firms

where he started his career, obtaining his AAT accounting certificate and bookkeeping diploma. The company treats him well and they've just signed off his ACCA, a globally recognised accountancy qualification. It's a badge of quality and professionalism certifying that Dan's knowledge and skills are of the highest standard.

Doc is also about to specialise further. She's a research scientist and team lead working on a new treatment for pain relief. The medication is tailored to an individual's genetic make-up. Doc and her staff use computer simulations to develop bespoke opioids that only become active at sites affected by injury or inflammation. The objective is to increase effectiveness while avoiding side effects and addiction.

> " TO ATTAIN SAFETY AND SECURITY, HE SEEKS TO CREATE AN ORDERLY, PREDICTABLE, STABLE, UNCHANGING WORLD – ONE IN WHICH THE UNEXPECTED DOES NOT HAPPEN. [C-1, 253] "

Currently, she is working with a test group of 30 participants for a three-year clinical trial. These are all individuals suffering from hip injuries. One person dropped out at the last minute and Doc was annoyed about how unreliable some people are. That day she spoke to her uncle from Wantabe. He recommended she contact Conan who was at home following a silly sports accident. Well, it wasn't the accident that was silly, but the sports, he said. It was quite a surprise when Conan's test results came back ticking all the right boxes.

He's quite a charismatic guy and reminds her of someone she nearly dated during her first semester at university, back when she was quite wild and lively. Conan, with his impulsive persona, big red car and youthful charm, brought back memories of the good old days. It was nice to have someone from Purpleshire in the group.

Just to be clear, strict procedures exist to avoid personal relationships influencing the results, and it's all above board.

Doc is based at the RC but she's hired by a pharmaceutical corporation. The setup is complicated because she works in a matrix; her boss, who has disciplinary responsibility, is based at PharmaCorp LLC HQ and the RC's Head of Research at the RC is her functional boss. The latter is part of the faculty of science, which belongs to the university. The institution and PharmaCorp together employ more than 10,000 staff and have devised their 'one way' of doing things, which is consigned in lots of standards, procedures and manuals. You may believe there's only one right way, yet if others refer to different details developed in various parts of the world and have their own 'one right way', [C-1, p.257] then confusion can arise. She wonders whose is the 'right way' anyway. Conflicts were more frequent in the beginning but Doc got to understand that some issues can be pre-empted. Most steps and criteria are documented, easily accessible and therefore can be managed. It's only when personal interests and interpretations come into play that things can get complicated. As Doc knows, we can't have it all and life does have its limitations. All in all, this arrangement allows her to engage in truly innovative research while leading a normal life.

Doc's world is complicated enough as it is, although the Descartes have an efficient setup.

They're involved in one of the national political parties, which generates a lot of work. Dan is the regional bookkeeper. Despite an endless list of legal procedures to consider, they both see their role as part of their civic duty. They strongly believe in the power of democracy and value local, independent units of political institutions. They view safety, security and stability as universal drivers. It's all too easy to fall back into a world led by power and fear, which ultimately brings about instability, unpredictability and chaos. As the old saying goes "He who sleeps in democracy awakes in tyranny."

Doc's also engaged in her local school and has responsibility for educational standards. She likes the idea that every child has the same starting point and an equal chance to progress in the world.

AUTHOR'S COMMENT:
A sense of duty is a professional or ethical obligation. For example, this value translates to a person carrying out a job or task for which s/he feels responsible. In a 4th (Blue) stage environment, a general sense of duty can be expected – people will endeavour to fulfil tasks they've taken on or been assigned to.

Doc is very clear that her world has many positive aspects worth safeguarding:

- **MANIFOLD UNITS AND ROLES GUARANTEE A BALANCE TO SERVE ALL;**

- **JUSTICE IS HIGHLY VALUED AND PROTECTED;**

- **ROLES, TITLES, STRUCTURES, HIERARCHIES AND PROCESSES PROVIDE CLARITY.**

On the other hand, she realises that her world isn't perfect; some negative sides need addressing:

- **SOME PEOPLE DON'T SEEM TO WANT TO FIT IN**

- **THE MATRIX SYSTEM, WITH ITS MULTIPLE UNITS, GENERATES CONFLICTING GOALS/ INTERESTS;**

- **PEOPLE STRUGGLE TO FOLLOW A PROCESS MADE COMPLEX BY TOO MANY STEPS;**

- **WHEN A SYSTEM GETS TOO COMPLEX, IT CAN BECOME SELF-SERVING AND FAIL TO WORK IN THE INTEREST OF ALL.**

The insight she gains from league tables and academic standards helps her challenge the school to strive for continuous improvement. It's important to enhance efficiencies, reduce costs and make things, well, better. There's always something to do and she feels it's her duty not only for her daughter, but for society as a whole.

Doc has a clear list of values:

STABILITY
LAW & ORDER
CLARITY
SENSE OF DUTY
RELIABILITY
COMPLIANCE

Overall, this is a good life that provides some stability and certainty; everyone knows where they belong. As long as everything remains the same, this is a comfortable level. No one goes to extremes nor oversteps boundaries. People plan ahead, live their lives and everyone is content.

INDIVIDUALS

> **SACRIFICE THE DESIRES OF THE SELF NOW IN ORDER TO GET A LASTING REWARD LATER.** (C-1 . P. 252)

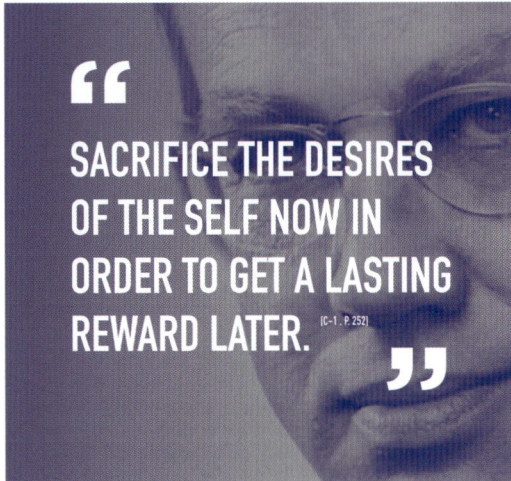

It might seem an overly orderly world that Doc lives in, but she likes it that way. Why put up with chaos and unexpected situations when you can avoid that altogether?

Also, Doc is a calm, diligent and well-organised character. She has her life in check and it suits her. Her home and office desks have a nearly identical layout. The documents might be different, but the colour codes and stationery are very much alike and in the same places; just the way it should be. She has many duties, lots of lists and will gladly sacrifice her desires and interests for the greater good. She admires her own level of discipline and believes that the Queen of the UK herself would approve. The Carltons, who are her neighbours to the left, say she's incredibly accurate and comes across as conventional. Doc thinks it's a fair description.

Looking at their front garden and their not-so-white fence, it seems they could benefit from taking a leaf out of her book.

For now, let's stay on this side of the fence. With all her duties, Doc still makes time for family.

It works when you organise it all properly. She loves their summer holidays in Mallorca. They found this family-friendly, well-managed retreat the year before their daughter was born. It's close to the beautiful city of Palma and the lively resort of Magaluf, though not as big. They know the staff well and are on first-name terms with Biel, the deputy manager. He's a real local and his family used to live where the building now stands. The pool and hotel area are enclosed and private, which means the little one can't get away; the security guards make sure of that.

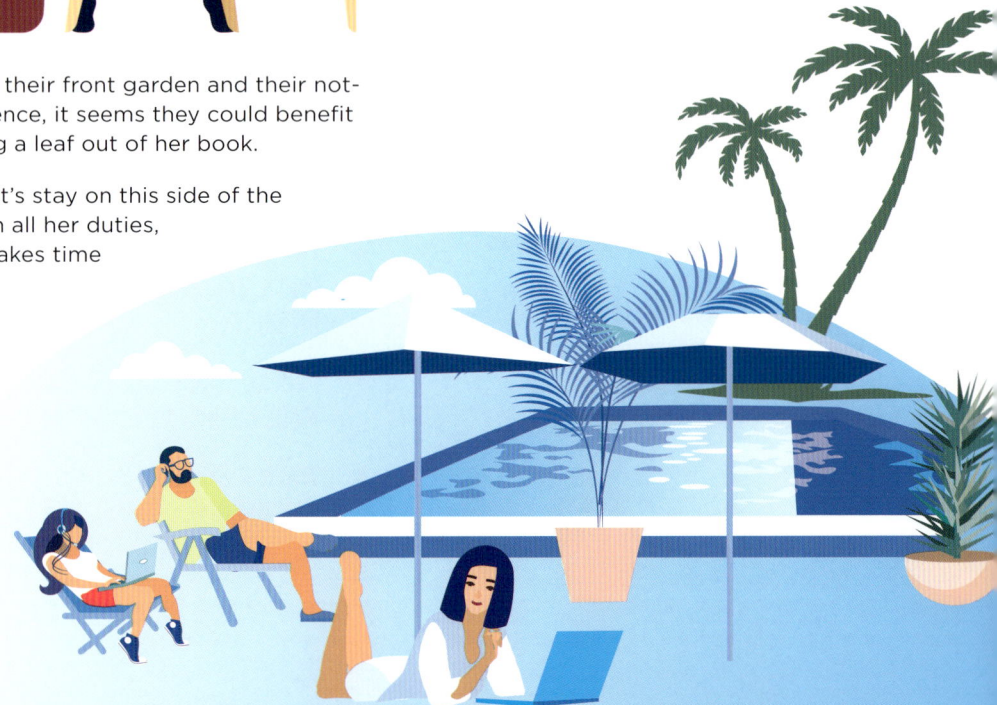

Next year they're thinking about going away with friends who have a daughter of the same age. It's tricky though making arrangements with people you don't know that intimately. They met most of their friends via their professional groups or through the children. They came across the Detsons at the school where Doc works. Maybe it would be good for the girls to spend next summer together. Who knows? If only children weren't so unpredictable.

She wonders whether the Detsons play board games as much as they do on holidays, if they like Scrabble, Codemaster and Codenames too. Doc has started a game of Sudoku, her favourite solitary activity to distract herself and stop worrying about all the 'what ifs'. She has 25 minutes to go before the end of her lunch break. At 5p.m. she'll be off to the gym. She goes twice a week for 60 minutes, Tuesdays and Thursdays right after work. It's important to her to keep mentally and physically fit. Life is full of challenges, distractions and desires, and it helps to be strong.

Doc has modelled this attitude from her 'heroes'. All the historical figures she looks up to are strong and controlled characters. The first one to stand out was Arab scholar and mathematician Al-Kindi. He pioneered a method to decipher encrypted messages based on how often letters occur in a text, nowadays known as frequency analysis [4-2]. Doc is in awe of what some people achieved in those bygone eras.

She admires Marie Curie for her endurance and devotion. She was the youngest of five children born to poor school teachers, and she lost her mother at the age of 11. Marie couldn't afford a proper education, but, through her insatiable appetite for learning, she still made history discovering the elements polonium and radium. She's the only woman to have received two Nobel prizes. The journey to the breakthrough was long and arduous. Like her idols, Doc believes the way of progress is neither swift nor easy, and nothing in life is to be feared, it is only to be understood.

Another hero is Ada Lovelace, an English mathematician and writer, chiefly known for her work on Charles Babbage's proposed mechanical general-purpose computer, the analytical engine. She recognised that the machine had applications beyond pure calculation and published the very first algorithm. [4-3] She's considered one of the earliest programmers. She was born in 1815!

Doc is pleased that Hollywood pays homage to many scientists and inventors nowadays, which means there's always a good movie to watch on Sunday evenings. Her favourite ones are 'A Beautiful Mind', "The Imitation Game", and 'The Theory of Everything', as they reveal the human side and struggles of great achievers. She even liked 'Becoming Warren Buffett' although business never really appealed to her. Buffett is a level-headed and shrewd investor well-known for the incredible returns he offers shareholders thanks to his patient, conservative and data-driven investments. Even more than his humble lifestyle in the face of such financial gains, Doc is impressed by his approach to philanthropy, which was heavily influenced by his late wife and long-time activist Susan Thompson Buffett. Buffett's love for her and her unfortunate passing led him to pledge $37 billion of his $44 billion fortune in the form of company stock to the Bill and Melinda Gates Foundation. This is the largest philanthropic donation in history.

Money doesn't motivate Doc. She has enough to be content and responds to:

PURPOSE
Stability & safety
Predictability, organisation and discipline

MASTERY
Ability to become in-house specialist, possibly external expert of field
Dedication and potential focus on a specific area

AUTONOMY
Space and freedom to work within a defined role
A set and ascribed framework
A predictable career path

What frustrates her are people refusing to make decisions or holding others back. Devina, the head of research, is a classic example. She always tries to go by the book, which isn't a bad thing. However, if something isn't spelled out in detail, a professional, especially a leader, should take the initiative. But not Devina. She escalates matters very quickly and refers to her boss most of the time. The team have nicknamed her the **Bot** or **Dot**, depending on the situation. She relies on electronic communication, requests information by email and responds online like a **bot**. She seems to lack emotional sensitivity, avoids critical feedback or discussions, especially those involving people and soft skills. When confronted, she picks on those with less expertise or refers to the hierarchy. She will sometimes use the political correctness card to get her way or block others in their tracks.

On other occasions, she gets hung up on concepts and drafts if the i's and t's haven't been **dot**ted and crossed properly. She focuses on her research department, at the exclusion of others or the corporation, without which this work wouldn't be possible financially.

When things get difficult, Devina's natural response is to point out that dealing with issues isn't in her job description. Of course, she'll consider it when her duties are updated accordingly. She always says that with a grin, as she knows that more responsibilities mean higher pay.

The organisation has a lot to answer for, having allowed Devina to be the dot in the mornings and the bot in the afternoons. Everyone wonders how she'll cope with the upcoming change programme.

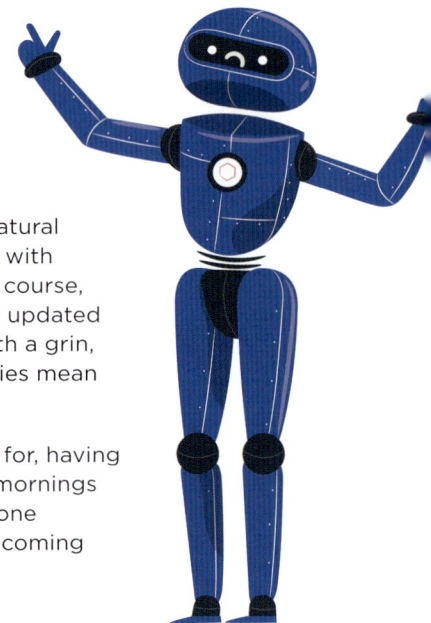

LEADERSHIP

Doc understands Devina when it comes to management, as nearly everything is defined. For example, the university has the ISO 30408 in place to ensure professional handling of human resources (HR). This norm provides the guidelines for a human governance system that can both respond effectively to operational needs and manage HR risks. If anything's unclear, HR Business Partner (HRBP) Darius is an expert in ISO 30400, which spells out the fundamental HR management terms.[4-4] Not only is everything perfectly described and documented, but one is well advised to stick to the official manual; procedural mistakes can have severe consequences!

Doc prefers reading more inspiring materials to inform her role as team leader. The HBR paper 'Seven Transformations of Leadership' [C-4] highlighted two suitable leadership styles for her.

First she's the **Expert** in her department, having all the necessary qualifications, certifications and experience. Doc leads with logic and know-how, she uses facts and figures to gain consensus and buy-in. Her division is a strong contributor to the overall research output. When needed, she helps rationalise and effectively manage complicated scenarios.

As a **Diplomat**, she seeks harmony and avoids open conflict. She strives to foster a sense of belonging but also respects her people, views them as complex individuals. She listens to the team and will give in if something is important to them. Doc is very loyal to her direct reports, looks for consensus and tries to ensure everyone gets along.

She's good at shielding her team from outside intrusions. She sends out a clear message with Archimedes's quote above her door: 'Do not disturb my circles.' We know who that is intended for.

> " THE LEADER VALUES THE LIFE THAT ENABLES HIM, IF NECESSARY, TO SACRIFICE HIMSELF IN THE PROTECTION OF THE FOLLOWERS. THOSE WHO FOLLOW VALUE SACRIFICING IN SUPPORT OF THE LEADER. BOTH LIVE BY A DIFFERENT "SCHEMA" VARYING FROM THE SAME "THEMA". [C-1, P. 268] "

TEAM COLLABORATION

Doc works best when she can refer to formal instructions. The ISO 30405 and 30409 ensure clarity and alignment in recruitment and workforce planning. As you'd expect, everyone in her department has a written overview of their roles and responsibilities, linked to yearly performance reviews. This highlights the connection between company and individual accomplishments.

Duties are clearly linked through processes and flow charts. That means anyone taking over a new job knows what to do. In a world where things change rapidly, the challenge is to find ways of giving people influence beyond their usual sphere, allowing them to step out of their defined roles and take matters in their own hands.

As is the case in a few large organisations, job descriptions are written by HR, quickly become outdated, and many are so specific that individuals stick to their remit to avoid causing friction. When conflicts arise, Doc observes the following simple logic to resolve them:

1. **Minor:** put on diplomatic hat and sort it out directly

2. **Medium:** include another person, possibly an expert or her boss

3. **Serious:** follow disciplinary procedures and include HRBP or one of the in-house mediators.

> " **THOSE WHO FAIL TO PLAN, PLAN TO FAIL.** "
>
> **ANONYMOUS**

PLANNING & STEERING

Managers in large organisations find themselves planning for all sorts of things, as Doc knows all too well. 'The manager's role, in this person's mind, is to provide the routine, structure the task, define and clarify the regulations, and represent the organisation.' [C-1, p. 268] In Doc's case, the executive teams of both firms are responsible for setting company goals. Doc is loyal to her employer and focuses on the objectives of PharmaCorp, but she could equally be loyal to the RC or the research itself.

PharmaCorp's current strategic goal is to integrate all the different units and brands into one global company called OnePharma. She's bringing David, a new researcher, up to speed and sharing the direction of travel with him.

> " **THESE ARE THE PEOPLE WHO BELIEVE IN "LIVING BY THE TEN COMMANDMENTS", OBEYING THE LETTER OF THE LAW, ETC. THEY WORK BEST WITHIN A RIGID SET OF RULES, SUCH AS ARMY REGULATIONS.** " [C-1, P .258]

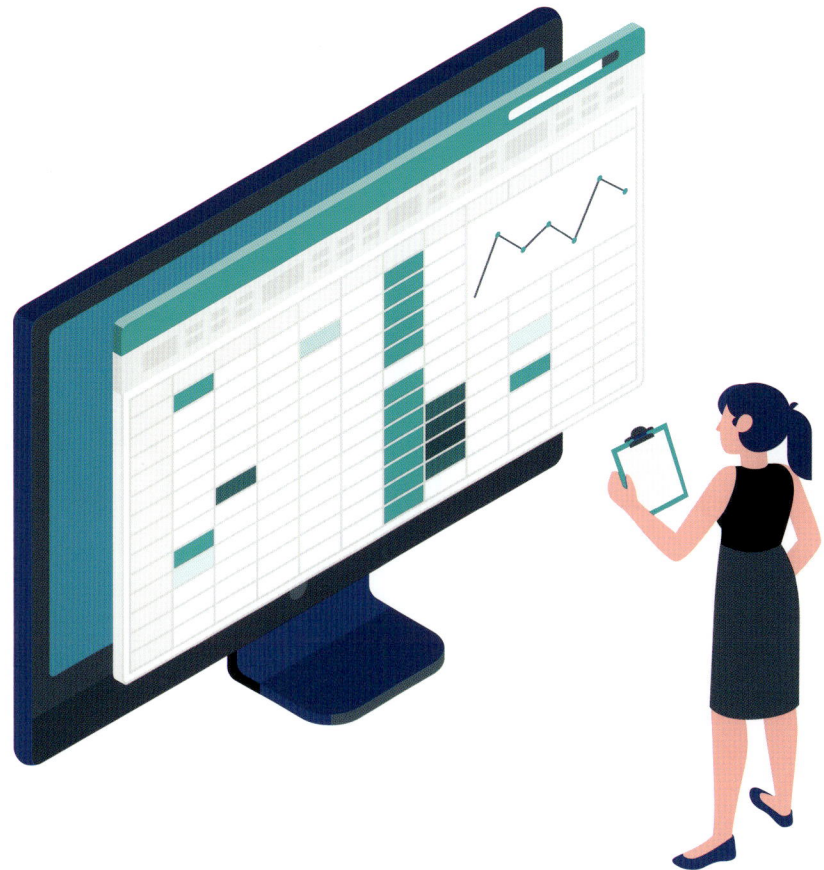

> **THE MANAGER'S ROLE, IN THIS PERSON'S MIND, IS TO PROVIDE THE ROUTINE, STRUCTURE THE TASK, DEFINE AND CLARIFY THE REGULATIONS, AND REPRESENT THE ORGANISATION.**

Part of the 'becoming one' strategic objective breaks down into tactical plans outlining the aims of the various functions. For example, what does IT need to do differently to enable the organisation to operate globally? What does marketing need to change to consolidate all national brands into a global one? How are Doc and her team going to collaborate and share resources with colleagues they've never met?

She describes how cascading works. Managers use four main types of plans in the pursuit of their goals: strategic, tactical, operational and individual. Doc thinks of these four planning levels as downwards stepping stones – she can see clear links between them, leading to the realisation of the overall goals.

These tactical plans are then translated into operational plans, like Doc's new scheduling project to include an increasing number of virtual sessions with her staff. Her daily work is very much organised through project management. This involves initiating, planning, implementing, controlling, and finalising her own and her team's work to achieve specific tactical targets within given timeframes. Her primary challenge is to realise all project goals within the constraining golden triangle of time, cost and quality.

She prioritises meetings, based on her position and research area, and only adds essential ones to her e-calendar.

This usually requires lots of planning, data, endless Excel sheets, and it all boils down to avoiding risk. Some of her days consist of meeting after meeting so she needs to be highly organised. There's also contingency planning, but now David's eyes are glazing over, a sign that he's getting overwhelmed; she doesn't want to lose him on day two. The project portfolio management tool, budgeting application, task lists, RACI matrices, timesheets and all other forms and templates in the ERP system will have to wait.

ORGANISATIONS

Doc feels that the organisation itself requires a lot of planning, but there's no other option to manage over 10,000 employees. She remembers the time when the business had fewer than 50 people. Work days weren't very well organised and she had to deal with constant distractions. That's when she discovered another one of her heroes.

The individual that most influenced her understanding of people management is Frederick Taylor. Trained as a machinist, the engineer became well known as an efficiency expert in the early twentieth century by publishing *The Principles of Scientific Management*. Taylor's philosophy focuses on the belief that making people work hard isn't as efficient as optimising the way they work.

While Taylorism in a pure sense isn't used much today, scientific management positively and significantly influenced management practice. It introduced systematic selection and training procedures, provided a way of studying workplace efficiency, and encouraged the idea of standardised organisational design.[4-5]

> " THE MANTRA IN BUSINESS IS PROFIT MAXIMIZATION. A COMPANY'S GREATEST CAPITAL IS NOT ON ANY BALANCE SHEET. IT IS THE LOYALTY AND SINCERITY OF EMPLOYEES WHO ENSURE CUSTOMER SATISFACTION. "
>
> ANDREAS MUELLER,
> SENIOR VP EMEA @ ARAS

FACT:

Frederick Taylor is also known as the 'father of industrialisation'. Henry Ford was heavily influenced by his thinking. He based his conveyor belt manufacturing process on Taylor's main principles.

These can be summarised as follows:

1. Using scientific methods to study work and determine the most efficient way to perform specific tasks;

2. Matching workers to jobs based on ability and motivation, and training them to work at maximum efficiency;

3. Monitoring worker performance while generating data, and providing instructions and supervision for efficient working;

4. Allocating work between managers and workers so that managers spend their time planning and training, to allow workers to perform their tasks efficiently. [4-6]

Doc's performance in the company back when it was still small helped improve its ways of working. Essentially, Taylorism breaks tasks down into manageable steps and focuses on how best to perform them. This structure and logic enabled Doc to make a name for herself. She learned a lot during that time, her contribution was recognised and she secured her first team leader role.

Doc doesn't agree with Taylor's concept that people are only motivated by money. She understands and appreciates that today's employees are driven by purpose, mastery and autonomy. This wasn't a common viewpoint 100 years ago.

Doc believes her work output partly contributed to her company being acquired by another player a year later, which was then taken over by PharmaCorp five years ago.

It seems to be where this world is heading, because Doc can see a pattern when it comes to organisations, and it has to do with size. Firms acquire other businesses to increase their economies of scale, which also eliminates competition, drives down costs per unit and enhances gross profits. This means you can sell cheaper per unit and keep afloat. Along the way, data is used to understand and analyse cost structures. Entire departments concentrate on entering data in spreadsheets which then go somewhere – where and why we don't always know. Every function and unit follows its own targets and generates its own data.

In a company exceeding 10,000 employees, not one person recalls the bigger picture any more. The problem is that by pushing through cost reduction (race to the bottom), the customer focus effectively disappears from sight.

On the sales side, companies start off with mass production to drive down cost per unit. At some point advancements in technology allow mass customisation and, eventually, they can even deliver mass individualisation.

Doc notices similar patterns everywhere and wonders where it's all heading.

MARKETS

Doc first got to understand economic patterns from reading W. W. Rostow's book *The Stages of Economic Growth* for a school project. It places modern economic history within a comprehensive framework and offers a taxonomy that he called 'Stages of Economic Growth' in 1960 [4-7]. Modern economic growth, according to Rostow, means that all countries go through the following stages as they develop:

1) TRADITIONAL SOCIETY

2) PRECONDITIONS TO TAKE OFF

3) TAKE-OFF

4) DRIVE TO MATURITY

5) AGE OF HIGH MASS CONSUMPTION.

The final stage is a mature market where demand is stagnant or growing insignificantly. The pie chart on the PowerPoint has reached its maximum size and David refers to it as a state of equilibrium. Mergers and acquisitions (M&As) become more frequent along the way.

With only a handful of big players left in an industry, anti-trust or anti-monopoly laws prevent the final consolidation chapter, as it would only result in a single company sooner or later. PharmaCorp recently tried to acquire the second biggest competitor in the sector, but, after lengthy discussions with government representatives, ambitions suddenly came to a halt with the appointment of a new CEO. Doc and David agree on the importance of promoting fair competition in business. Consumers need to be protected from predatory capitalistic trade practices that would force them to pay higher prices for a limited supply of products and services.

The political system at this Blue level interferes heavily with the economic and business worlds. Separation of powers, as a model of state governance, isn't a recent idea. Some 2300 years ago, in ancient Greece, the philosopher Aristotle formulated the concept of a 'mixed' government [4-8].

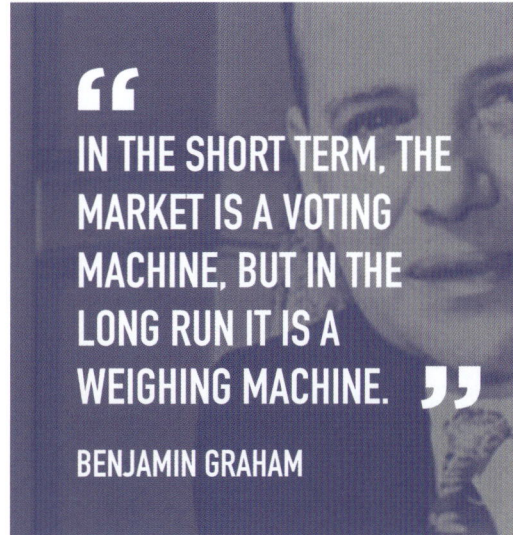

> ## IN THE SHORT TERM, THE MARKET IS A VOTING MACHINE, BUT IN THE LONG RUN IT IS A WEIGHING MACHINE.
>
> **BENJAMIN GRAHAM**

Citizens can then rest assured that no one is taking advantage of them and that all is in order. Doc loves this achievement and often thinks about how Aristotle too was so ahead of his time.

LIMITATIONS AND GROWTH INTO NEXT LEVELS

The 1st (Beige) stage is all about survival. The 2nd (Purple) already provides some stability, as long as you're a valued member of the group. In the 3rd (Red) stage, the young and restless break out of the traditional mould to find or create something new. In the 4th (Blue), one learns the hard way that an ego's appetite is boundless and fierce. A system needs to be put in place to limit individual greed and serve everyone more equally.

The 4th (Blue) stage is based on a top-down system with 'one right way', remember? Taylor's thinking enabled Henry Ford to scale his automotive production.

Doc gets it and she really likes efficiency but she's not sure if doing it on such a large scale is sensible. With an organisation of thousands of staff, you have hundreds of departments working on their specific, often isolated, goals and targets. This requires devising endless procedures and guidelines to keep everything under control. At this level of complexity, the focus becomes sticking to the rules and doing things right, rather than doing the right things. It's no longer about people but 'human resources', 'human capital' or 'FTEs'. The system takes over. It gives the 'self-righteous woMan', someone like Devina, the opportunity to thrive, to stick blindly to the rules and not only get away with it but get promoted. After all, she's not going to 'rock the boat'.

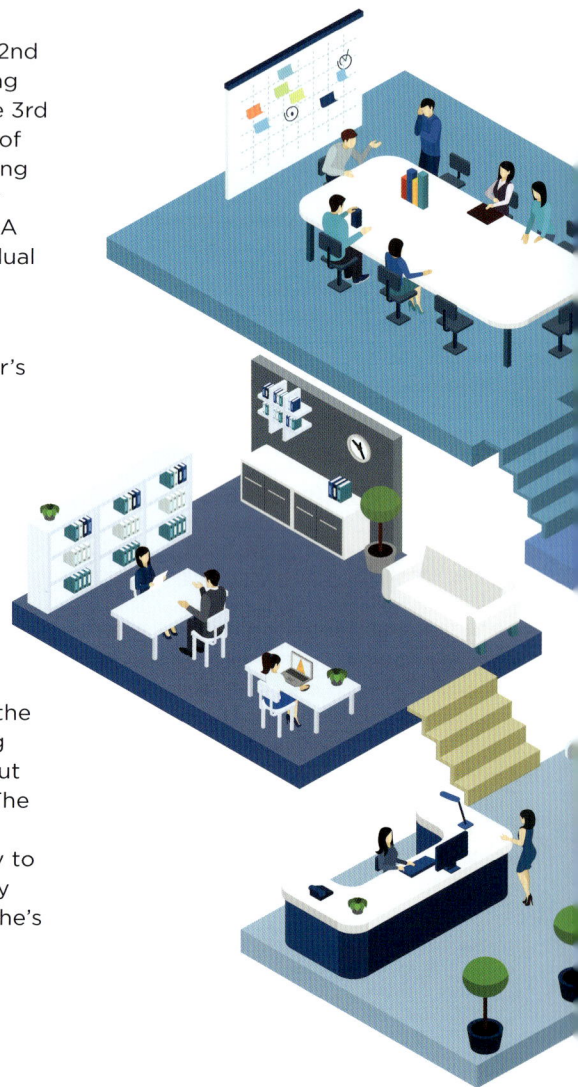

We often confuse effectiveness with efficiency. The difference can be summed up shortly and sweetly — being effective is about doing the right things, while being efficient is about doing things right. Efficiency is a core characteristic of the 4th level, whereas the following, 5th (Orange) stage focuses on effectiveness.

A system that stays in place too long and relies on efficiency will start developing resistance to change. Holding on to certainty becomes the objective, rather than challenging the status quo, and experts fiercely defend the one truth they have established or built their world around. In a world where politics and science have adopted such a mindset, real progress is at risk. The dismissal of Rupert Sheldrake's curious questions and the taking down of his TED talk proves the power of a system that wants to believe in nothing but what it knows.

Humans have a natural desire to be part of something that they can help shape. If they're discouraged or punished for looking beyond their defined responsibilities, lack of ownership becomes a problem. If people's ideas are dismissed, some will keep their head down in 9-to-5 jobs and others will leave.

If an employee makes a mistake, a rule or guideline is put in place to avoid repeating the same mistake. It's a clever way of dumbing people down and hindering innovation and proactivity.

This is also true of politics where politicians become disconnected from the public and start creating and driving a self-serving system. Disconnect is the key issue when this 4th level concept is taken too far. When people work against each other and focus on their own good, the intended balance has turned into a stalemate.

This breeds a certain amount of mediocrity that does everyone a disservice. Corporations comprise of a growing number of departments and management levels; the more levels, the further away decisions are made from where it matters. And so much of what we call management consists in making it difficult for people to work. This creates stagnation while the rest of the world keeps moving.

In the meantime, mass consumption leads to mass production and mass exploitation of limited natural resources. Planned obsolescence allows mass consumption to carry on, but this must end sooner or later.

Yet again, one must break out of the Blue conformity to overcome the limitations of this level. Time to promote individual responsibility and push decision-making and progress through all levels of the organisation.

The characteristics of 4th level Blue markets look as follows:

'MARKETS ARE STABLE AND PREDICTABLE'

POLITICAL
- Constitutional state, often democracies (different political parties)
- High levels of bureaucracy and regulation
- Lobbying possible (due to Red/Orange players)
- Measures to avoid abuse of individual players

ECONOMIC
- Minister/secretary for economics
- Government interventions and considerable taxes
- Low growth rates
- Subsidies/grants to bolster existing structures

SOCIAL
- Various ministers/secretaries (health, education, housing, etc.)
- People are comfortable and passive
- Social welfare and health system
- Widespread learning and development (e.g. institutions)
- Personal freedom (e.g. freedom of speech)
- Work-life balance is considered

TECHNOLOGICAL
- Many big players
- Old economy (steel, coal, automotive)
- Slow innovation, mainly driven by individuals and small businesses
- Generates lots of data, but doesn't make bigger sense of it

ENVIRONMENTAL
- National public bodies exist (e.g. water, energy, waste)
- Environment used as a resource (e.g. landfills, water reservoirs)
- Industries controlled and governed by national bodies

LEGAL
- Rule-of-law principle (Blue achievement)
- Highly regulated and lots of laws
- Individuals enjoy equal opportunities
- Often a high ratio of lawyers per capita

5th STAGE
ORANGE: LIFE IS ABOUT ACHIEVING GOALS

THIS LEVEL IS ABOUT AMBITIOUS GO-GETTERS, OFTEN ENTREPRENEURIAL, WHO WORK WITH A TEAM BUT APPRECIATE AUTONOMY AND COMPETITION. THEY CAN SEE THE BIGGER PICTURE AND ARE VALUED FOR THEIR ACHIEVEMENTS. THEY ENJOY STATUS SYMBOLS AND INNOVATIVE OR UNIQUE BRANDS.

TEAMS FOLLOW TOP-DOWN DRIVEN KPIs; EMPLOYEES ARE GIVEN THE WHAT AND LEFT TO FIGURE OUT THE HOW. INDIVIDUALS ARE WILLING TO SUPPORT OTHERS IF IT HELPS THE TEAM PROGRESS AND MEET ITS TARGETS. EVERYONE HAS TO PULL THEIR WEIGHT.

THE PERFORMANCE-DRIVEN COMPANIES HAVE A CLEARLY DEFINED ORIENTATION (E.G. CUSTOMERS) AND DATA-DRIVEN GOALS. THEY OFTEN HAVE PRESTIGIOUS OFFICES/ADDRESSES AND ENGAGE IN HIGH-STATUS EVENTS. DATA DRIVES COMPETITIVENESS. TYPICAL ORANGE COMPANIES ARE THE MANY INVESTMENT OR MANAGEMENT CONSULTING FIRMS. AMAZON, GOOGLE, AND GENERAL ASSEMBLY ARE ALSO PRIME EXAMPLES.

NO COUNTRIES ARE PURELY ORANGE YET BUT SOME HAVE AN ORANGE INFLUENCE, LIKE SINGAPORE, CANADA AND NORWAY. THEY EFFECTIVELY OPERATE LIKE STRATEGIC PLAYERS IN THE GLOBAL ARENA, FOR EXAMPLE BY ATTRACTING INNOVATIVE INDUSTRIES AND DEVELOPING CITIZENS EFFECTIVELY TO TAKE ON MODERN PROFESSIONS.

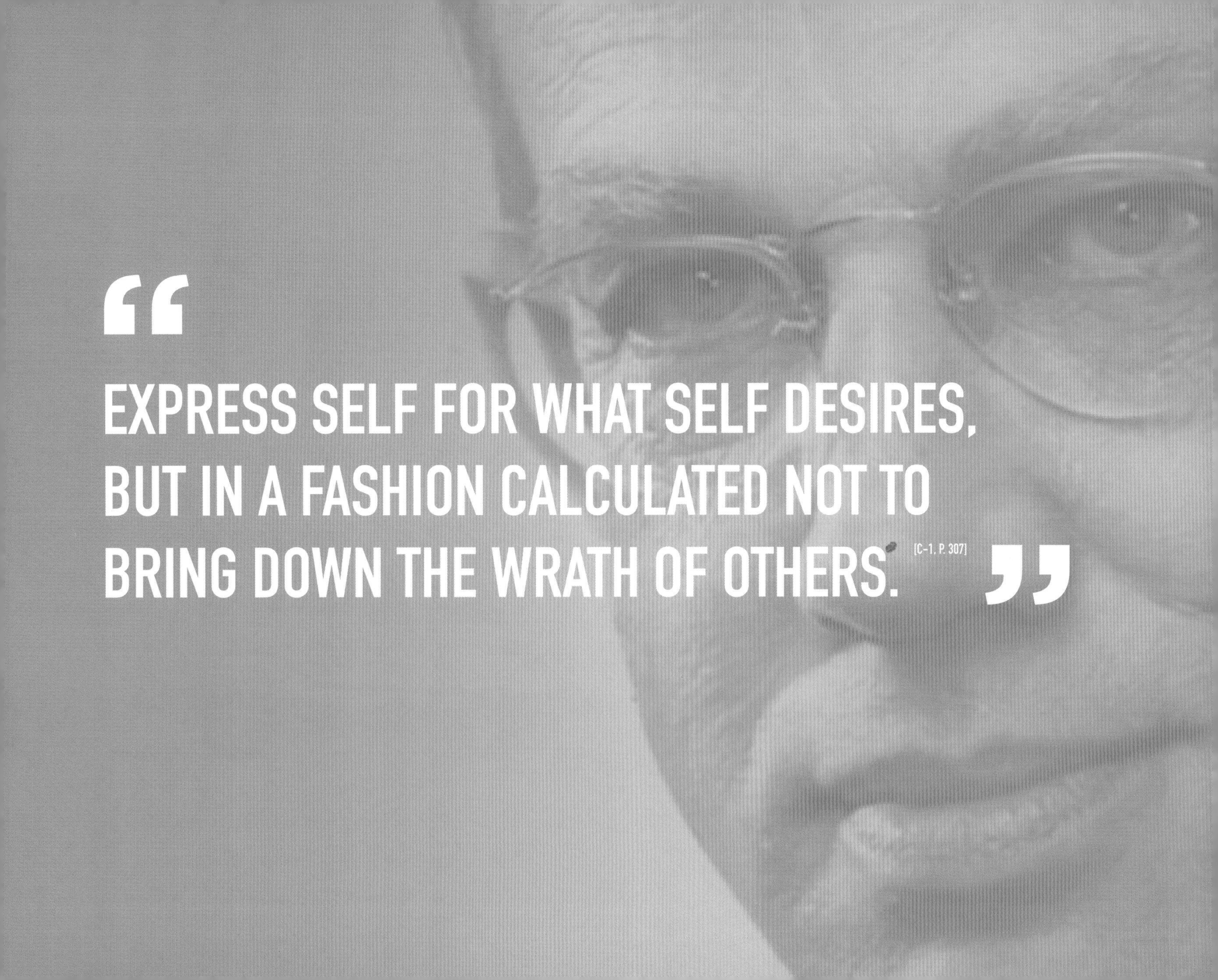

"

EXPRESS SELF FOR WHAT SELF DESIRES, BUT IN A FASHION CALCULATED NOT TO BRING DOWN THE WRATH OF OTHERS. [C–1, P. 307]

"

ELI'S SPHERE

You can easily tell where we are by the high-powered and prestigious glass cathedrals of capitalism. We're back in the city, at the very heart of the financial district, where Eli is swiftly zooming past some cars to get to his meeting. He loves the way the electric engine of his orange Tesla Roadster accelerates effortlessly, and how easily he can overtake people without them realising until they see his supercool flashing backlights. He's rushing to attend an important partner meeting in 20 minutes at

his company, medium-sized PerformVentures SARL. The firm started as a management consulting firm, then began acquiring stakes in struggling businesses in return for guidance to reach their performance goals. In the next 2–3 years, PerformVentures will make its major profits from straightforward investments, mostly in tech.

This company, like many, if not most in this world today, lives and breathes data. That data is turned into information and applied to business scenarios to provide customer, product, competitor and market intelligence. This approach is typical of businesses, with a 50+ headcount, that survived the digital wave.

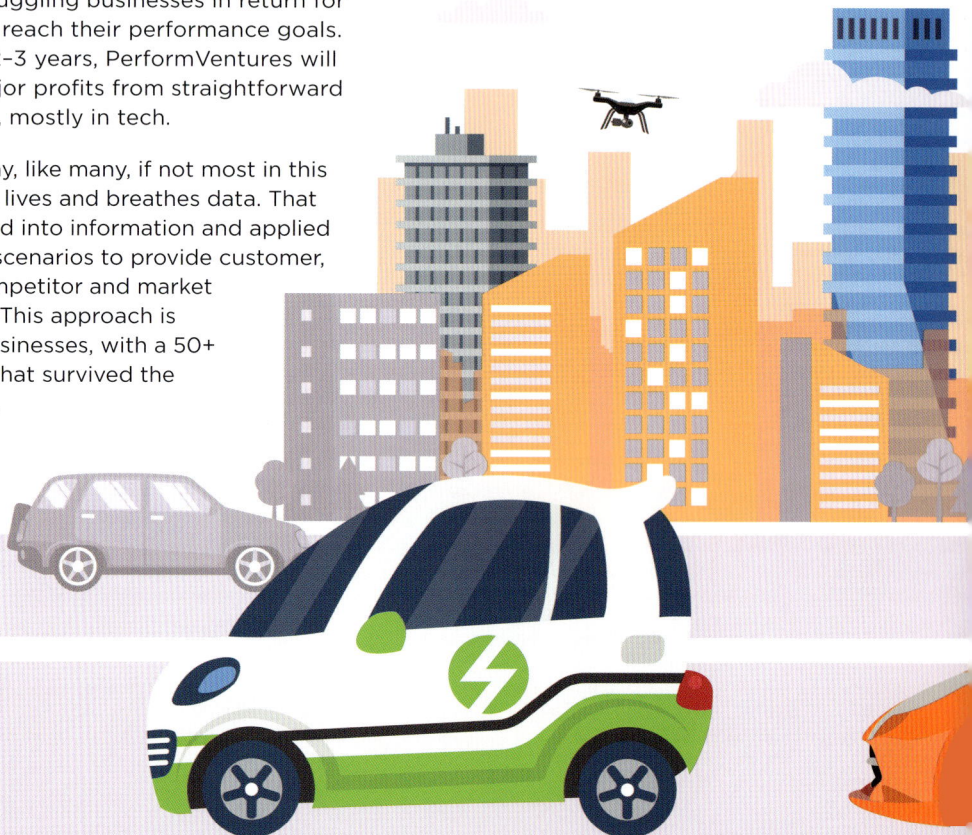

> " THERE ARE MANY DIFFERENT WAYS YOU CAN THINK ABOUT SOMETHING, BUT THERE IS JUST ONE GOOD WAY YOU SHOULD THINK ABOUT THINGS. [C-1, P. 308] "

The discussion about digitalisation has been going on for decades. However, it has so far mainly revolved around technologies and the impact on business and day-to-day culture.

The digital wave has been building up since the latter half of the 20th century and will eventually reach a catalytic tipping point that will impact everyone. The wave metaphor illustrates a force that ebbs and flows, but rather than ebbing away, digitalisation is here to stay. It will hit a huge percentage of well-known companies, which will either break up or go into demise. Many of us will be shocked to see the average lifespan of companies listed in Standard & Poor's 500 drop to a single digit in the years to come (1950s = 60 years, 2019 = 19 years). Then again, business is about survival of the fittest, so if you don't think ahead, adapt and change, why bother at all? If the data shows you're wrong, then you should change accordingly.

The problem isn't technology, but politicians, executives and organisational cultures that are unwilling to adapt and take advantage of tech-enabled acceleration. The onus is on people to use technology to its fullest potential.

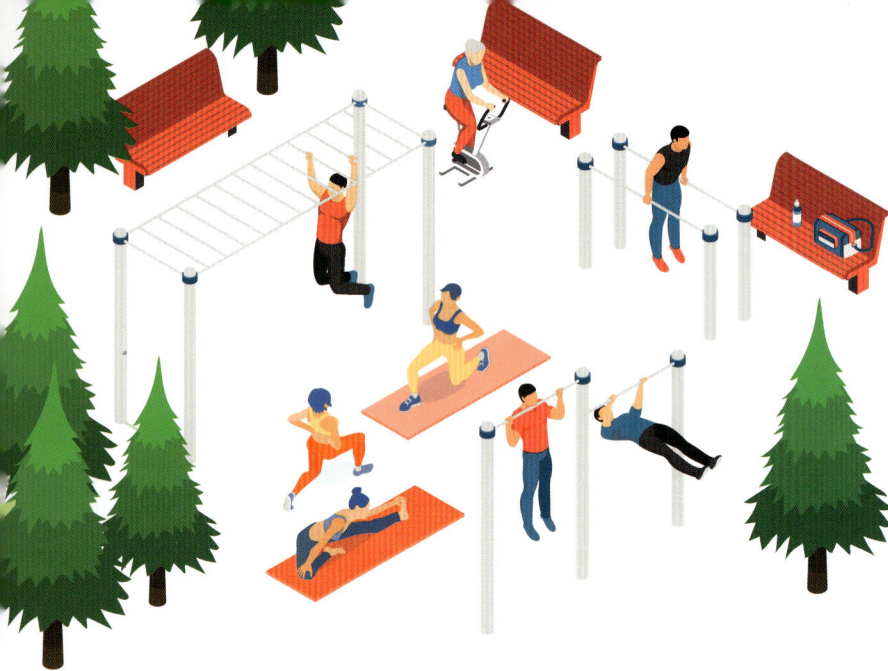

Eli's district has changed significantly since he's moved his family into a cool penthouse in a local high-rise. The top floor was designed to accommodate six penthouse apartments. They live in a cleverly constructed maisonette that is more than big enough without the children. Eli's eldest son is off making a name for himself, and the younger one is at boarding school. In the evenings, Eli loves a bit of peace and quiet, and spending time with his wife Evangeline and their Samoyed dog Evander.

He likes the breed for its stamina and determination. These are values he also appreciates in people, because "winners never quit and quitters never win", as Vince Lombardi once said. It has always been important to Eli to be clear about his goals and go for them. Other values that drive him are:

1.	PERFORMANCE	5.	COMPETITION
2.	ACCOUNTABILITY	6.	INDEPENDENCE
3.	PERSONAL AND OVERALL SUCCESS	7.	STATUS
4.	RESULTS	8.	VALUE CREATION

Employee engagement is usually assured as remuneration is related to individual, unit or organisational performance, depending on your current level.

Even politics has changed for the better, in Eli's opinion, though not as fast as the business world. Change-resistant politicians have had to give way to new thinkers and doers. As long as you combine data with transparency, set goals and promote open communication, people will deliver and accept accountability. It does help that nearly all engagements are done or tracked digitally. You have online voting, for instance, where different channels inform you about topics relevant to you. This makes it easier to do things on the fly. While in the lift, Eli is able to quickly provide mobile feedback to the Council to request more outdoor places for fitness and training in his district. Many former business spaces have been turned into housing complexes, and Eli thinks it would be great if people could train outside more. A fit population benefits society after all.

Eli thinks the world is relatively good. He doesn't believe in a higher power and sees it as crucial that everyone learns through their efforts and determines their own goals. Some people set high goals for themselves, take risks, show resilience and succeed. Those that fail will find leaders to support. This means everyone gets to enjoy the fruits they deserve in life, which ultimately improves the conditions for all.

These values have helped drive this Orange world, and a lot needs protecting:

- TRYING OUT NEW IDEAS;
- EVERY INDIVIDUAL CAN PERFORM AND ACHIEVE;
- DATA BECOMES AN 'OBJECTIVE' MEASURE FOR IMPROVING LIVES;
- DATA AND INFORMATION GUIDE DECISION-MAKING;
- LIFE CHANGES, BUT ONE CAN ADAPT AND CONTINUOUSLY IMPROVE.

Eli knows there are always things to improve. He can identify negative points and notices when people go off the right track:

- SOME PEOPLE PLAY TOO HARD TO WIN AND BREAK THE RULES, RATHER THAN BENDING THEM;
- PEOPLE BURN THEMSELVES OUT TRYING TO REACH TARGETS THE SLOGAN IS 'UP OR OUT';
- MONEY AND POWER BECOME THE ONLY FOCUS;
- NUMBERS PREVAIL AND SOFT TOPICS ARE NEGLECTED.

INDIVIDUALS

He had switched to a purely plant-based diet three months earlier. It changed his life to learn that some of the fastest, strongest and most successful athletes on the planet are vegan. It started with people like Formula One champion Lewis Hamilton, top-ranked tennis player Novak Djokovic, and nine-time NBA All-Star Chris Paul, to name just a few.

The diet gave Eli a performance improvement of approximately 25%, a complete revelation.

> **POWER IS VIRTUE. IT IS BETTER TO ACT AND FAIL THAN TO SUFFER THE IGNOMINIOUS SHAME OF NOT HAVING TRIED.** [C-1, P. 309]

However, he got so power-hungry that he kept on pushing his body and overdid it. To his surprise, the plant-based diet helped with recovery too, but he won't be able to compete professionally again.

This story is part of Eli's journey and made him the man he is today. We sometimes have to learn the hard way. Eli always knew he was destined for great things. It is in his name after all – Eli is of Hebrew origin, meaning 'uplifted', 'high' or 'my god'. He's aware he isn't the latter, but then again, who knows? He never shared his ambitions to increase his wealth and achieve complete autonomy with anyone at PerformVentures.

Currently, Eli is heading the 10|1000 Venture, the business unit investing in the latest research and tech around human performance. The objective is to become the market leader and achieve 1000% ROI in ten years. Eli knows all too well what it means to set goals, break them down into achievable sub goals, and relentlessly work towards them. If you can believe it, the mind will help you achieve any goal. You might fail repeatedly, but that ultimately contributes to your success.

He's currently working on science-based tech and software, an area close to his heart. It targets athletes and ultimately anyone who needs to perform at their best. The front of the brochure lying on his desk captures this nicely:

- **Scientifically determine an individual's constitution to maximise physical performance levels**

- **Set seven main KPIs and 49 specific, personal parameters per athlete**

- **Enable the athlete to nurture and drive the body to maximum performance.**

Eli has strategically invested in a portfolio reflecting the seven key areas for driving human performance. He and his team nurture big ideas, set high targets and work towards them. After all, success is where hard work and data-proven insight meet.

When you can employ and collaborate with the best in the field, the sky is the limit. Eli was nearly late earlier on because a meeting with Doc ran over. Remember Doc from the previous chapter? PharmaCorp has developed innovative pain relief medicine and, on the back of it, has built a huge database on human pain points and drivers. The data provides great insight into pain levels; they can map out an individualised chart from a single person's DNA. The latest artificial intelligence can identify when perceived pain crosses over to a different 'wavelength' that results in damage. It is a breakthrough for Eli and, if the results come back as expected, he and Doc will have made a major leap within one of the seven performance areas.

Evangeline will be happy too as she has been annoyed at Eli losing sleep over how to crack this nut. He believes that the size of a challenge matches the level of satisfaction derived from its successful completion. They will celebrate this evening with one of the prized Champagnes Eli recently purchased.

Evangeline understands him, as she has been present through most of his professional journey. She worked as a successful sports commentator before effecting a complete career change. She's now an expert at understanding financial trends in modern art, with a personal interest in progressive art. She also spends a lot of time with Evander.

The Samoyed comes from one of the best breeders in the world and is a dog to be proud of.

The official story Eli tells people is that the dog was named after his wife. However, the truth is that his dog had a run-in with a terrier called Tyson at the breeder's home. It was all a big drama and Evander was left with a tiny scar on his right ear. The thought still makes Eli giggle, as he believes Evangeline has no clue that this is a reference to Mike Tyson's infamous fight with Evander Holyfield.

Eli and Evangeline spend most of their time on professional ventures now that the kids are mainly away. Fin, the eldest, went off to work for one of the blockchain-agnostic software development companies. He has just obtained his XCSM scrum master title. The firm believes in the good that blockchain can achieve, and develops mainstream solutions to solve social frictions and imbalances. The younger unplanned son, Chester, lives for playing hockey and football, chasing girls, and constantly gets into trouble. God knows what he's up to at this moment. Sending him to a sport-focused boarding school has been Eli's best outsourcing decision to date.

At home, they know the owners of a few prestigious nightspots where they don't need to queue. It's always nice eating or drinking in establishments where chefs and bartenders try to impress with the latest trends in culinary arts and drinks.

Eli has just put the Champagne in the fridge and still has time for a proper tour on his MLQ Spinning Bike 99X before gorgeous Evangeline comes home. He likes to exercise and particularly enjoys swimming, but the pool is always busy at this time.

Swimming reminds him of Michael Phelps and Katie Ledecky, who are not only incredibly talented swimmers, but also hard workers. After all, to give any less than your best is to waste a talent. He also likes Christian Pulisic, a great footballer who is always at the heart of the action, and Los Angeles Dodgers outfielder Mookie Betts who is fun to watch on the big screen.

The new TV with immersive tech is ideal for watching sports games. Drones, robotic cameras, and cameras with high-powered zooms are connected, automated and driven by AI in stadiums. This provides seamless and dynamic experiences from all angles.

Eli is partial to most of the latest action movies where human heroes win battles against human androids through sheer will and power. Willpower is like a muscle – the more you work it, the stronger it gets. He also enjoys classics like Limitless, The Matrix, Sneakers, or Game Changers, because they always make for good conversation starters.

The highlights of Eli and Evangeline's personal lives are their holidays. They have visited all the modern cities like Singapore, Bangalore, Seoul, and Beijing. It can be tricky finding outstanding places that are on the up, but still affordable. Then again, if you earn top dollar, you might as well spend them on the best. They combined lovely Cape Town with a personalised safari getaway. It turned out to be an eco-conscious tour, which is usually well received in conversations. Cape Town triggered their interest in Loisaba, Kenya, which is on the list for this year. Then there is Niyama in the Maldives, or they could just go old school and visit Cipriani in Venice. They are spoilt for choice.

Anyway, the 60-minute cycling tour is over now. Eli managed to get close to his 40-kilometre goal once again; in a few weeks, he will have to set a new target or change the resistance. A quick shower and Evangeline will be back. The Champagne should be chilled by now.

Showering is an opportunity for Eli to reflect on what motivates him beyond the ever-increasing bonuses he receives:

PURPOSE

Glorious success

Achievement in exposed, public areas

Status and perks

Contributing to success

Wealth

MASTERY

Opportunity to shine as a person

Goal orientation

Stardom

Being respected as an achiever

AUTONOMY

Setting high and measurable goals

Being responsible and being held accountable

Constant career drive (progress)

Adventure

Identifying your true motivations brings out the best in you. Eli is a big fan of the recent improvements of Kaizen in business development and growth. These have played, and still play, a major part in his continuous development. It's great to see how far the concept has come. He once doubted the timeliness of Kaizen, but then passionate experts continuously refined the ideas. Eli found this very appropriate and authentic.

Some say that something good always comes out of something bad. When people face outlandish obstacles, they go above and beyond. When your life is on the line, goals become crystal clear.

In life and business bad examples always exist. In Eli's case, performance at all costs is one of them. In his previous company, he experienced a business culture purely centred on hitting the targets; you either moved up or out. Meanwhile, you had to deliver like a machine, were constantly kept on track, and never allowed to think outside the box. What of brewing battles for power and material gain? This made for lavish, sometimes outrageously bombastic parties, but you couldn't trust anyone.

AUTHOR'S COMMENT:
Kaizen principles are still in line with the work of Masaaki Imai, the Japanese organisational theorist and management consultant partly responsible for making this practice so popular. Today's high-end solutions draw from the plentiful data and predictive analytics that enable leaders to see what might be coming. It's fascinating to know that all this comes from the initial steps of 'define, measure, analyse, improve, control'.

What most people ignore, though, is that the concept of Kaizen was born during WWII. One of the challenges during this terrible war was that neither time nor resources were available for large, innovative advances in the production of war equipment. Instead of encouraging radical changes to achieve desired goals, these techniques recommended that organisations introduce small improvements, preferably ones that could be implemented on the same day. This incremental work improvement approach was developed in the USA. Its aim was to make better use of the workforce and technologies.

In Eli's opinion, one partner was responsible for instilling this kind of culture. His name was Machiavelli [C-1, p. 323], but everyone called him 'Engineer'. This was officially for being so good at engineering short-term deals, but, unofficially, it was more about him being cold-hearted, calculated and power-driven. He's still known for being an achiever, but at what cost? Once a target is set, nothing can stop him. He irritates people by ignoring established organisational structures and processes.

Eli thinks the 'Engineer' is a psychopath. Not like a murderer, but he has a certain brain structure and an uncanny ability to seize opportunities with an unexpected level of ruthlessness. Psychopaths usually have superficial charm and a need for stimulation. They show a high level of empathy, but lack remorse or guilt. They possess a brain structure that reveals a propensity for violence and criminal behaviour if violence was present in their childhood. Most psychopaths live amongst us and work in a nearby corporation or strategic enterprise. [5-1]

Research shows we're four times more likely to meet one of them in the corporate world than in everyday life. The world of advanced capitalism, and specifically venture capitalist firms, are perfect breeding grounds.

LEADERSHIP

Doc shared a paper with Eli, that described empirical research carried out to identify seven leadership types.[C-3] It was an interesting read and Eli decided not to consider too many types, because two of them work very well for him.

Firstly, he is an **Achiever** who promotes teamwork, juggles managerial duties and responds to market demands to achieve goals. This person is well suited to managerial roles, because they can drive change, get things done and relish accountability. The more competitive the environment, the better. It is all about hitting the targets; even if this means bending the rules.

Secondly, he is an **Individualist** who interweaves competing personal and company action logics with ease. He can also create unique structures to resolve gaps between strategy and performance. These leaders are effective in venture and consulting roles. They put personalities and ways of relating into perspective and communicate well with people who have other action logics.

What sets Individualists apart from Achievers is their awareness of a possible conflict between their principles and their actions, or between the organisation's values and its implementation of those values.

For example, Eli modified the ROI calculation for his 10|1000 venture by excluding overheads and general costs, and listing investments only.

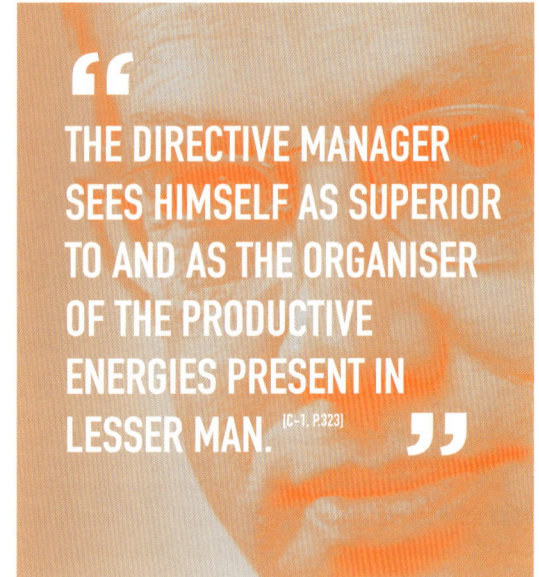

> **THE DIRECTIVE MANAGER SEES HIMSELF AS SUPERIOR TO AND AS THE ORGANISER OF THE PRODUCTIVE ENERGIES PRESENT IN LESSER MAN.** [C-1, P.323]

No one is likely to question the initial numbers because the baseline is now established. This little initial twist will pay off in years to come. If the other partners find out, Eli can always refer to having used the templates, which hadn't been updated at that point. His motto is play hard and smart. Business is often like playing chess and it helps to plan some moves well ahead of time.

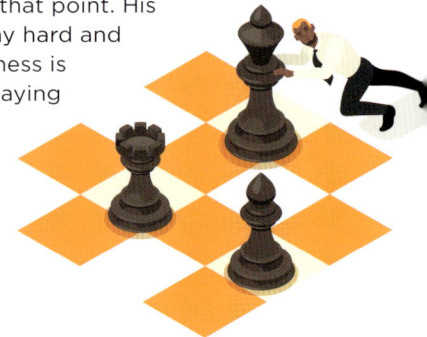

Eli invests a day a week in giving individual performance feedback to his team. He understood early on that making time for this helps align expectations, and accelerates performance and business results. He knows that the number and quality of KPIs have a strong influence on ways of working in his unit; they are crucial.

Furthermore, he makes good use of Objectives & Key Results (OKR), a pragmatic framework for defining and tracking objectives and their outcomes. OKR is relatively simple, because its format has been standardised. The **O**bjective is qualitative and the **KR**s quantitative (Eli usually uses three). This lets him focus a group or individual around one of his bold goals. [5-2]

He likes to keep a simple hierarchy in his team, similar to that of PerformVentures. Hierarchies have shown a negative effect on people's motivation and therefore overall performance.

TEAMS

Eli's team members are a great bunch. He has organised his unit into seven functional areas and ascribed clear responsibilities. The overarching target for the several business functions was set at group level, and sub-targets were agreed with his leads on signup; no room for excuses. Then the same was done for the remaining levels.

Everyone has clear targets recorded on and accessible in real time from the performance dashboard. The detailed view reveals 12 sub-targets.

This data also informs the financial department because employee paychecks consist of 35% performance-oriented flex pay.

There are clear expectations of employees and full transparency about the reward system, sanctions and defined boundaries, with latitude within the latter. The goal is to achieve and the team is here to figure out how to do that.

The organisation can sometimes become an obstacle, so Eli looks out for his team in their interactions with others. He's not afraid of modifying processes and procedures that get in the way of reaching goals. For example, last week, they were chasing an investment in a small startup doing innovative work in predictive data intelligence.
The normal process follows a clear due diligence checklist. Investments exceeding one million require each partner's approval. However, the strategic match and initial data looked promising and there wasn't enough time to wait for partner approval. So Eli had a word with the other partners who closed the deal even before the 'Engineer' could act. Eli feels good, as this will strengthen his reputation. The 'Engineer' and his company offer fierce competition, and outdoing them is always an extraordinarily sweet victory.

As the great Muhammad Ali said, "He, who is not courageous enough to take risks, will accomplish nothing in life."

> ## GET OFF MY BACK. I DON'T WANT YOU TELLING ME WHAT TO DO. [C-1, P. 323]

Healthy competition also exists amongst and within teams, and Eli likes that. He just ensures it doesn't get out of hand. He believes people perform best in a competitive environment – look at sports.

Here, everyone benefits and can feel proud to be part of Eli's successful team. He can offer loans at favourable rates to his best performing colleagues. For example, Esther wanted to buy a cool flat in an area that she normally wouldn't be able to afford. She can now, which makes her friends slightly envious and boosts PerformVentures' reputation. At the same time, this secures Esther's full dedication; everybody wins.

Each year, the team's top two performers get to enjoy an all-inclusive weekend away in one of the cool resorts with which the firm has deals; results pay off all around.

Eli's team run a tight ship and he's convinced they will outperform most of the other business units next year. They're on their way to the top.

PLANNING AND STEERING

Each business unit at PerformVentures has a clear, streamlined value chain and focuses on the customer or, in Eli's case, on the identified market opportunity. Projected numbers give him an idea of future market size, allow him to calculate his market share and, from this, to establish target numbers and the scalable size of his unit in the years to come.

It all starts with attention to detail. This is key, as you need a rock-solid foundation if you rely on numbers. They don't need to be as accurate as Doc's scientific ones, which would be too onerous, but the more accurate, the better. Eli recently had to let go of a team member who wasn't playing ball. He didn't understand that cutting corners repeatedly jeopardises the work of the entire unit. Without self-discipline, top achievements are highly unlikely.

A lot of the data is managed by the company's state-of-the-art, digitally empowered balanced scorecard, which not only translates downwards, but measures and analyses upwards. In the past, firms concentrated on measuring financial figures, but nowadays they also consider customer, people and organisational performance drivers. This influences leadership style and decision-making processes. For example, if Esther receives an updated target,

she has to figure out how to reach that mark. The entered information is turned into measurable data, which produces a cost-benefit analysis. If the outcome is within the decision-making power of the individual, in this case Esther, she can go ahead. The system forecasts short, medium and long-term perspectives, but predictions can be a bit uncertain with some strategic long-term aspects. If Esther cannot decide, she consults her colleagues, or Eli as a last resort. She knows how busy he is and wants to shine by delivering results without taking up his time. This is cost-benefit thinking in action.

However, the goals are top-down and Eli steers this catamaran. Esther loves sailing.

> ## THE WORLD IS NOW AWASH IN DATA AND WE CAN SEE CONSUMERS IN A LOT CLEARER WAYS.
>
> MAX LEVCHIN, AMERICAN-UKRAINIAN SOFTWARE ENGINEER

ORGANISATIONS

Orange performance-oriented catamarans are different to Blue corporate tankers.

As a partner, Eli is also a co-captain on the big ship, responsible for the governance of their strategic enterprise. His approach is to focus and not get carried away. He keeps an eye on the performance of the whole business, as do other units, to be sure to achieve the required profitability targets; profit before turnover.

The way strategic enterprises plan and steer reflects their structure. A streamlined setup will steer and plan as effectively as possible.

The customer or market opportunity sits at the core of everything. Eli still enjoys using client-focused workshops and user-centred design. The findings are always valuable and the data generated is another step on the way to success. The value chain is organised all the way to the strategic suppliers, who are viewed as partners. After all, they also have insight and today's B2B suppliers truly enable their customers to perform better. Such an approach replicated across the value chain creates a truly powerful combination of forces.

The latest range of CRM-IQ cloud solutions makes this possible. They integrate the balanced scorecard thinking [5-3], and even connect directly with some strategic partners to generate and share valuable insight in real time. Figuring out what and how much data to share is tricky, but the small team of in-house consultants do a good job of it.

This provides real competitive advantages by offering a much wider perspective – additional insight facilitates innovation and prospect identification. Even employees are encouraged to identify new prospects and to present a Business Model Canvas. PerformVentures uses a set of tools and techniques, such as Strategy Maps, Design Thinking, Value Proposition and Empathy Canvas. They even refer to Tom Peters and Robert Waterman's 7S model [5-4] – a simple way of getting to grips with business structure, interdependencies, and how to stay ahead of the game.

> IF YOU'RE COMPETITOR-FOCUSED, YOU HAVE TO WAIT UNTIL THERE IS A COMPETITOR DOING SOMETHING. BEING CUSTOMER-FOCUSED ALLOWS YOU TO BE MORE PIONEERING. THE SINGLE MOST IMPORTANT THING IS TO FOCUS OBSESSIVELY ON THE CUSTOMER.

JEFF BEZOS, CEO @ AMAZON

Fully integrating the support functions into the balanced scorecard was tricky in the first few years. Eli remembers going through many HR people until he found one who understood not only what measurable results mean, but that everyone in the company needs to contribute to the business outcomes. It was still a stretch getting HR's full buy-in to personal accountability, but a bit of support and pressure gets you there with the right ones. The 7S model was of great help during this endeavour.

An integrated firm is only as strong as its weakest link. As a result, the company occasionally hires in performance consultants from specialist firms. They come with a high price tag, but bring specific skills and seniority to the table, which is essential to implement innovative practices and solutions. The consultants share insight with the employees to upskill them and allow them to carry out future modifications themselves. That is how you capture expertise, embed it in the learning organisation, and only invest into costly consultants when they can truly add something new.

Eli enjoys metaphors and has tried to find a suitable one for the two main dynamics of running a company. He thinks of an athlete who needs to stay strong and lean inside, whereas goals and real opportunities lie on the outside. He's not sure it's a good one, but then again he isn't paid for that.

MARKETS

Eli's country has become a true buyer's market. This is a logical consequence of focusing on customers and harnessing the power of analytics. Consumers and customers enjoy a high level of personalisation, which means they can have products and services inscribed with individual names and designed to their own specifications.

Consequently, customers and markets generate boundless data and metadata, which, combined with AI and unseen computing powers, allows companies to understand and forecast customer trends and market opportunities.

"INFORMATION IS THE OIL OF THE 21ST CENTURY, AND ANALYTICS IS THE COMBUSTION ENGINE."

PETER SONDERGAARD, VP @ GARTNER (2003–2019)

Over the years, companies have formed strategic alliances with suppliers and partners, and integrated data systems across the value chains, helping everyone involved to respond faster to market changes. They have also kept an eye on direct competitors and competitive forces, thus leading to a continuous improvement drive.

This also means focusing on what is truly relevant and having the confidence to leave out what isn't. Advancements in data IQ, predictive software and analytics have created new possibilities. Tech itself doesn't provide answers, but can highlight trends and suggest abnormal developments. The trick is then to get the right people together and run design workshops. Eli believes data can go a long way, but it helps to have human minds in the equation that will interpret the insight, put it into context and come up with realistic solutions. This step may not appear logical, but bouncing different ideas around can suddenly get you there. It might also allow you to realise that your product is a good fit for unexpected customer groups, like fire fighters and surgeons, who also need to perform at their peak.

Besides, data facilitates accountability. The world of marketing is a prime example of how larger companies have not just requested cost-benefit calculations before spending money on marketing, but demanded to see real-time data on ROI progress.

Eli laughs, wondering if politicians will ever seek his services to achieve peak performance. Maybe some presidents and prime ministers, but, in his eyes, they lack discipline and willingness to invest time. That said, politics has improved overall. The time of the big parties is over. Parties are now numerous and much smaller, none close to anything like a majority. This means they cannot talk others down without discrediting themselves. This sense of competition makes for a more constructive atmosphere. Any elected party has to form temporary alliances for shared interests and combined action.

The process brings them to consider the measurable goals that got them into power, and to decide which party takes the lead. At that point, politicians from other parties can join the cause. It's usually because they bring valuable experience or skill sets to the table. Here again, data helps enormously and provides accountability. Orange teams like these usually agree specific timelines and are accountable. This can help sieve out non-performers over time and improve results and player calibre.

It isn't perfect, as there is still a lot of room for improvement, but then again that is always the case. You just need to keep going.

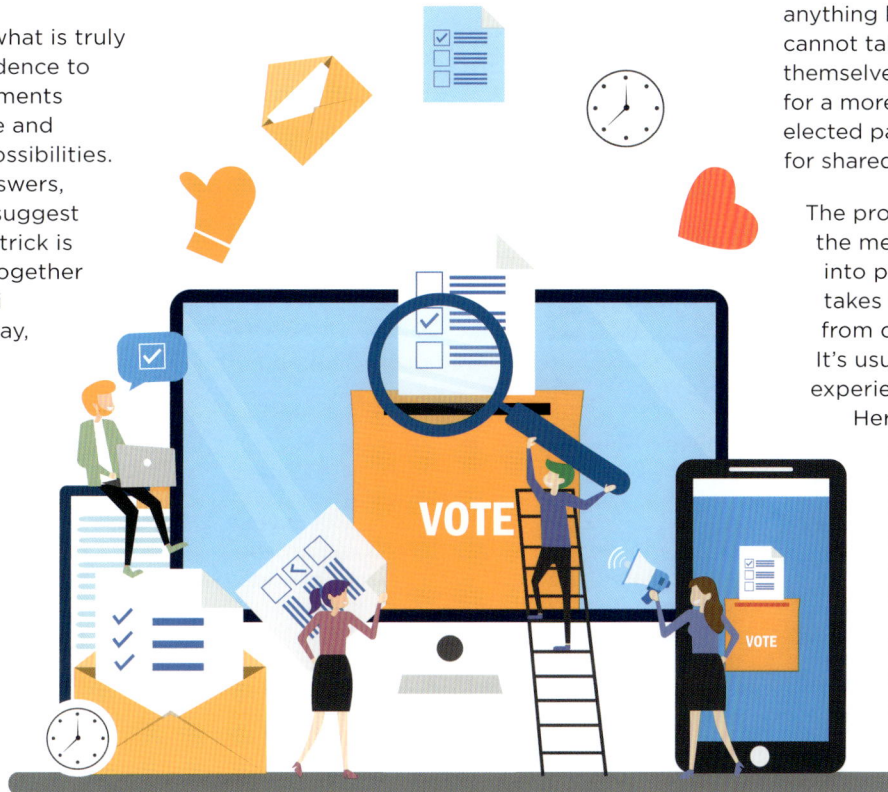

LIMITATIONS AND GROWTH INTO NEXT LEVELS

The 1st (Beige) stage concentrates on daily survival. The 2nd (Purple) stage provides safety, comfort, and peers for support and company. The boundless energy of the young at the 3rd (Red) stage often proves overwhelming for the tribe; the elders keep repeating themselves and it is time to move on. The 4th (Blue) stage had to learn the hard way that constant change and too much 3rd (Red) stage power can be more destructive than useful. Therefore, what the Blues perceive as Red chaos needs to be brought under control; a little bit of discipline has never harmed anyone. Mature, 5th (Orange) stage individuals free themselves from the restrictive generic structure. Independence is their watchword and they will approach authorities to negotiate rules that are hindering progress – 4th (Blue) stage 'one size' doesn't fit all anymore.

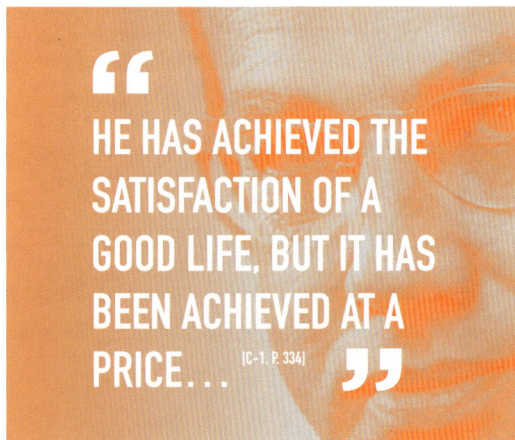

> " HE HAS ACHIEVED THE SATISFACTION OF A GOOD LIFE, BUT IT HAS BEEN ACHIEVED AT A PRICE… [C-1, P. 334] "

Driven, entrepreneurial individuals like Eli want control over their life and environment. They often love competitive settings; they most certainly are in it to win it. But after a while individuals start to realise that accumulation doesn't enhance their lives, at least not in any proportionate way. Some will come to see, as Eli did, that material self-satisfaction isn't enough. They feel they can achieve a lot more. You can boast about the big yacht that you only get to use twice a year, but it's more headaches than it's worth. It once felt great to be respected and envied by others for your material status, but over time, you get to understand that this isn't real respect. Besides, children who grow up in this environment often reject their parents' materialistic values. Suddenly, life seems to be so much more about humanity than status-driven materialism. Eli has come to "see that satisfying self alone, in a materialistic way, is not enough." [C-1, p. 327] So, if this isn't it, what should Eli be conscious about in his life?

Companies at this level perform well in a capitalistic world. They are customer and market-driven; they are adaptive, dynamic, and good at driving measurable profits. This is very suitable for venture capitalists and investment firms, where the bottom line is all that matters. Businesses focus on financial opportunities, no matter what. These firms are vigorous thanks to clear performance goals, which make objectives and decision-making rather straightforward.

Many companies rely on customers as well as suppliers and partners, all of whom will play along while the Orange business partner provides a benefit. However, resentment grows

and problems arise over time, quicker still if you treat them harshly. The same applies to employees who, at some point, go off financial rewards. They may no longer buy into the 'up or out' mantra. Employees working cross-functionally tend to be treated like 2nd-class citizens in unhealthy Orange environments. There's only so much money can buy.

In the '90s, many programmers in the software industry weren't in it for the money. They didn't want to be driven by measurable results. They claimed their creative freedom and the space to develop something that made sense to them. As the industry was becoming more of an employee market, programmers were in a better position to choose their employer. Soon after, the Agile Development Manifesto was written and a new level of management became more appreciated and acceptable. [5-5]

Society goes through similar developments. Some people get richer while others lag behind. Does all that accumulated wealth make you happy once society has declared many practices and status symbols unjust? Perceptions change – a CEO's performance bonus, which is more than his PA's lifetime salary, is suddenly no longer acceptable. How can someone have a net worth of $180 billion? [5-6]

Citizens start to challenge authorities about what is right, wrong, good, bad and acceptable. Individual performance, self-gratification and materialistic consumption have enabled some to achieve something they believe to be great, but wealth disparity has alienated them and envy has turned into resentment. It's time to move on.

The characteristics of 5th (Orange) stage markets are as follows:

'MARKETS ARE QUANTIFIABLE OPPORTUNITIES TO BE SEIZED'

POLITICAL

- Democracy as a pragmatic solution
- Parties compete for the best solutions
- Use tech to improve effectiveness (e.g. online voting)

ECONOMIC

- Easier entry for players adds competitive edge
- Idea of global position, core competencies and niches
- Predictive market developments
- Encouragement to succeed (clear performance measures)
- Government invests strategically into future trends, skills and infrastructure
- Companies and government collaborate to strengthen country's competitive advantages

SOCIAL

- Support individual performance = benefits communities/all
- Shared/participative decision-making – only if it makes sense ('tried & tested')
- Service model in social areas/often privatised (i.e. outsourced)
- Flexible working hours are common

TECHNOLOGICAL

- Highly developed
- Drive cutting-edge tech = competitive edge
- Use tech to optimise developments and decision-making
- Enable individual development

ENVIRONMENTAL

- Regulated, but open to investment
- Optimise resources, cost-benefit calculations instead of dogmatism
- Waste seen as a valuable resource
- Recycling done cost effectively

LEGAL

- Regulated, but pragmatic, and willing to make changes 'if benefits outweigh risks'

6th STAGE
GREEN: RELATIONSHIPS & MEANING

TEAM-ORIENTED INDIVIDUALS WHO BELIEVE IN RELATIONSHIPS, HIGH PERFORMANCE, BALANCE, WORKING TOGETHER FOR THE GREATER GOOD, CONSENSUS, FAIRNESS, AND TRANSPARENCY, POPULATE THIS STAGE THEY ENJOY BEING PART OF A TEAM THAT DETERMINES ITS OWN FATE. SOME INDIVIDUALS VALUE RELATIONSHIPS, INTERACTIONS AND THEIR COLLEAGUES MORE THAN THE JOB ITSELF – THEY LIVE FOR OVERALL GROWTH AND WILL GO OUT OF THEIR WAY TO HELP. 'ALL FOR ONE, ONE FOR ALL' IS THEIR MOTTO.

COMPANIES SEE THEMSELVES AS PART OF VARIOUS ECOSYSTEMS AND RESPONSIBLE FOR THE WELLBEING OF THEIR EMPLOYEES AND STAKEHOLDERS. THEY WILL EVEN ACCEPT TEMPORARY FINANCIAL LOSSES UNDER CERTAIN CIRCUMSTANCES. THESE ARE OFTEN LESSER-KNOWN FIRMS, DUE TO THEIR SMALL HEADCOUNT (50-250 EMPLOYEES), AND BECAUSE BRANDING AND SALES ARE ACHIEVED ORGANICALLY RATHER THAN THROUGH MARKETING CAMPAIGNS.

SOCIETIES COMPRISE DIFFERENT CELL-LIKE STRUCTURES AND OPERATE IN AN ORGANIC WAY, WITH HARDLY ANY CENTRALISED POWERS. INSTEAD, PEOPLE COLLABORATE ACROSS DEPARTMENTS ON SHARED INTERESTS, WITH INFORMATION FLOWING AS NECESSARY. HERE, CONCEPTS SUCH AS AN IMPROVED VERSION OF UNIVERSAL BASIC INCOME (UBI) TAKE CENTRE STAGE, AS DO HUMAN FACTOR KPIs, LIKE PERSONAL GROWTH AND HAPPINESS (E.G. GNH), RATHER THAN GROSS DOMESTIC PRODUCT (GDP). TRANSPARENCY AND TECHNOLOGY MAKE IT POSSIBLE TO FOCUS ON PEOPLE WHILST GUARDING AGAINST INDIVIDUAL ABUSE AND SEEING MOTHER EARTH AS PART OF SOCIETY.

HUMANKIND IS STARTING TO LIVE MORE SUSTAINABLY AND TO CONSIDER NATURE MORE PROACTIVELY, INCLUDING THE IMPACT OF OUR LIVES ON THE SURROUNDING FLORA AND FAUNA.

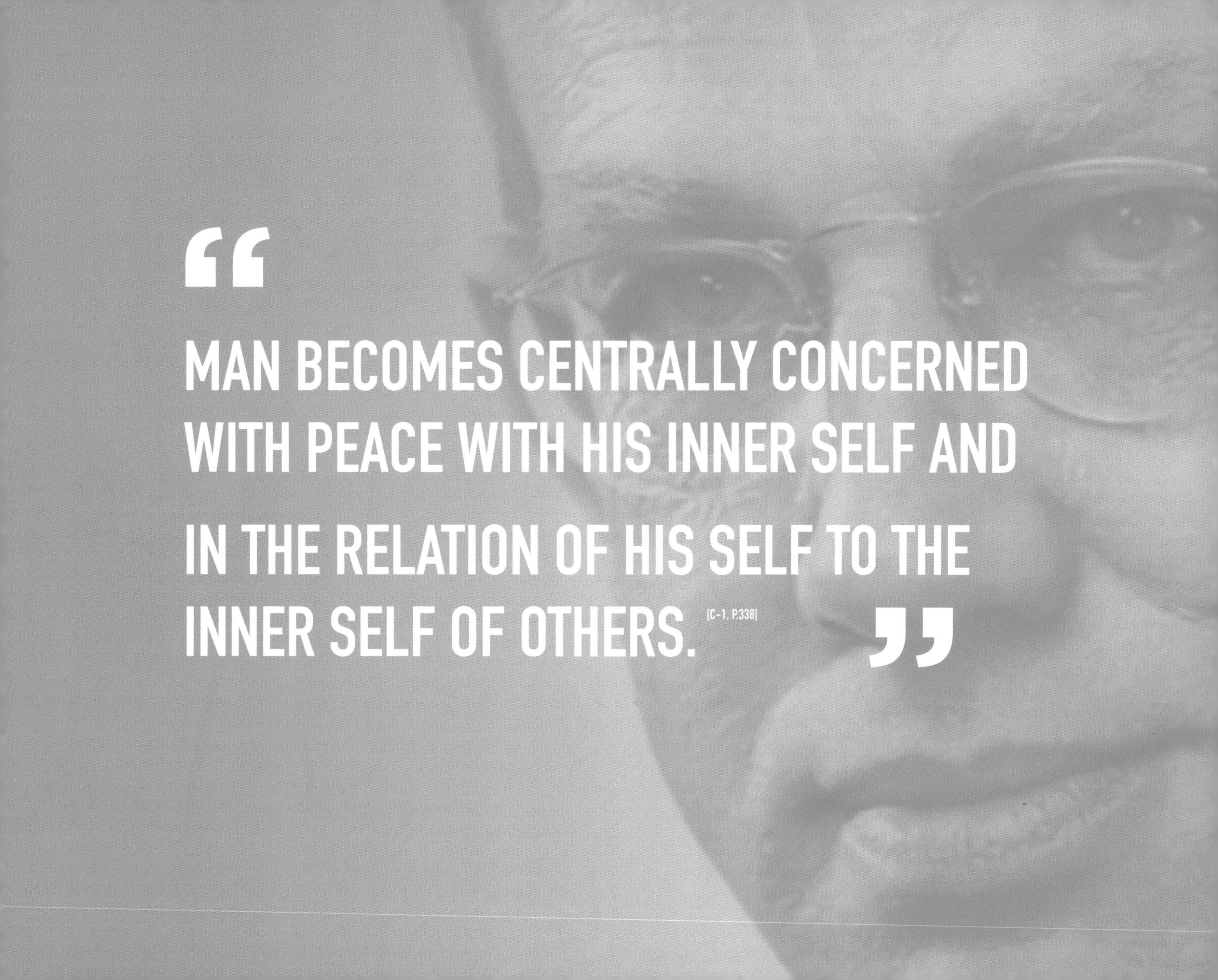

"

MAN BECOMES CENTRALLY CONCERNED WITH PEACE WITH HIS INNER SELF AND IN THE RELATION OF HIS SELF TO THE INNER SELF OF OTHERS. [C-1. P.338]

"

FLORENCE'S WORLD

Florence is sitting with Eli (our dynamic hero from the Orange chapter) in Fusion, the only restaurant they could agree on, just round the corner from Eli's posh district and Florence's former neighbourhood – the "alternative hippie quarter" as Eli calls it. Edward and Fae, two polar opposites, set up Fusion together – Edward is all about branding, strategic positioning and image, whilst Fae is interested in healthy food, sustainably sourced and served in visually appealing ways. Both believe in putting the customer first and they have separated their responsibilities rather cleverly. Edward is front-of-house and Fae handles the kitchen and suppliers. This is a great example of two styles coming together harmoniously.

Florence and Eli used to work together and respected each other's expertise and professionalism. However, Florence now realises how much they have grown apart on a personal level. Eli chases financial goals and drives business at all costs. To what extent? Florence asks herself. She tries to get Eli to consider that many of today's problems have their roots in profit maximisation and the exploitation of human and natural resources.

Eli fails to acknowledge any of the oppression, injustice, capitalistic exploitation of people and resources, racism, mass farming, or animal cruelty. In his world, life is what we make it and he refuses to listen to Florence's concerns. Therefore, she decides to put her business hat on again, to keep the focus and harmony.

In the old days, when they worked together, Florence was a user experience (UX) designer and

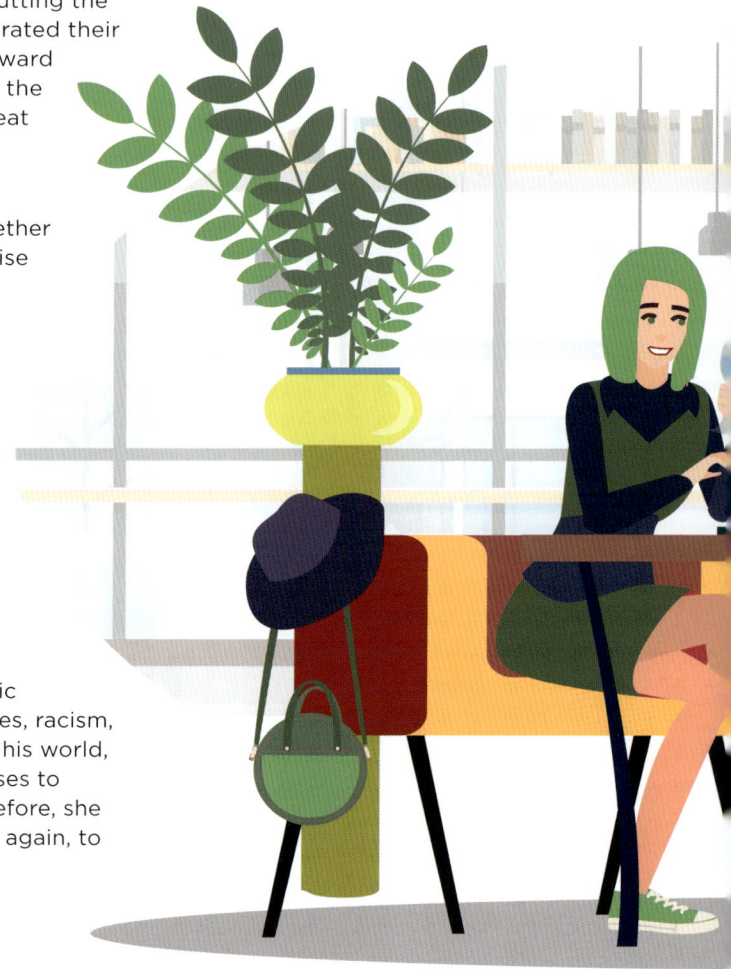

> "SUDDENLY THE PERSON OPERATING AT THE SIXTH LEVEL BEGINS TO REALIZE THAT EVERYTHING HUMAN BEINGS HAVE BELIEVED IN IS BY AND LARGE WRONG — THAT IT HAS REALLY LED TO MORE TROUBLE THAN GOOD." (C-1, P.330)

maximised the purpose and functionality of Eli's product portfolio. Still passionate about UX, Florence is now a SCRUM Master, responsible for promoting and supporting a framework designed to develop and sustain complex products. She and her team are pushing the boundaries of interactive, digital customer engagements.

We have entered a world where relationships exist between users and their devices. Imagine your tech device responding to your biometric and facial characteristics – let's call it user relationship (UR). This is exactly what Eli is looking for. He has developed an app that measures and monitors how far you can push your body without harming yourself. For example, the app can advise a bodybuilder when they have reached optimum muscle ratio. You can imagine how successful this is amongst professional athletes. Eli is now targeting other professionals seeking peak performance. Market research identified fire fighters, surgeons and ambulance services.

However, the initial feedback shows they have little interest in biometric data, but are keen on user-friendliness.

That is where Florence comes in. She decided to work with Eli and PerformVentures, because they have the means to drive cutting-edge solutions, and her team enjoys opening up new horizons. Human-centred innovations are an interest they all share. Of particular interest to them are approaches that involve biomimicry and biomorphism, as a way to ensure they learn from nature and pay tribute to naturally occurring patterns or shapes. Taken to its extreme, this work attempts to force nature's intelligence and shapes onto functional devices.

Despite access to all kinds of fancy meeting tech, Florence and Eli feel it is important to meet in person occasionally to clarify situations and expectations, especially before kicking off big projects. For now, they have agreed to bring their teams together on Friday, via a virtual reality (VR) session, to mark the official start of the project. VR technology facilitates a three-dimensional (3D) video conferencing experience with enhanced collaboration opportunities. The two still need to agree basic terms and conditions, but the discussion went well. Eli is easy to please when you support his ambitions.

The Graves levels we are entering here do not fully exist yet. A growing number of individuals are striving for the 6th (Green) stage and some companies, like Valve Corporation (aka Valve Software) and Semco Partners, opt for people-centric, organic operating systems. However, there are no fully fledged 6th level societies. I imagine worlds of this kind will emerge in the near future. The Nordic countries are certainly front-runners, in my opinion, for they are closest to this level.

For the time being, I have created scenarios that personify characteristics typical of this level while still being believable. It is unchartered territory and I hope I have found the balance between what is and what could be.

In the future, it would be great to collaborate and co-create with futurists, visionaries and philosophers on what the upcoming levels might look like in more detail, blending the framework with research, projections and imagination. This can provide roadmaps on possibilities for societal progression. I truly believe a shared global approach will benefit us all.

Florence Fellows, who lives in the countryside, enjoys returning to the city occasionally. It gives her the chance to catch up with friends from her old university, Team Academy [6-0]. She likes to see how everyone is and what they are up to. Florence has enough time to meet three friends at the station before taking the high-speed train home. She can use the four hour train ride to outline the project details and upload them to the virtual workplace, where everyone will be able to review and contribute to them. Her team comprises 14 high-calibre people, who are an integral part of Peopl-eUR, a 120-strong software company specialising in easy-to-use, enjoyable tech. With its human-centred touchpoints and seamless people journeys, Peopl-eUR is a typical company of this region and era.

Along her train journey, Florence crosses many regions. People have started to organise territories in a different way, with localisation and communities in mind. National states, as defining characteristics of societies, are no more and countries decentralised their federal powers a long time ago. Nowadays, local regions consist of around a million people and meet certain cultural and geographical factors. Florence lives in the South East Ocean region.

Within the regions, people live in self-organised holonic systems (aka SOHOS) [6-2] of up to 20,000 people. Florence's SOHOS is called Navitas, Latin for energy, its theme. People there pioneered the designing and building of local SOHOS, many of which are themed to bring out the natural shared bond between their inhabitants. SOHOS break down into two to five clusters of three to nine holons, each counting 500-1500 inhabitants with similar values, while still allowing for healthy diversity. Florence's holon, one of seven in her holarchy, is named Anahata. At the heart of each holon lie hubs of 100-200 people, who form the local neighbourhoods.

The logic very much follows the Australian idea of *20-minute neighbourhoods* where people work and socialise close to their homes.

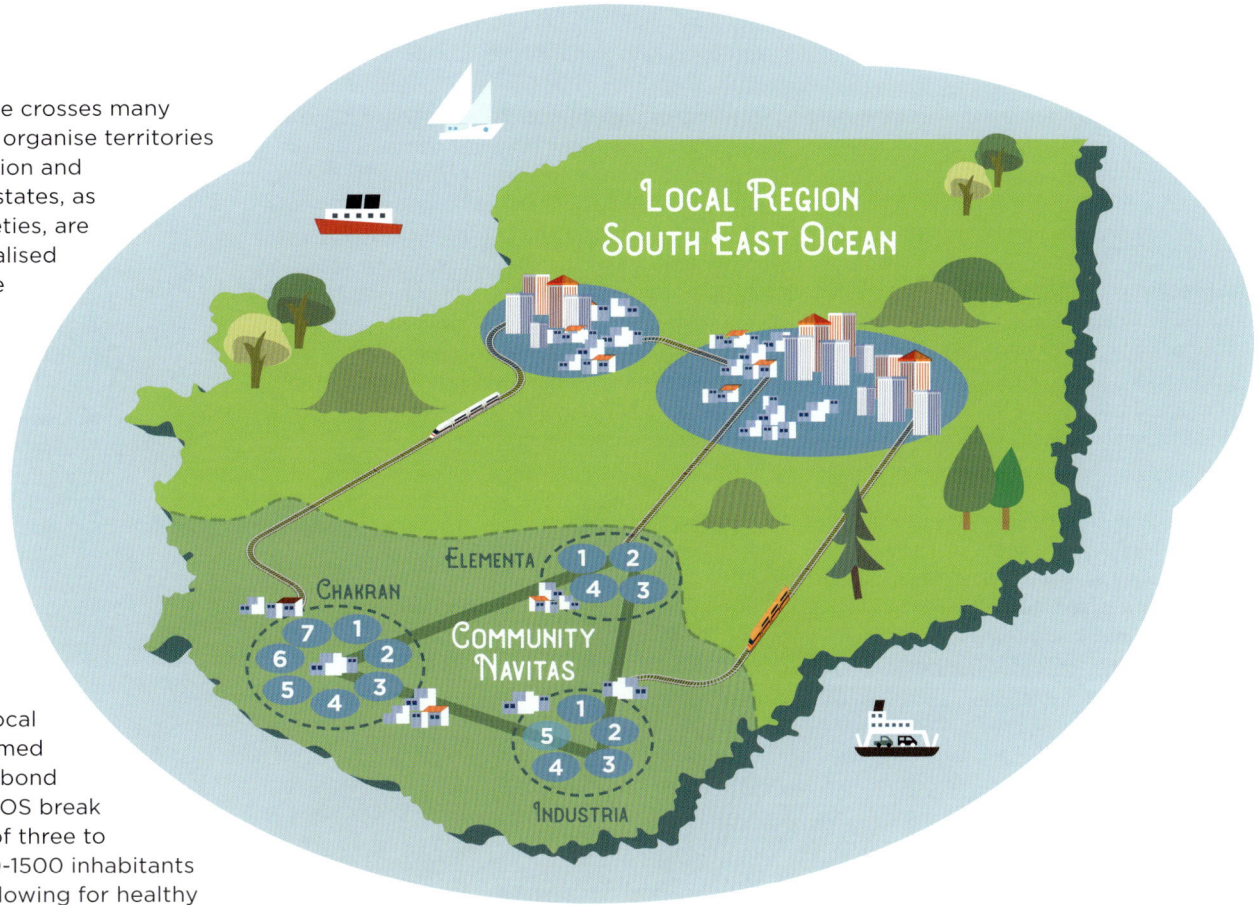

LOCAL REGION SOUTH EAST OCEAN

CHAKRAN

ELEMENTA

COMMUNITY NAVITAS

INDUSTRIA

1ST SOHOS	2ND SOHOS	3RD SOHOS	
CHAKRAN	ELEMENTA	INDUSTRIA	
1. Muladhara	1. Terra	1. Eget	
2. Swadhisthana	2. Ventus	2. Mechanica	
3. Manipura	3. Ignis	3. Magneticus	
4. Anahata	4. Aqua	4. Electrica	
5. Vishuddha		5. Pre-designed, but not named	
6. Ajna			
7. Sahasrara			

SOHOS can shield themselves, individually or collectively, from any threats such as diseases, fires or floods. Conversely, authorities can requisition them to contain outbreaks when and where needed. They can also be relatively independent. Automated underground pathways transport supplies to and from holons. This facilitates the implementation of hygiene measures. Provided there is no contamination within, many of the holons and holarchies can continue operating relatively normally during a crisis.

SOHOS exist within holarchies. From space, holarchies look like streams of cells with the ability to shut themselves off during emergencies. In many ways it is like circles within circles. The term holon is an essential part of the concept as it implies the parts and the whole are inevitably interconnected. Every holon is both a part and a whole, or the other way around: an individual is part of a family, which is part of a hub, which is part of a holon, and so on.

Topics that matter to people are handled within the most relevant circle (e.g. family, hub, holon) and coordinated with the other circles. A lot of the thinking behind these circles comes from human physiology – a science of the mechanical, physical, and biochemical human functions.[6-4] As a discipline, physiology connects science, medicine and health; it creates a certain logic for understanding how the human body adapts to stress, physical activity and disease. [6-5]

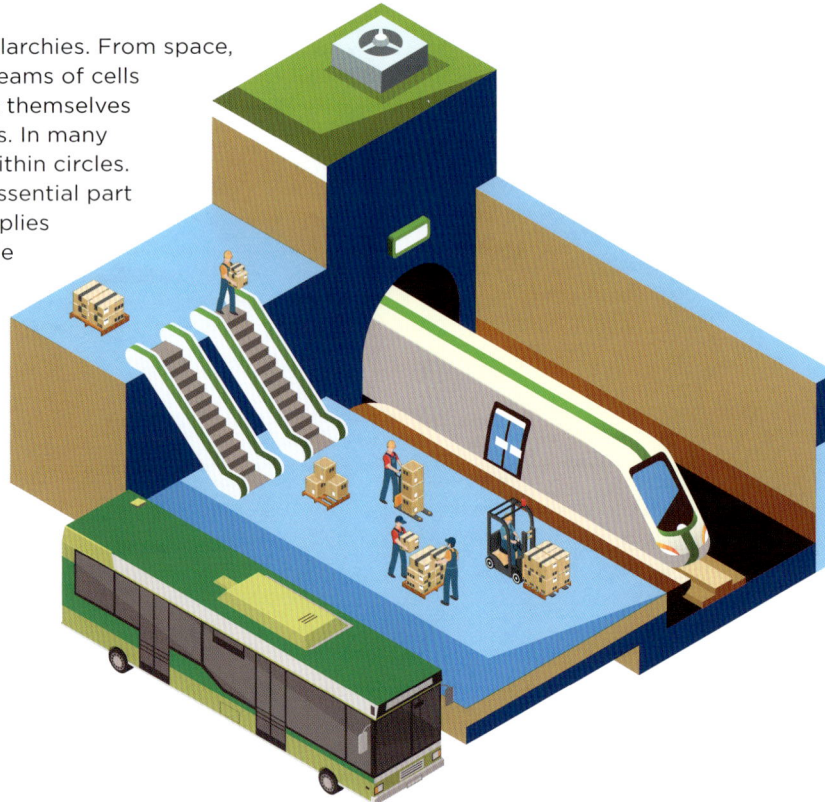

THE HOLISTIC CONCEPT

The terms holon and holarchy were coined in the 1967 book *The Ghost in the Machine* by Arthur Koestler [1905-1983], a Hungarian British author and journalist. A holon is an evolving, self-organising system composed of other holons, the structure of which exist at the balancing point between chaos and order. A holon is simultaneously a whole and a part. A holarchy can be a connection between holons. Koestler defines a holarchy as:

1. a hierarchy of self-regulating holons that function first as autonomous wholes in supra-ordination to their parts;

2. dependent parts in subordination to controls on higher levels;

3. entities in coordination with their local environment.

This is sometimes also discussed in the context of self-organising holarchic open systems (SOHOS), which confirms the organic nature of these systems. [6-3]

In Florence's world, everything is coordinated from within, not top-down. This means hardly any centralised political and government offices exist, and decisions are made where they matter.

Florence is looking forward to going home because, as convenient and buzzing as cities are, she enjoys living in her local hub. She joined her community when she married and is very much involved with and attached to it. She feels truly at home there, partly thanks to a clear match in values:

1. CONSENSUS

2. COOPERATION

3. RESPONSIBILITY FOR THE OTHER

4. HUMANISM

5. SELF-DETERMINATION

6. EQUALITY AT ALL LEVELS
   (E.G. GENDER, RACIAL, ETHNIC, ECONOMIC, SOCIAL...)

7. COMPASSION

8. PACIFISM

+ She believes that from the values grows the right kind of strengths, as follows:

- ACCEPTING WHOLEHEARTEDLY THAT ALL PEOPLE ARE DIFFERENT AND DESERVE TO BE HAPPY;

- GIVING PEOPLE THE OPPORTUNITY TO STRIVE FOR MEANING AND PURPOSE;

- CONSIDERING AND LOOKING AFTER PEOPLE AND RESOURCES;

- CREATING MORE SUSTAINABLE SOLUTIONS WITH WIDER INVOLVEMENT OF PEOPLE AND STAKEHOLDERS;

- POSSESSING GREATER SELF-DETERMINATION AND CONFIDENCE IN PEOPLE, WHICH, IN TURN, LEADS TO A GREATER LEVEL OF PRODUCTIVITY, HEALTH AND HAPPINESS.

− That said, she knows nothing is perfect. There are also downfalls to this community:

- PEOPLE BURN OUT IN THEIR SEARCH FOR ACCEPTANCE — THEY HELP OUT CONSTANTLY AND WORK FOR THE GREATER GOOD OF THE TEAM, HUB OR SOCIETY (ESPECIALLY TRUE FOR UNBALANCED GROUP SETTINGS);

- TRYING TO KEEP THE PEACE AT ALL COSTS AND NOT WANTING TO ROCK THE BOAT CAN MEAN MISSING OUT ON NECESSARY CLARIFICATIONS, TOO MANY MEETINGS, AND A LACK OF PROGRESS;

- TOO MUCH IDEALISM (E.G. ULTRA-ALTRUISM) CAN BECOME UNREALISTIC AND CAUSE FRUSTRATION WHEN PEOPLE FAIL TO REALISE THEIR POTENTIAL — ESPECIALLY IN ENVIRONMENTS WITH STRONG DYNAMICS FROM THE OLD RED, BLUE OR ORANGE WORLDS;

- GROUP CONFORMITY CAN STIFLE INDIVIDUAL INTERESTS AND GROWTH BEYOND WHAT MATTERS TO THE COLLECTIVE.

Florence enjoys living here and feels very much part of a bigger, connected human community. This part of the world has come a long way: people, businesses and social leaders now put humans or customers at the heart of everything. That is where she and her husband Finn always wanted to be. They only moved once within the community to a new holon – when they were expecting a baby and wanted more space and other families around them.

The planet is still suffering from the aftermath of actions by previous generations, but people are starting to act more responsibly and sustainably by consuming less and living more balanced lives. Florence and Finn rejoice that humankind is reaching a level that affords real hope to them and their children's future.

INDIVIDUALS

Florence has arrived back home and is happy with the amount of work she has done along the way. Thanks to the latest tech solutions, she can work simultaneously on different devices, and collaborate in real time with partners whilst travelling at optimum speed. Virtual co-creation is productive and fun. Welcome to the era of work-life integration.

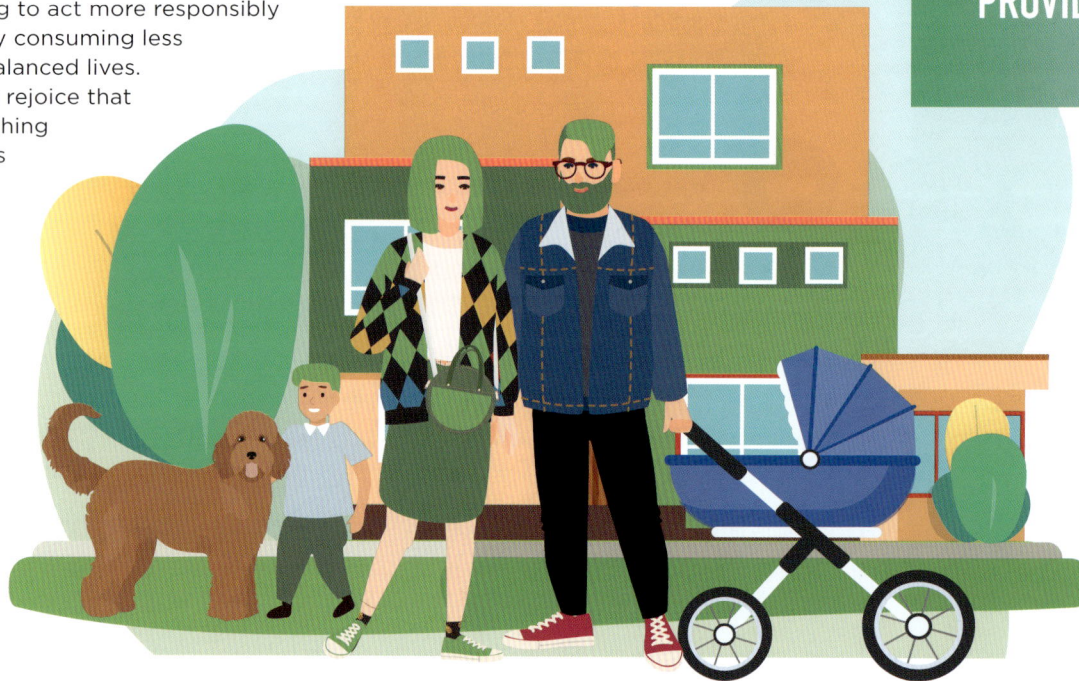

> " IS IT BAD TO ASPIRE THAT ALL SHARE THE FRUITS OF WHAT THE CUMULATIVE EFFORTS OF MAN HAVE PROVIDED? [C–1, P. 347] "

Florence and Finn had no trouble choosing the most fitting community and hub to live in, as the regions prioritise transparency about demographic, environmental and economic data. The couple made a conscious choice to move to Manipura. They felt it would give them the best opportunity to focus on their development.

Florence is truly grateful to previous generations who worked hard and endured a lot to create societies like this one. It is fantastic to live in a time and place where people can blossom and make the world around them more vibrant. This fits nicely with her name – Florence's parents named her after Saint Florentin (from Latin *florens/ florentius*, meaning 'blossoming'). To her, flourishing in life also means accepting, appreciating, and honouring what her generation has inherited.

In many ways, she is doing the same for her two children. As she did, they attend a Montessori school where they have the opportunity to grow and develop to their fullest potential. In today's Green world, schools do not adopt the one-size-fits-all approach; instead, they let children learn independently and collectively based on their specific talents and needs. Every flower grows and blooms at a different pace; humans are the same. Here, teachers have become facilitators, managing group dynamics and trusting children to find out what is important to them. At times that might also mean taming egos, providing discipline and helping children understand how the little steps are part of bigger achievements. In their school, life is not about things, but people, meaningful bonds, and growth.

Both Florence and her husband hold these beliefs. The Fellows shared the responsibility of bringing up their children. Florence only took time off to raise their first child and Finn for the second one. In places like Navitas and companies like Peopl-eUR, an equal and more extended approach to childcare is standard. The Green society has worked out that it takes young children a few years to develop deep human bonds, trust, emotional stability, and a sense of belonging. Every human needs strong roots. Finn loved the early years with their youngest and it worked well with his professional career –

he is a drummer and lives for jazz. Music is very much part of the family vibe. Finn missed a few lucrative opportunities whilst being a stay-at-home dad, but so did Florence when she was a stay-at-home mum. Luckily, everyone in South East Ocean receives a Universal Basic Income [UBI], which makes life much easier. With basic needs covered and healthy environments provided, personal life and growth take on a completely new dimension.

UBI in a Green society comes with a performance-related element and a high level of accountability. Early attempts at UBI missed these vital aspects and many people took advantage without contributing to their society. In order to make UBI work, people needed to develop a certain level of maturity and understanding of how and why this approach works.

For example, when Finn does not earn enough and relies on UBI, he has to help in various areas to support the community. He loves this as it usually means getting involved in a community or environmental project for a few weeks or months. You start by learning about the topic at hand, you then do the work and, finally, provide feedback to others and the organisation. It is a great way to get familiar with different fields and share that learning with others. It reminds Finn of a bee buzzing around and exploring some of the (bio)diversity around it. You can end up taking on very different roles. For example, last time Finn's brief was to set up a group to explore what agile development has in common with child development, and how jazz can serve as a metaphor. It hit many sweet spots for him and he learned a great deal. The insights and new friends he gained were the best part of the experience. He realised that, in diverse and focused settings, people blossom just like wildflowers. In addition, being able to share most of the ideas at home means everyone gets to learn and grow.

AUTHOR'S COMMENT:

The UBI (Universal Basic Income) provides everyone with a set monthly income, regardless of means. Supporters believe an unconditional safety net can help people out of poverty, by giving them the time to apply for jobs or learn essential new skills. This is particularly important in the age of digitalisation and automation, with the constant need for adaptation. Additionally, it provides room for more meaningful and often community-oriented engagements.

It was once politically unpopular. The idea that everyone in society would get an unconditional source of revenue, which they could use as they wished, seemed unthinkable. However, UBI has gained traction in recent years. [6 - 6]

Although it is enjoying renewed popularity and trial runs are taking place all over the world, the concept is not new. In fact, it dates back to the early 16th century when Sir Thomas More's book *Utopia* depicted a society in which every person receives a guaranteed income.

In Switzerland, the introduction of a national UBI was voted down by close to 80% in 2016. Finland's scheme ran in 2017 and 2018, and attracted widespread international interest — 2,000 randomly selected unemployed people across the country received a regular monthly income. This trial was a bit different as it focused on individuals who were out of work, and sought primarily to test whether a guaranteed income might encourage people to take up low-paid or temporary work without fear of losing benefits. The security of a basic income generally allowed people to do things that are more meaningful. [6 - 7]

However, no country has yet fully bought into it. This is a good example of a concept that would work very well in a society with a 6th level mindset, where people have gone through 5th level values such as performance, measurability, continuous improvement, and personal accountability. These values are not lost at the 6th level, instead people have become more community-oriented, more social and supportive. With this level of maturity, the logic of UBI would thrive.

Even Bond, their dog, benefits from a healthy and lively home, and you can tell by her relaxed nature. Bond is a good-tempered, unflappable Labradoodle, which looks a bit more like a hairy retriever than a poodle. Nearly all of the neighbours love her, which is good as the Fellows live in a small, but suitably sized flat within a three-storey *earthship house*. None of the holon dwellers live in one place forever; instead they move according to their life circumstances and needs at any given time. People are not as materialistic as they used to be, and digital solutions facilitate a truly shared economy. It is a reminder of Kate Humble's first edition book "*A year living simply*". Once upon a time this was just a set of examples, then these became a trend, and nowadays living simply is a lifestyle choice; ultimately, owning products doesn't make one happy in the long run. Many tools, home utilities and machines are shared, which means less baggage and easier moving. Even car owners sign up to one of the established services to add their vehicle to the local hub carpool. Life in general is about sharing.

Likewise, most of the sports equipment is available for all in a hub like Anahata, organised via mobile devices that keep track of times and usage. Tracking solutions within the holon and the internet of things (IoT) encourage people to look after the equipment and advise when it needs servicing. There are many team sport activities on offer, and automated tech solutions can even help initiate games and exercise. For example, when a holonic baseball field has a free slot coming up, the system contacts a certain number of people to check whether they are up for a game. If interest is low in Anahata, the system contacts people in neighbouring holons. This is great for Finn who loves getting together for a good basketball game. Florence is more into Bikram and Vinyasa yoga. All she needs is a pair of Lululemon yoga pants, a shirt, and a mat.

Florence and Finn made friends and met like-minded people through sport. There is always an activity they can join in the hub or holon. Their friends come from different parts of their life – work, musical groups, and neighbours. The lines between personal and professional lives are often blurred.

Included in their extended community are friends from further away. They can stay in touch easily thanks to modern tech solutions. For example, Florence and Finn regularly meet for virtual cooking classes with friends who live 1000 km away. The virtual sessions come in the form of holograms, affording them a 3D experience. It is not the real thing, as you cannot swap spices, but you can still cook and eat together.

Overall, digital tech has moved towards shared experiences. Florence likes to watch movies with her university friends during virtual movie sessions – they are all big fans of anti-hero movies.

Their favourites include *Paths to Glory, Gran Torino, Erin Brokovich*, and *Biggest Little Farm*. They order the same food, ice cream, bubbly, and synchronize deliveries. It is fun on the occasion, but Florence usually streams content around her specific interests – like jazz, child education, and nature – from whatever services are most suitable.

The new trend in crowd-financing means that even niche topics can be professionally produced once funded. Florence and a few like-minded people have just kicked off a production about one of her early school-day heroes. It's the French philosopher and writer Auguste Comte [1798-1857], the founding father of sociology who formulated the positivism doctrine. She is fascinated that someone in the first half of the 19th century could be so forward-looking and really wants this programme to come to life.

Florence is fond of many people. The one person that stands out currently is Greta, who lives across the road. She lives with a cool husband, three kids – one of whom is slightly disabled – and her in-laws. Florence likes Greta's passion for social solutions. With her small consulting firm, Greta works in many different areas and develops innovative social solutions on the back of interdisciplinary insights. The company regularly features as one of the influential players in the regional news.

Furthermore, Greta supports three social initiatives around mindful living, multicultural integration, and the LGBTQ community. Her latest achievement consisted in bringing a version of the Burning Man festival to her local region.

AUTHOR'S COMMENT:

Auguste Comte grew up after the French Revolution and during the industrial one. Hierarchical belief systems were changing, scientific findings questioned religious dogmas, and social inequalities widened, giving rise to new ideas about democracy, political rights and living together. It was a time of far-reaching social and political upheaval.

Auguste Comte was born into a strict Catholic family, but also had the privilege of receiving a highly progressive education. Looking at the world around him, he became obsessed with the idea of building a new kind of society or nation. He was a visionary, eccentric, and only intermittently sane. This is no surprise considering how far ahead he was of the people and world around him. [6–8]

He believed societies operate according to their own laws, much like the physical world. Some people copied his term social physics, and thus he coined and protected the word sociology. He posited a world where knowledge needed the positive proof of science, observation and/or experimentation. He applied this rigour to social studies and gained insight into social dynamics — what aspects of societies change and which ones remain the same. His idea of 'live for others' comes from 'vivre pour autrui' and is the origin of the word 'altruism'.

He had the courage to stand up to the established powers in Europe and suggest a new form of society to suit the intellectual and emotional demand of modern men and women. Some established religious beliefs and practices no longer worked — atheists were growing in numbers and a multicultural society required 'different ways'.

For example, he wanted to build Temples of Humanity where people could come together and discuss religion, science, philosophy, art, and so on. He also suggested a shared calendar with each month dedicated to an important field of endeavour — like marriage, parenting, science and art, among others — and each day to a person who made valuable contributions. These are even modern ideas by today's standards. [6–9]

It is a global phenomenon and Florence is so thankful to Greta for establishing a local version. Why travel when you can have a mindful event locally? Florence thinks of herself as incredibly good at balancing different matters, but Greta takes this to another level. You have to admire people like her.

Florence is also involved in a few communal initiatives. Currently, she is participating in a movement called She Leads Change. [6 –11] It began with a few women coming together in a peer group to encourage each other to step up into new leadership roles, in new ways. Their core aim is to support people from all walks of life to find generative ways of leading positive change. They offer programmes that focus on helping change-makers build more courage, confidence and competence. Nowadays, it is open to everyone, men included, but the organisation has kept its name to stay true to its roots of embracing and adding "female" leadership characteristics to develop more balanced, well-rounded leaders. These sessions do away with power differentials – between those who have the questions and those who have the answers; everybody has something to contribute and to learn. What Florence loves about the programmes is the energy that arises from within each individual, and then generates ever-changing,

FACT:

Burning Man takes its name from its finale, the symbolic burning of a large wooden figure.

Baker Harvey, an artist, philanthropist and activist, and his friend Jerry James initiated it in 1986. The festival started small and was a summer solstice evening ritual where they would burn their creation of a man's effigy.

This event seeks to encourage fellow visitors to be kind to each other and to Mother Earth. A crowd of people coming together at the height of summer in the middle of a desert, where no exchange of money or formal currency is allowed, may have no choice but to be compassionate and look out for each other's needs.

This ongoing experiment in community and art follows ten main principles: radical inclusion, gifting, de-commodification, radical self-reliance, radical self-expression, participation, immediacy, communal effort, civic responsibility, and leave no trace. It supports its global participants to manifest its ten principles through six interconnected and aspirational areas: arts, civic involvement, culture, education, philosophy and social enterprise. [6-10]

self-determined individualistic and group dynamics. In addition, every session and cohort is different. You just have to learn to let go, trust the people, the process, and the dynamics. After all, we can all learn from each other, and the collective is smarter than the individual. [6 -11]

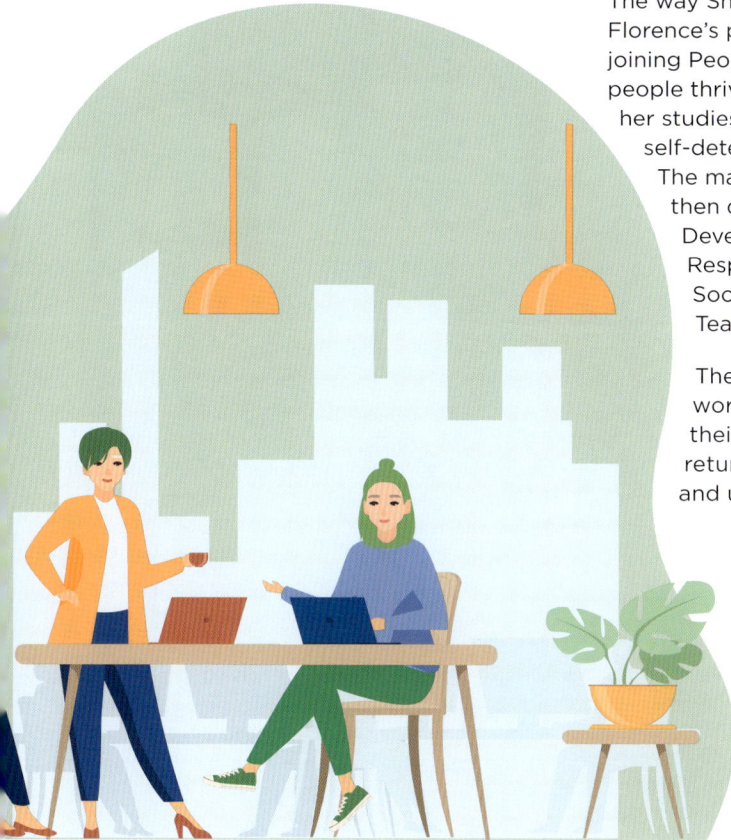

Florence would like to see this approach embraced in secondary schools. Instilling a true sense of being and connecting early on could lead to conscious, responsible teenagers and adults. Her children will need more attention as they grow older – this could be one of her next projects.

The way She Leads Change operates matches Florence's preferred way of working since joining Peopl-eUR and understanding how people thrive in the right environment. During her studies, she looked into the origins of self-determined, people operating systems. The many practices she came across then did and still do fascinate her: Agile Development, Holacracy, Lean Startup, Responsive.org, Semco Style Institute, Sociocracy 3.0, Google's re:Work, and Teal Organisations. [6-12]

The creators of these concepts and working styles were pioneers of their times, who helped business return its focus to people (customer and user centricity).

Flourishing in this Green world requires the following motivations:

PURPOSE

Fun and satisfaction

Self-determination

Work-life integration

Positive contribution to the collective (e.g. team)

MASTERY

Balanced, human growth

Team development

Experts with strong social skills

AUTONOMY

Joint creativity

Interpersonal dependence

High level of personal freedom

Self-directed career path

AN ANALOGY

The principles Florence employs in her work share many similarities with jazz: keep the rules to a minimum, create a high level of transparency [6-13], trust the process and people, mistakes allow you to learn and grow, and friction isn't necessarily a bad thing. Florence is a passionate pianist and plays mainly trios, like her idol Bill Evans. His use of impressionist harmony, creative interpretations from a traditional jazz repertoire, and his uniquely independent melodic lines influence her style greatly. [6-14]

Florence knows that rules are sometimes necessary and established for a reason. However, she feels they can also hinder creativity and change. If people focus too much on the what, they forget the why and run the risk of applying rules to the wrong context. At the onset of her career, rules would occasionally crop up because of the 10% of people who were misinformed or made mistakes. What a great way of restricting the remaining nine out of ten professionals! Consequently, Florence calls rules guidelines that come together in recipes, much like her freestyle cooking. Teams discuss the guidelines when needed, use them to work around rigidity, and occasionally adapt them to roll with necessary changes.

Openness and transparency matter to Florence for they enable useful feedback. Constructive criticism and mutual learning can be very empowering and have brought her where she is today. Instinctively trusting others

is part of her mindset, though one has to earn respect. She still possesses a healthy level of scepticism, but believes that people have earnest motivations.

There is a lot of experimentation going on in both her jazz trios and her company. We naturally all make mistakes, but Florence sees these as learning opportunities. You never know where life might take you and how opportunities shape that path. For example, she had an interesting moment during a performance for a rather large audience with her current trio, only a few months after they had come together. She was really getting into the swing and it was taking shape nicely. Suddenly, at the height of the performance, Florence played a chord that was completely off. It was painful to

hear and she felt she had let everyone down. Miles, a member of the trio, briefly stepped back, took a deep breath and played a few notes that complemented Florence's chord. This slightly bizarre sequence became their signature sound. Friction is a force that can hold back a movement, but, with the right level of trust and openness, it is just what is needed to adapt and get things moving forward again. It is also a way of staying alert. As Adrian Cho points out, "being able to improvise is crucial in today's business climate, and so is having the collaborative agility demonstrated by a good jazz combo." Many people have built on his 14 principles of the Jazz Process ever since [6-15].

Flexibility, trust and commitment enable Florence and her musician colleagues to be quite mindful. However, she can sometimes sense a drawback. It is often difficult to figure out the recipes for success and repeat them retrospectively. When the flow is right, it is like magic. Florence thinks the great jazz musician Miles Davis put it nicely when talking to Ben Sidran in 1986: "The albums '*So What*' or '*Kind of Blue*', they were done in that era, the right hour, the right day, and it happened. It's over now. What I used to play with Bill Evans, all those different modes, and substitute chords, we had the energy then and we liked it. But I have no feel for it anymore – it's more like warmed-over turkey." [6-16]

Neither Navitas nor Peopl-eUR are perfect. Florence knows this, but what is perfection? Is there a perfect jazz tune? Do people need to be perfect in order to be valuable team members or friends?

Florence looks at Feena, one of her relatively new peers, who just entered the room. Feena is petite, kind, caring, and tremendously considerate. Still, Florence feels Feena is too idealistic and tries too hard to make everyone like and be nice to each other. It is as if she had no friends of her own, and it is just a bit too much for Florence.

Here is an example of how over the top Feena can be. The organisation is seeking to pilot a new in-house initiative: creating project teams with colleagues who do not often work together. To initiate this, Feena is keen to run a whole day on values, developing shared professional and personal interests. She pushes for this to happen by trying to convince everyone. However, a whole day is a lot of time and colleagues at Peopl-eUR already share a common ground. As a result, people push back and their lack of enthusiasm for her idea offends Feena.

At the same time, Feena struggles to meet her own deadlines and often seems to make up for it on the weekends. Florence respects her dedication, but believes Feena lacks performance-oriented pragmatism at times and is overly critical when it comes to creating temporary hierarchies, generating profits and making money. Florence agrees that you should not generate money at the cost of others, but, if you provide value for money and generate a healthy profit margin, you can invest that back into your employees and society.

AUTHOR'S COMMENT:

I would like to point out that rules in music have relaxed and become fewer over the years and centuries. For example, between 500 and 1500 AD, the Catholic Church ruled musical composition. Rulers had strong opinions about what was "holy" and what was not. During early medieval times, they only allowed perfect intervals in harmony; all other intervals were considered impure and, therefore, not fit for church. You might forgive these religious leaders for having lived at completely different times in history.

Leadership did not really progress in the following centuries if you consider what German rulers tried to do in Czechoslovakia during the 1940s: Goebbels deemed jazz "degenerate" or "jungle music".

In his short novel, The Bass Saxophone, Czech writer and dissident Josef Skvorecky published the Nazis' ten bizarre rules on how to restrict jazz. They are well worth a look, if only for their absurdity. They are all rather amusing, but my favourite one, simply because of the exception, is:

Rule six: "Also prohibited are so-called drum breaks longer than half a bar in four-quarter beat (except in stylized military marches)." [6-17]

LEADERSHIP

Peopl-eUR is an agile organisation in every sense of the word. Florence loves that and has been with the company for more than four years since the merger of her own boutique consultancy with Peopl-eUR. Day-to-day work is lively, as was her previous work environment, but her current employer has more method in the madness. Working in a larger organisation can be tense at times, but at least she has access to more opportunities.

At Peopl-eUR there are no formal leadership levels – who cares the most takes the lead. The founder, Fred, is still in the business, but the employees now own the firm. There is no top-down approach here; leadership bubbles that follow a star logic drawing on experts from specific, professional areas determine leadership. The star is made up of the four main forces: future, people, organisation, and tech. These translate into 12 strategic bubbles, each headed by a bubble hat who works within the strategic core bubble with a support bubble. The support bubble ensures the representation and consideration of all directly related areas. The rest of the employees make up the base bubble. Thus, every employee belongs to a bubble and leadership becomes a shared experience. Everyone can attend any bubble session, even if strategic decisions are being shaped. People trust each other to focus on the bubbles to improve their company's overall competitive position.

For example, Fred wears the hat for the core bubble 'Long-term Strategy' (i.e. future). In parallel, he attends all three tech support bubbles to understand how technologies are progressing. Furthermore, he also keeps abreast of general people and organisational matters by attending basic bubbles. He would love to be in all twelve core bubbles, but then he wouldn't have enough time to get his work done.

This takes Florence back to her early days. When she joined Peopl-eUR, she was suddenly interested in participating in so many different areas. It was also a great way of meeting all these interesting and knowledgeable colleagues. However, due to her initial lack of focus, she quickly fell behind targets that linked into her colleagues' work, and consequently had to tame her professional curiosity (at least a bit). Balancing engagement and delivery is one of the initial lessons Florence had to learn the hard way. Ultimately, the company is performance and target-driven, and needs to meet economic realities. It is great being friendly and seeking harmony, as long as you deliver; otherwise someone else has to pick up the slack. There is always a lot to do.

> **ANYBODY CAN PUT ON THE HAT OF "THE BOSS" TO BRING ABOUT IMPORTANT DECISIONS, LAUNCH NEW INITIATIVES, HOLD UNDERPERFORMING COLLEAGUES TO ACCOUNT, HELP RESOLVE CONFLICTS, OR TAKE OVER LEADERSHIP IF RESULTS ARE BAD AND ACTION IS NEEDED.** (6–18, P. 114)
>
> **FRÉDÉRIC LALOUX**

Overall, L&D duties take up little of Florence's time as she pushed for additional peer-to-peer support right from the outset. Green firms often practise leadership as followership. In this case, the 14 employees chose Florence as their formal leader. Every 6-12 months, all disciplinary and circle leaders go through this selection process.

Florence's second hat is that of Scrum Coach for one of the key projects. She was also a team coach in her previous company, dealing mostly with methodology and processes. Nowadays, her focus lies on people and social interactions. As team lead, she empowers members to manage themselves rather than taking on these responsibilities herself. She is a so-called servant leader, in touch with the customer-facing product owner, and overseeing the circles and dynamics to allow team members to succeed.

Florence spends a lot of time facilitating interests, empowering people to optimise processes, ensuring the team has the resources it needs, and managing circles overlapping with hers.

She is an expert in her own right in both roles. Everyone is aware of the direction of travel and of their respective goals. Florence leads with questions and acts as a sounding board when and where needed.

Nowadays, Florence has two big hats (i.e. leading roles) and even more small hats (supporting roles). First, she is the disciplinary leader for a team of 14. This is still a legal requirement, as employees need to have a person to turn to, for example, for people or Learning and Development (L&D) matters, and in case of conflict. Employees are generally encouraged to take matters into their own hands. With L&D, Florence follows the common V-Rake model and advises her colleagues to develop either vertically, by adding depth in a specific area of expertise, or horizontally, by adding companion skills to their key ones.

People tend to figure out what skills to develop to match their personal interests and align with future demands and developments. Peopl-eUR offers some assistance with an extensive database that manages people's skills, as well as their interests and business demands directly related to the firm's growth strategy. Additional predictive software solutions enable employees to gain insight into future demands from every angle.

According to Torbert's seven leadership styles, people at the 6th (Green) stage fall under the category of Strategist with the following attributes: [C-3]

CHARACTERISTICS
Generates organisational and personal transformations; exercises the power of mutual inquiry, vigilance, and vulnerability for both the short and long term.

STRENGTHS
Effective as a transformational leader; good at handling people's instinctive resistance to change, and comfortable dealing with conflict. They can naturally engage with people at all levels of an organisation.

What sets them apart from Individualists from the 5th (Orange) stage is their focus on organisational constraints and perceptions, which they treat as negotiable and changeable.

A Strategist works less with method and processes and more with people and interactions.

At Peopl-eUR, leadership roles can change quickly, if necessary and the parties involved agree. Here, it is not about ego, but joint effort. Florence sees this as another similarity with jazz. Jazz performers routinely take the initiative and temporary lead in response to other players and sequences, often creating shifts that result in novel sequences. A band's musical leadership often changes during a set, keeping the sound fresh and surprising. Agile rather than top-down leadership can be healthy for multi-circular teams with expert members.

As mentioned, in addition to her two big leadership hats, Florence wears a lot of changing hats. Over the past six months, she has worked for different projects as an independent tester, as an integrator, and even got involved in consultative and team selling. She might want to take on a role as product owner later on in the year, but first she will invest a bit of time in shadowing her colleague Fatima, who is great with clients. Her clients become real partners, taking on a natural lead in her projects and becoming an intrinsic part of its success. In a weird way, they constantly redefine their success and are very happy with what they co-create.

TEAMS

How do you define a team? For many years, companies have tried to train groups of individuals working alongside each other to form teams. There is a difference between a group and a team. A team is a bunch of people coming together to achieve a common goal. At Peopl-eUR, that is everyone. Florence recently discussed whether some long-term external partners could become part of the team, but for now, they have decided to stick to employees.

Numbers are a natural barrier to meaningful relationships. This is down to a sense of belonging – to one another and, in business, to the company. Early pioneers like the US-based online retail company Zappos – which originally thrived with an agile Green operational model (Holacracy) approach – tried to scale into the thousands, and had to learn the hard way that running an organisation in a Green way has limits. Florence sees this limit in the region of 150-250 employees, but that is just a hunch. She believes you can stretch it a bit, but while you might gain quantity, you can lose quality, which could push disillusioned employees to leave in droves. [6-19]

Consequently, Peopl-eUR invests a lot of time in making sure they bring the right people into their circle. It is not just about professional skills (e.g. qualifications), but also social ones (e.g. communication, feedback) and personal characteristics (e.g. self-awareness, discipline).

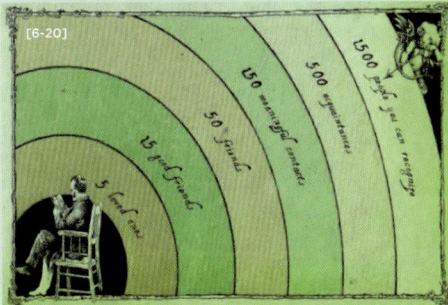

Potential recruits are invited to work in the company for a few weeks with up to three different teams, or to come in for an "Innovation Circle" with Peopl-eUR employees. Team feedback is essential in the decision-making process and usually ensures the right fit. Florence loves Innovation Circles in particular, because so much new thinking emerges from these. Needless to say that Peopl-eUR pays interested people for their time and input, even if they do not hire them. As Mao Zedong said, "Let a hundred flowers bloom, let a hundred schools of thought contend."

Florence was also involved in an initiative to employ young professionals with Down syndrome. She and Laura, the project lead, hired two professionals earlier in the year and brought two more on board recently. People who are somewhere off the normal range on a spectrum can also have outstanding skills. Two of the newcomers are very good with data. Furthermore, Florence recognises the positive contribution they brought to the company culture. Two of them recently fell in love and are planning to get married. Somehow, this filled the whole company with love and pride. One of the reasons why Florence enjoys working here.

When Florence came on board she had been collaborating with Peopl-eUR for months and it felt like a natural fit. Initially, she struggled a bit with the culture that she found, in her words, co-opetitive. Despite all the collaboration and peer support, colleagues occasionally try to outsmart and outperform each other. The better you perform, the more recognition and attention you gain. Having said that, the company did learn from previous bad experiences and competition is now limited. Doing something that works against the greater good is frowned upon big time – the emphasis is definitely on the 'co-op'.

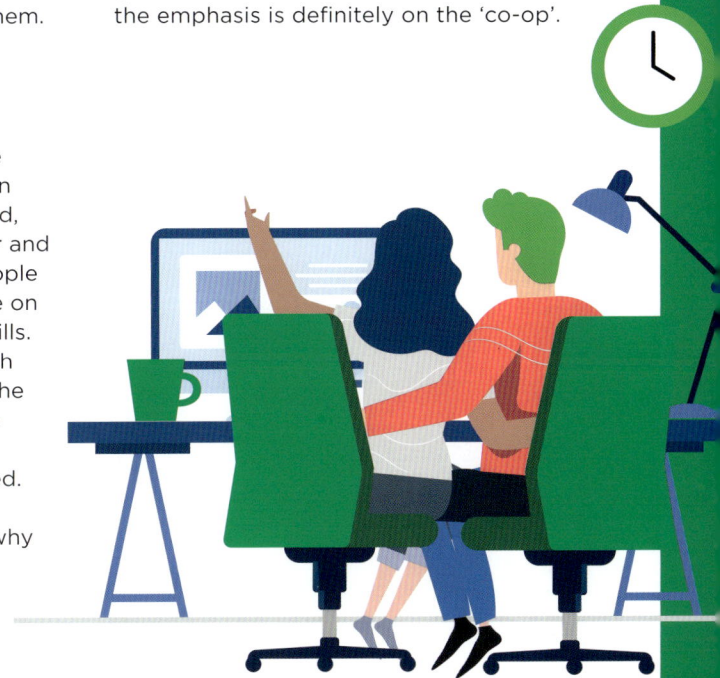

> ❝
> **I MIGHT BELIEVE A PERSON HAS WHAT IT TAKES TO ADD VALUE IN THE FORM OF A SPECIFIC ROLE, BUT IT IS NOT MY DECISION. THE PERSON NEEDS TO SHOW THE TEAM THAT THEIR JOB OR ROLE IS VALUABLE TO THEM. ALTERNATIVELY, ONE CAN ALWAYS CHECK IF USING A FREELANCER IS MORE USEFUL FOR THE JOB IN QUESTION.** ❞
>
> JULIAN WILSON, OWNER @ MATTBLACKSYSTEMS.COM

Florence recently experienced a conflict with a relatively new employee. He was wearing the big hat of the domain owner at the time and clearly overstepped his responsibility. As in 70-80% of cases, it turned out to be a lack of understanding and clarity. Through this incident, Florence gained insight into how domain parameters had changed over time without anyone noticing, and recipes needed updating. We live, learn, and adapt.

Change is constant anyway. This is not surprising as employees work with different teams, at different times, in different roles. Employees often determine where and whom they want to work with, although they cannot always have it their way. Florence expects to be called in to certain situations because of her expertise in a particular field, like performance coaching.

AUTHOR'S COMMENT:
Co-opetitiveness is a mix of cooperating and competing. At this level, this also happens between organisations. A good example is the collaboration between otherwise competing pharma companies in developing a new vaccine for Covid-19. There is an overall humanitarian objective, which is finding a vaccine. During times like this, fiercely competitive pharmaceuticals will help each other out for the sake of the greater good. There is hope.

shared goal

Whilst she might not learn a lot, she is flattered to be asked, as with her current role as mediator in a conflict situation. She does not particularly relish that job, but recognises the importance of finding the best way forward and ensuring everyone learns from this. Florence feels a high level of responsibility towards her team members. As co-owners, they all benefit from a positive outcome.

Thankfully, these incidents do not happen often. There is a buzzing harmony most days and Florence actually enjoys creative conflicts. As long as professionals trust each other, have clear targets, and seek a shared way forward, it is usually about the how and not the who or what. It is often "just" about communication. Peopl-eUR places an emphasis on continuous feedback because it can lead to continuous improvement and personal growth – something Florence has had to get used to. Feedback is collected both electronically (similarly to social media comments and likes), and in person when the occasions arise.

A good example of personal feedback is project reviews, an opportunity to celebrate team successes. It is a great way for people to gain recognition, find out more about colleagues, and give feedback in a social setting. There is no "blame culture" at all, but a willingness to hear what others have to say, to understand what they mean, put it into context, and come away enriched.

Florence had some reservations in the beginning, but with her burning desire to improve and to become a valued member of Peopl-eUR, she wants to continue learning and developing in necessary areas. There are downsides to this level of collaboration though. In cases where collaborators operate at different mental stages or where the individual work sprints are too long, the experience can get quite frustrating. Just last week, Florence did quite a lot of work without receiving any update about the latest changes. She realised, during the circular, that she had created a detailed flowchart that was now surplus to requirement. Nothing and no one is perfect.

Florence loves working in a company where individuals and teams are encouraged to take ownership of their work and of the organisation as a whole. No one can complain since everyone contributes to making things better. Love it, leave it, or change it.

PLANNING & STEERING

Peopl-eUR puts its employees first and keeps a strong focus on customers, so that Florence often wonders which is more important. But, in a balanced relationship, does it really matter?

> " WE LEARN OUR WAY INTO BEING THE LEADERS THE WORLD NEEDS NOW. WE ARE WHOLEHEARTED, TAKE AGENCY AND WORK TOGETHER TO CO-CREATE TRANSFORMATIONAL EXPERIENCES – AND IN DOING SO TRANSFORM OURSELVES AND EACH OTHER. "
>
> NICOLA MILLSON, CO-FOUNDER @ SHE LEADS CHANGE

Well, it does. Looking back at the past five years, Florence recognises that Peopl-eUR has not been driven by profit maximisation or customers, but by the company's professional purpose and where people wanted to take it, professionally and personally. The company continuously reviews strategy development and future direction, and several circles make any necessary incremental adjustments. Thinking about it, it is clear to Florence that working with others and the journey itself are what matters, rather than getting somewhere in particular.

Of course, Peopl-eUR needs to be profitable, and that is where customers come in. The company focuses on customer experience and provides personal recommendations, based on algorithms and the customer data generated. Most customers share personal data to enable personalisation and suggestions to make their lives easier. In-house experts analyse the abundance of data with the support of circles concentrating on customer satisfaction. They will not only follow a logical approach, but also listen to their gut and favour intuition over logic. These are the magic moments Florence loves experiencing.

As with its development, strategy implementation is part of day-to-day business. Circles gather information along the way and feed it back to others. If there is a shortage of people in one area, colleagues from other areas will be informed, join in and support as necessary. You cannot really tell people what to do, but you have to attract them. This only works, in the end, if people

know you will return the favour when the time comes. This is no place for takers.

One mindset or technique Florence had to learn is thoughtful experimentation.[6-22] Employees use it to answer questions, or to inform and guide decisions. They regularly stress test beliefs or theories in a playful manner by combining data and intuition with Edward de Bono's Six Thinking Hats®. This simple, but powerful technique helps Florence and her colleagues to explore different perspectives for tackling a complicated task. It simplifies thinking by limiting focus to one viewpoint at a time.

It allows individuals to take on different hats and challenge their thinking without offending others. Florence likes wearing the black hat and playing devil's advocate, because that is usually not her nature at all.

Like in many other organisations, there is the expectation that teams with mature experimentation programmes will implement at least 50% of their learning. In so doing they increase the quality of strategy implementation. This comes around full circle and is particularly powerful when sharing the main insights directly with the circle working on strategy development.

With all these exchanges going on, the danger is that planning and steering will take up too much time. Decisions are reached through dialogue, reconciliation and consensus, and technology can be of great help, but it cannot solve all problems. For example, if a person or project loses momentum, or has difficulties attracting followers, support will start to dry up. Ultimately, this is a kind of natural selection that has shaped Peopl-eUR for years and will hopefully continue doing so.

ORGANISATIONS

Peopl-eUR founder Fred never struggled to relinquish control. He is passionate about technical aspects and future trends. However, he always saw a business as needing to be responsible for people and local communities. Right from the start, he designed the business as a BCorp – a business as a force for good. It has always been important to him to meet high standards with regard to social and environmental performance, public transparency, and legal accountability, and to balance profit with purpose.

This practical approach to making a business not purely profit-driven also provided fertile soil for transforming Peopl-eUR into a fully employee-owned business over time. It is quite common in today's Green world to have employee-owned firms, because they have higher levels of commitment, satisfaction, and have proven to be more resilient during economic downturns.

> " UNDER EMPLOYEE OWNERSHIP, THROUGH GREATER ENGAGEMENT, TRUST AND LOCAL DECISION-MAKING, IT IS POSSIBLE TO MANAGE GREATER COMPLEXITY WITH ALL THE SYNERGIES THAT COME WITH IT… AS IN NATURE…THERE ARE NO MONOCULTURES. "
>
> GUY WATSON @ RIVERFORD, BCORP

FACT BOX

The BCorp certification is to businesses what Fair Trade is to coffee.

The B in BCorp is open to interpretation. It originally derived from "Benefit Corporation", a type of US corporate structure that binds itself to benefit all stakeholders. However, BCorp means many things to many people now – for example, "be the change you wish to see in the world" (original quote from Ghandi) or "better business", which is what companies with BCorp status are aiming to be.[6-23]

So what does that mean in practice? Well, BCorp certified companies strive not only for profits, but also for a better world. This includes their employees and customers, as well as society and the environment at large – both locally and globally.

BCorps are transparent about their operating practices and held to a high standard of legal accountability. Companies have to be re-certified every two years, or risk losing their BCorp status. Not only that, but criteria are dynamic, to make sure that BCorps are always moving with the times.

BCorps form a community of leaders and drive a global movement of people using business as a force for good. [6-23]

This also means Fred is not visible within the business as such. As a recognised expert in the field of digital user relationships, he acts as a link between upcoming trends and the business. This is crucial because the firm has links with many different outer circles. They are a reflection of all the interests that exist within a business. How many of these do we share with other people? Therefore, it is mission critical to keep employees somehow focussed on the business at hand; it is premise and purpose.

Two years earlier, Florence and Fred attended a learning journey where interested people visited other firms to gain inspiration about internal organisational setups. The journey was inspired by the 7S model that suggests that, for an organisation to perform well, seven in-house elements need to be aligned and mutually reinforcing.

Vital in the model is to understand how the separate aspects of an organisation relate to each other, and how change affects each aspect differently to create performance improvements and sustainable growth. The 7S is also part of the underlying fabric at Peopl-eUR and the purpose of the trip was to gain inspiration. With a few like-minded people and after a few bottles of fermented grape juice, Florence, Fred, and a few others decided to take this logic to the next level. The question they asked was: What if a group of like-minded organisations work together to develop and sustain growth, and help directly related organisations to do the same?

When they agreed that it could only be a good thing, the Agile Business Development Group (ABDG) was born. Its main principle was the idea that people and organisations are far healthier and more productive when working with and for people who share the same values and vision. ABDG members developed best practices, clarified interdependencies, and grew individually and as a team.

Like most companies in this Green world, they recognise the power of tech, but put people before it. It is not so much about what is possible, but what makes sense. The days of developing robotic nurses are long gone, but automated electronic trays to support nurses make sense. In a world where Artificial Intelligence is present in every aspect of the business and powered by quantum computing, it is clear that you need to put people before tech to avoid enslaving yourself. [6-24]

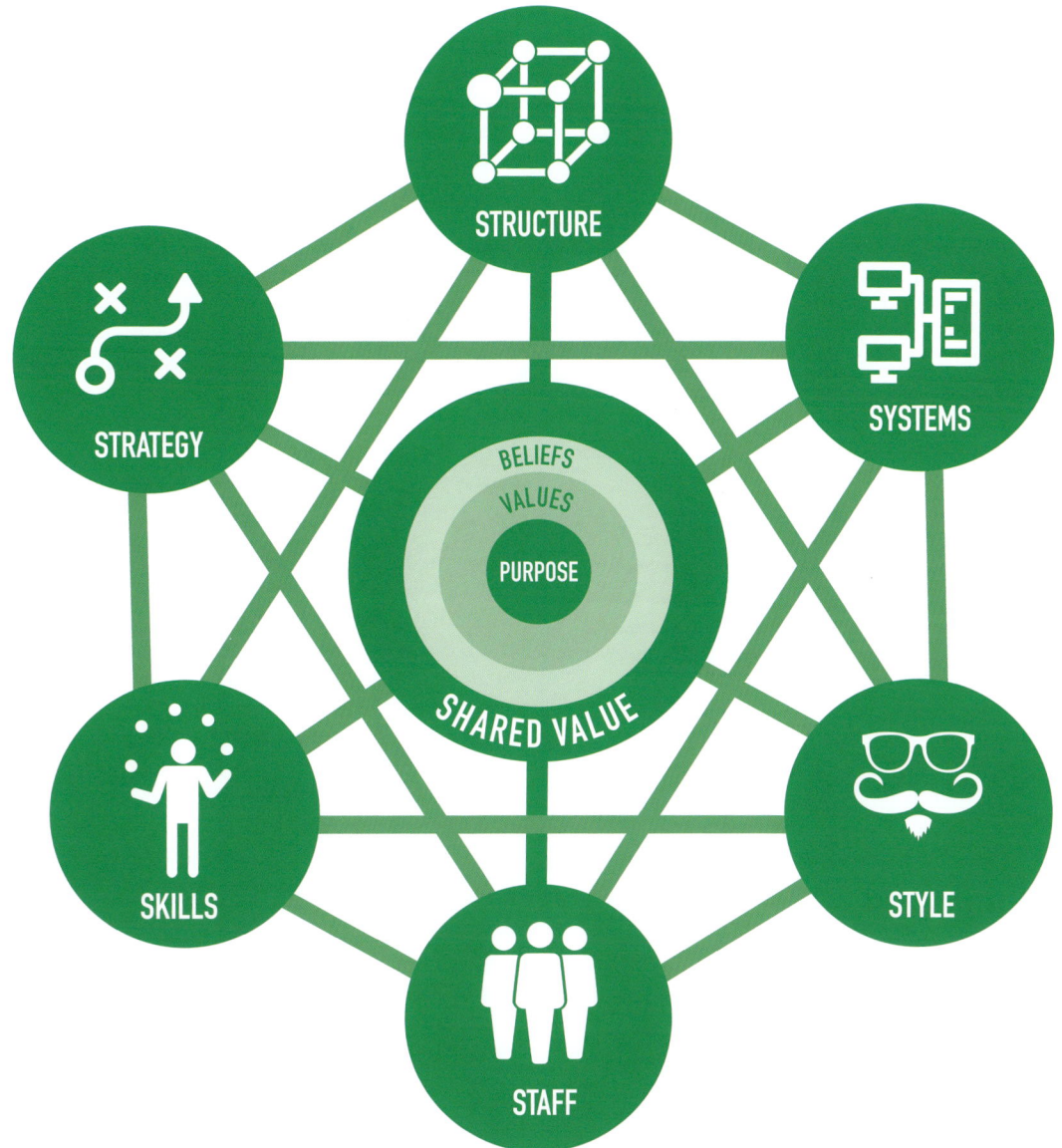

STRUCTURE

STRATEGY

SYSTEMS

BELIEFS
VALUES
PURPOSE

SHARED VALUE

SKILLS

STYLE

STAFF

Transparency is key to healthy business growth. This applies to salaries, as well as documentation and decision-making. For example, Peopl-eUR employees define their own wages every year. They have access to comparable roles within the company and the local region. They can also take the economy and their personal situation into consideration. This means every time you want to bring in a new member into the circle, you can quickly calculate how that affects the cost-benefit scenario. Employees act very responsibly if you educate and treat them as entrepreneurs. Peer and work pressures ensure people look out for and challenge each other. The overall benefit is that employees see themselves as an integral part of the organisation and ecosystem, they feel responsible for the well-being of their colleagues and are even willing to accept financial loss under certain circumstances. Florence thinks this is great, but also knows this can only work when people's basic needs are satisfied.

People do not usually have a hidden agenda; they just want to have a good time while creating cool stuff. This encourages diversity, because many of us are interested in so many different things. Florence notices this when she sits on the Kan-ban board, where people choose tasks of interest to them and quickly explain why they will do a specific job and how they will go about it. There are plenty of other tools around with a similar human-centred approach. Florence likes design-thinking[6-25] with empowered individuals, anything related to co-creation, and many tools from the company IDEO, which manages to constantly learn and reinvent itself.

In general, at this Green level, personal growth is deemed essential and people prefer a growth mindset, believing that we are not designed to shrink, but to blossom. Learning is a social endeavour that allows the sharing of interests and responsibilities. Florence involves the community in personal development, which enriches everyone. Her team measures the time invested into learning and development [L&D] and it is just around the 20% mark. This means she and her team spend on average 1 day a week on L&D. She often wonders how they get all the work done, but entering a state of flow is much easier with highly developed and aligned people[6-26], and that is where the magic happens.

However, people do not attend L&D sessions just for the fun of it. For example, Florence wears a big hat for the Agile Business Development Group (ABDG). When she attends a professional 1-day course, which the company pays for, she automatically commits to offering a 1-hour session to colleagues interested in this particular area, and a further half day to people needing deeper insight. She does this as she recognises that teaching is the best way to learn. The time involved means she selects L&D sessions cautiously.

People growth follows a well-rounded approach and employees take it upon themselves to champion specific topics. Secondments and paid sabbaticals for personal reasons and social causes are common.

Peopl-eUR is a good example of a company acting as a living system, organising and empowering committed employees to define their goals, and supporting them to deliver. Florence and her colleagues are like entrepreneurs interested in responsible and sustainable solutions, and helping humankind to advance. They look for meaning in what they do, collaborate, co-create, act sustainably, and in so doing contribute to a world where people and resources come before profits.

MARKETS

Florence is also a typical consumer in this Green world. Not perfect, but conscious and informed. She reads magazines like Pebble Magazine or Ethical Consumer to keep up to date with the ethical and environmental practices of brands. She places importance on standards like biodynamic, organic, and Fairtrade, which promote workers' rights and animal welfare. She likes buying products from employee-owned companies or co-operatives. She is big on organic, because she wants to protect the natural environment and mitigate the negative impact of various industries on the planet.

Florence still eats animal products, but preferably from places that guarantee the above-mentioned standards and animal welfare. With many regions developing their own standards, it can be difficult to understand the exact criteria. This is especially true for regions that are further afield, but you have to start somewhere.

The good news is that there is a growing trend towards more localised production. After a series of pandemics exposed the weaknesses of global supply chains, first countries have started to enforce more national autonomy and local regions are now taking this to the next level. Waste is another thing that holons, holarchies, communities, and local regions have to get to grips with. The mantra is reduce, reuse, recycle – a slogan that has been around for a while and is now truly lived by. It is fascinating to see how people can make use of reusable resources. For example, Finn signed up to a new group earlier this year and is becoming quite the specialist in upcycling clothes and household items.

Technology at this Green level has become such a powerful force that, at some point, humans asked themselves how to keep the focus on people and humanity. Florence thinks it is a bit ironic that we needed technology to clarify our purpose.

We use tech to improve people's lives. For example, robots can execute jobs related to the three Ds: the dumb, the dirty, and the dangerous. Digital tech was also very useful in uncovering the devastating consequences of planned or inbuilt obsolescence in products. In the old days, most products were designed to break after a while – think about light bulbs or washing machines. This eventually led to the exhaustion of resources and poisoning of our planet with thousands of landfills.

> ## TO LOVE SOCIETY IS TO LOVE SOMETHING BEYOND US AND SOMETHING IN OURSELVES.
>
> EMILE DURKHEIM [1858–1917, 6–8]

Consequently, consumers have reduced the amount of products they own, choosing instead to share or lease them. For example, they lease their fridge or oven from the manufacturer who services them. The positive outcome is that companies have started manufacturing reliable products again, which are easy to repair, and use digital solutions like predictive maintenance software to keep track of it all. In addition, tech like Artificial Intelligence (AI), Virtual Reality (VR), Augmented Reality (AR), and Quantum Computing (QC) enable a completely new dimension of sharing. Florence will never understand why people did not always do this.

Markets are more fragmented and follow the regional and holon setup. There is a relatively high level of autonomy. In many of the more modern holons, like Anahata, commercial spaces and shops are owned by holon dwellers. This ensures that services offered match the needs and desires of the community. In Florence's view, this provides even greater localisation and strengthens the community, but it can also mean less money for the holon. It often saddens her when certain shops lose their space to something she isn't personally interested in. However, it is a natural way of managing supply and demand, and it ultimately serves the community.

Just because one thing ends, does not mean it needs to be the end. Life goes on. When a convenient community space was taken over by one of the regional sports equipment manufacturers, tech came to Florence's rescue with additional space. Thanks to tech-communication solutions, other like-minded inhabitants came together and the group now meets in different locations, which means Florence gets to visit all these places. Opportunities are like flowers, they open up when the time is right. Life is a journey.

LIMITATIONS AND GROWTH INTO NEXT LEVELS

The 1st (Beige) stage doesn't look too far and only knows one way. The 2nd one (Purple) looks back and emulates the way of their ancestors. The 3rd (Red) stage is impatient, driven, wants to break away from the traditional "we have always done it that way", and says convincingly "I do it my way". The 4th (Blue) stage uses science to identify ultimate truths, creates a universal system to run society, and therefore only has one way for everyone. The 5th (Orange) stage can see various ways, but, with clear goals in mind, there can only be one best way.

At the 6th (Green) stage, "the sociocentric state begins to develop, the person begins to think in terms of being different to others, as living in different situations and in other terms than 'the one and the only way to behave', not in terms of 'the best way to behave', but in terms of 'the most appropriate way to behave in that particular situation.' He and she have found that some people survive living one way; some people survive living in another way." [C-1, p.348].

Now, people can conceive circumstances that imply the redundancy of standards of absolute and universal application. This relativistic thinking means the most appropriate way depends on the specific situation in space and time. [6-27]

> " SIXTH-LEVEL THINKING THAT CAME IN ABOUT THE END OF THE 19TH CENTURY SHOULD, IF THERE'S ANYTHING TO THIS THEORY AT ALL, BE AROUND FOR THE SHORTEST PERIOD OF TIME OF ANY OF THE WAYS OF THINKING THAT WE HAVE HAD PREVIOUSLY. [C-1, P. 347] "

The challenge people face at the 6th Green level is living in a habitat that has suffered dramatically as a result of 3rd level capitalism, with growing mass-market production, demand and supply.

After centuries of destructive wars, exploiting natural resources, mistreating the environment, the habitat and climate, pluralistic Green thinkers understand that we, as a community on this planet, cannot continue like this. People at this level have such a good understanding of the diversity and implications of modern life that they start to believe that what people have done so far is not sustainable.

People like Florence can see that, but with such a large population, it is difficult to make quick and necessary changes for the better. It is a bit like switching off the oven and leaving the cake in – when is it too late?

The same is true for markets and societies at the Green level. Slowing down is not necessarily going to reverse the downfall within a reasonable time frame. Companies are increasing their efforts to reduce their consumption and waste. However, this is not true of all companies and markets.

Florence is torn between her mature level of individuality and her community thinking. Realising we are all one community and wanting to bring these together is a constant challenge for her. After years at Peopl-eUR, Florence also realises that, while her work is dynamic and fun, she cannot see herself in this field for many more years. She has dipped in and out of enough areas over time to understand there is more to life than UR.

Life is about following one's curiosity. It would be naïve to think that Florence would be content with a single field all of her life. It is great having a bunch of flowers from one variety, but the real beauty comes from combining different flowers, thus making it truly diverse. Life is no different. The more diverse and colourful it is, the better.

Florence thinks it might make sense to start her own business again at some point. She also keeps asking herself this burning question: how can we develop sustainable solutions to our systemic challenges? Maybe there is an opportunity to combine the two?

The characteristics of 6th (Green) stage markets are as follows:

"PEOPLE FORM COMMUNITIES AND DRIVE OVERALL GROWTH"

POLITICAL

Governance groups and businesses collaborate to benefit society

"Widespread" involvement to form opinions (advanced online solutions)

Liquid democracy concept within circles

Measures to avoid abuse of power

Transparency is important (e.g. public access to everyone's income)

Government uses advanced KPIs (GNH > GDP)

ECONOMIC

SOCIAL

Self-determined individual growth to grow society

Everyone has a duty to help

Many groups collaborating, co-creating

Concepts such as UBI are openly discussed/practised

Work-life integration practices are common

Shared responsibilities

Shared business governance (e.g. sociocracy, agile principles)

Free flow of goods and services to benefit all

Trying to involve all stakeholders

TECHNOLOGICAL

ENVIRONMENTAL

Sense of sustainability

Represented by different groups who have a say

Nature seen as part of society (e.g. green living spaces)

Solutions to benefit society

Enable individual growth

Innovation by group collaboration (vs. individuals)

Green tech is seen as responsible and necessary

LEGAL

Protection of people and resources

Mediation as a starting point

"Warranty" of human integrity

A MOMENTOUS LEAP

"

I HAVE STOPPED FINDING FAULT WITH CREATION AND HAVE LEARNED TO ACCEPT IT. WE HAVE SOME POWER IN US THAT KNOWS ITS OWN ENDS. IT IS THAT WHICH DRIVES US ON TO WHAT WE MIGHT BECOME.... THIS IS THE TRUE MEANING OF TRANSFORMATION. THIS IS THE REAL METAMORPHOSIS. "

DAVID MALOUF, AUSTRALIAN WRITER

One might think that going from group-oriented 6th (Green) stage to individualistic 7th (Yellow) layer would entail yet another transformation. However, at this point, something fascinating happens that we have not yet fully understood. We are making a significant jump into Tier 2 (T2) that entails a true metamorphosis. As Ken Wilber explains:

The reason that Graves called second tier a "momentous leap" is that, unlike all first-tier waves (which imagine their values are the only correct values), second tier has an understanding of the crucial, if relative importance of all previous values— including Red, Blue, Orange, and Green. Orange thinks Green is mindless; Green despises Orange; Blue thinks both of them are going to burn in hell forever. Yellow, on the other hand, finds all of them necessary and acceptable, as long as none of them gets the upper hand and starts repressing the others. [M-1]

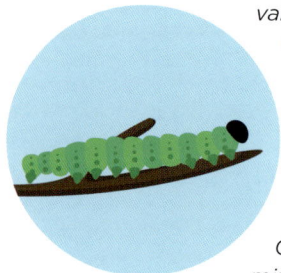

Looking at the current scenario we face on this planet, a momentous leap is necessary. Graves recognised decades ago that all life forms face a multitude of threats: "depleting natural resources, overpopulation, difficulties of too much individuality, and the like - problems which require tremendous change in thinking for humankind in order to solve them". [C-1, p. 366]

In many ways, the challenges at this point are an accumulation of our actions and reactions to various circumstances over the centuries. Our evolution is now endangering our very own existence. Creations once seen as advancements are now slowly and more widely being recognised for what they really are: toxic pollutants on the verge of leading to our extinction if left unchecked and not quickly reversed. "These are the problems of the threat to organismic life and rape of the world produced by the 3rd, 4th, 5th, 6th level existential ways." [M-2] So far, two characteristics that all levels share are that they are egocentric and often driven by fear. Hence, the challenges we face now are so complex and dynamic that we need to develop new abilities, such as systems thinking, to tackle them properly. Graves further explains: "It appears there are six basic systems of human behaviour. When they are lived through, and if the human being is going to continue to exist, the human has to begin to think all over again in some new and different manner." [C-1, p. 368]

The more simplistic logic and pattern of Tier 1 (T1) develops into a completely new way of thinking in T2.

We go from doing to being, binary to quantum computing, dualism to multilateralism, and so on. Christopher Cooke remarks "Everything that was believed to be true in T1 has to be questioned and possibly redefined."
Mankind now has the opportunity to "step over the line which separates those needs that man has in common with other animals and those needs which are distinctively human.". [C-1, p.367]
In T2, we finally start to get a glimpse of why our species is so different from others on this planet, and to understand the predesigned potential we hold within us.

At this point, it becomes clear that there is not just an evolutionary pattern as we see in T1, because we swing from being more individualistic to more group-oriented if we progress. Now we recognise that there is some kind of master plan:

"[At] the end of his first six-step trek, man finds he must return and begin again to travel the road by whence he has come. Man must return for some things to an autistic frame of reference. Thus, our 7th level of existence and corresponding value system are repetitions, in an advanced form, of his first level of existence and its reactive value system." [C-1, p. 367]

In other words, there are certain similarities between levels in T1 and T2: characteristics of the 1st (Beige) stage are mirrored in the 7th (Yellow); traits of the 2nd (Purple) stage are reflected in the 8th (Turquoise); and so on. Hence, as you will discover in the upcoming two stories, there are similarities between Amon (Beige) and G (Yellow), as well as between Bo (Purple) and Hortense (Turquoise).

For example, in a Purple environment forest farming was and is quite common. This is a technique dating back thousands of years, which was used by Native American Indians and many other tribes all over the world. It involves cultivating plants under a forest canopy, as opposed to wildcrafting or foraging, which is the practice of collecting wild plants and products from a forest. Forest farmers manage different layers in the forest structure to increase sustainable harvests of non-timber products from natural forests or tree plantations. The canopy trees, which serve as the top layer, provide timber, fruit and nuts, such as walnuts and hazelnuts. The middle layer might be full of berries or ornamentals. The forest floor can be cultivated for medicinal and culinary herbs, roots, mushrooms and landscaping or florist products, like flowers and ferns. The multi-layered structure of a farmed forest improves wildlife habitat and may increase the aesthetic and recreational value of the area.

That is a way of blending our abilities and interests with what nature offers us.

People did not always have a scientific explanation for their plant combinations. For example, it has long been common practice to pair up marigold and melons, tomatoes and cabbage, beans and corn. Nowadays, as we have gone through the scientific discovery and insight of Blue realms, we know that we plant marigold and melons together because certain marigold varieties control nematodes in the roots of melons, without any need for chemicals [M-4].

This is called companion planting or planting in guilds - something we find in the practice of permaculture farming. Here, humankind is designing the entire arrangement with nature in mind. The goal is to let nature take over the process so we have minimal work with optimum results. Planting the design is more work initially, but in the long term, it is more sustainable, productive, and effective.

Forest farming and permaculture farming follow a very similar logic and insight. Farmer Simon Cutter at Model Farm explains:

"It is a bit ironic that, after decades of 'modern farming practices', we are returning to what my grandfather already did and taught me. It is just that now we have the science explaining why these traditional practices make sense."

This is why some farmers are returning to ancient practices on their land. The only difference is that, now, they know why companion planting and other practices are beneficial. For generations, their ancestors acted with patience, watching the land, figuring out what worked well, and repeating what their own ancestors had done.

Another important factor worth noting is that people who share similar values, and therefore aspire to the same level, will naturally resonate with one another. That seems quite logical and we can observe this around us.

However, why people further apart on Graves' framework resonate with each other is more challenging to understand. Looking into the world of music can help explain this. For example, if you put two instruments next to each other – let's say a violin and a piano – and you sound the G key on the piano, the G string on the violin will vibrate as well. The same phenomenon happens between octaves, meaning the key in one octave resonates with its corresponding note eight tones up. Frequencies seem to be much more relevant to us than we understand at present. This is reflected in the GVS levels too, only here we see similarities and resonance on the same and every six levels, not eight.

In the here and now, living in a T1 environment, it is difficult to imagine what the future in a mature T2 ecosystem could look like. A world in T1 is relatively easy to map out, because some of the fundamental drivers are likely to prevail. For example, 3rd level capitalism evolved and reached its peak of profitability at the 5th level due to performance-driven measurability and

digital tech (think Amazon, the online retailer with a clear Orange footprint). We can also envisage, and in part experience group-orientated 4th level democracy becoming more transparent and localised to a communal level, creating a much more engaging group-orientated 6th level environment. However, it is still a form of digitally-enabled and localised democracy (think Switzerland or Sweden).

At the core of T1 sits money as a medium of exchange, in the form of coins and banknotes. It is very difficult to imagine a world without money and capitalism, because they are woven into the daily fabric. Money is rather abstract and its nominal value was ascribed to it by 4th level financial institutions. The value is not necessarily real. I too struggle to imagine a world without money. I am not referring to the transformation of money from coins to notes, then electronic cash, and eventually cryptocurrencies, which we can see happening now. I am talking about the transformation of money into a completely different form of currency.

I strongly believe that **value** will be the currency in T2. We will return to a world where we exchange goods and services for their intrinsic worth, not a physical currency deriving its value from its component material (e.g. gold or copper). Tech solutions will allow one party to ascribe a value to a service, and another to agree to an acceptable value. Here, "value" will have meaning.

I first came across this logic in its infancy when working with Consilience Ventures (CV), a tech-driven ecosystem that brings startups, investors, corporations, and experts together. Instead of investing money or providing paid consulting services within the CV ecosystem, everyone exchanges digital values - called tokens - with the mutual interest of growing together. Currently, living in the T1 world, no matter how much I am genuinely interested in growing the value of CV startups, I will at some point need to cash in those tokens to pay my utility bills and groceries. We are stuck in our current operating logic because the tokens are not widely accepted. Thus, it is difficult to imagine what the world will look like once it has morphed fully into T2. It is akin to imagining and creating a completely new operating system that you cannot run because it requires a hardware upgrade. For now, we are still fully grounded in world 1.0 (T1).

Now, imagine a T2 world where potential buyers ascribe value to everything that you offer as a seller, based on their own valuation. In time, advanced modern tech solutions, like quantum computing on the go, will support this more balanced approach to supply and demand, which will allow changes in value to adjust in real time. Like at CV, professionals will only be interested in delivering work where they can truly add value. There will be no money paid in a transaction, but rather a shared value that becomes effective when the delivered service or product contributes to the desired outcome.

Once this system is established between people (i.e. peer to peer), we will move away from static money to a more fluid currency, and exchange at the rate of value. This is why some people might refer to T2, for now, as Utopia.

So let us delve into two utopian scenarios and see what could unfold!

YOU AND I CANNOT MAKE MONEY!

As children, most of us received praise, from our parents and teachers, whenever we showed them something we made, whether a daub of paint or a box with holes in it...and this idea of making something has followed us into adulthood, as something to be proud of – whether it be tonight's meal, a work of art, or a house. Making something translates into a noble endeavour, something to be acknowledged.

In English, we often use the expression "making money". Of course, money itself is an artificial construct that only exists because we all accept its idea without question – we are indoctrinated in it. Even within this artificial construction, we forget that not one of us can actually make money. As individuals, the most we can hope for is to accumulate it. The more one has, the less someone else has. Paradoxically, we all participate equally in the initial creation of it, as we are all stakeholders in the workings of the central banks, which ostensibly are there to get money to everyone. However, as we have all witnessed around the world, whatever the nation, and whatever the currency, the vast majority are only connected to the money tank via very thin, fragile threads... whilst a few have large diameter, high pressure pipes.

Mansoor Ullah – British Citizen

7th LEVEL

YELLOW: A WHOLE NEW LEVEL OF EXISTENCE

INDIVIDUALS AT THIS LAYER ARE MAINLY ON THEIR OWN JOURNEY OF SELF-ACTUALISATION. FOR THE FIRST TIME, THEY APPRECIATE PREVIOUS STAGES AND ACKNOWLEDGE THAT THE SKILLS AND CHARACTERISTICS INHERENT IN EACH HAVE THEIR USEFUL AND APPROPRIATE TIME AND PLACE. HERE, PEOPLE LIVE IN A WORLD WITHOUT ECONOMIC PRESSURES OR FEAR FOR SURVIVAL, THANKS TO HAVING THEIR BASIC NEEDS MET. AS A RESULT, PEOPLE HAVE THE TIME AND FREEDOM TO LEARN AND DEVELOP ON THEIR OWN TERMS. CHANGING JOBS AND CAREER PATHS IS NORMAL, IF NOT COMMONPLACE, BECAUSE INDIVIDUALS SEEK CHANGE AND DIVERSITY. THESE INDIVIDUALS WILL OFTEN THRIVE IN AMBIGUOUS AND PARADOXICAL SITUATIONS, HALLMARKS OF A COLOURFUL LIFE WHERE ALL LAYERS ARE EMBRACED AND LEVERAGED.

PEOPLE TEND TO WORK TOGETHER IN TEMPORARY TEAMS FORMED WHEN AND WHERE NEEDED. THEY OPERATE IN INTERCONNECTED NETWORKS REFERRED TO AS "NETWORK ORGANISATIONS", WHICH ARE OFTEN ONLY TEMPORARY CREATIONS OF THEIR OWN. TECHNOLOGY AND ITS APPLICATIONS ARE SO ADVANCED THAT INTELLIGENT DATA SYSTEMS SUPPORT DECISION-MAKING, WHICH GUARANTEES A HIGH LEVEL OF TRANSPARENCY AND BUILDS UP TRUST IN THE POPULATION.

PEOPLE ASSUME VARIOUS ROLES THAT CHANGE ACCORDING TO THEIR POINT IN LIFE AND CIRCUMSTANCES. THEY RECOGNISE THEIR DEPENDENCE ON THE FLORA AND FAUNA AROUND THEM, AND THUS UNDERSTAND THEY MUST RESPECT IT IN ORDER TO GUARANTEE THEIR OWN SURVIVAL. THIS UNDERSTANDING FEEDS THE BELIEF THAT THEIR RIGHTS ARE INTIMATELY LINKED TO THEIR DUTY TO SERVE THE COMMUNITY AND THE GREATER GOOD. MARKETS AND SOCIETIES REGULATE THEMSELVES AND KEEP ANY DELIBERATE WRONG-DOING IN CHECK THROUGH CONSTANT, TIMELY INPUT AND MONITORING. THIS SOCIETY OBSERVES HIGH ETHICAL STANDARDS AND ENSURES COMPLIANCE THROUGH THE EDUCATION OF ITS PEOPLE, ACCORDING TO THEIR ABILITIES AND INTERESTS, AND THEIR CONNECTION THROUGH TRANSPARENT NETWORKS.

"

RELATIONSHIPS ARE ALL THERE IS.
EVERYTHING IN THE UNIVERSE ONLY
EXISTS BECAUSE IT IS IN RELATIONSHIP
TO EVERYTHING ELSE. NOTHING EXISTS IN
ISOLATION. WE HAVE TO STOP PRETENDING WE
ARE INDIVIDUALS THAT CAN GO IT ALONE. "

MARGARET WHEATLEY, AMERICAN WRITER

YELLOW LIFE

We are in Platonopolis, a place far away and very different from Purpleshire, the "old" world. It lies on a different continent and feels like it has gone through a time warp. At least that is how G thinks of it. G is short for Gregory, aka Greg in his previous life, but nowadays it's just G. When he came to this part of the world, he wanted to reinvent himself, make a fresh start, and felt that a new name (or nickname in this case) would help.

> **EXPRESS SELF FOR WHAT SELF DESIRES, BUT NEVER AT THE EXPENSE OF OTHERS AND IN A MANNER THAT ALL LIFE, NOT JUST MY LIFE, WILL PROFIT.** [C-1, P. 365]

G lives in a city that is a reminder of the past. Over the years, cities have been remodelled to create holonic environments (remember the holons and hubs from the Green chapter?). G was invited to move here on account of his expertise in structures and defence lines. These societal redesigns aim to shield from external threats and contain internal ones – like pandemics, fires, floods – to avoid them spreading to other holons. This also helps address the long-term, harmful effects of the destruction of previous biospheres and other natural systems. It isn't easy reshaping traditional structures while considering the implications on everything and everyone around it (e.g. local residents, infrastructure, and resource management), and that is where experienced, out-of-the-box thinkers like G come in. There is great value in having someone with his experience think through society's issues and build solutions into his designs. For example, since cars have been eliminated, many streets have been re-appropriated to create more open green spaces, walking gardens with different designs, themes and plants. These gardens managed by local residents are either full of life – with locals communing and children playing in them – or quiet, rather delicate and truly magical places. Also, all deliveries are done by bicycle.

AUTHOR'S COMMENT.
Graves assigned each of the eight layers a set of two letters: the first letter of each pairing represented the individual and used the first eight letters of the alphabet, A–H; the second letter (originally N–V) referred to the world around them. Initially, the 7th (Yellow) layer was thus given the letters G and T, and the 8th (Turquoise) layer H and U. However, Graves later changed this and ascribed the two T2 layers the letters A–N and B–O respectively (starting over with the first letters), to emphasize the similarities between these layers and the first two in T1 (e.g. Beige has parallels with Yellow, and Purple with Turquoise).

One of the main objectives of this book is to make the framework more accessible and facilitate use of the characters in future story-telling. Therefore, I have opted for the simplest logic I could think of and named the protagonists in alphabetical order, from A to H, to match the letters Graves ascribed to their level. Hence A is for Amon in the 1st level, B is for Bo in the 2nd, and so on.

Another phenomenon worth noting here is that the time it takes to evolve from one level to another shortens as we go along. One might think this is due to technology's influence in accelerating our "progression", and certainly that could be part of the story; however, the more important factor is that our conscious self reacts more quickly, as a matter of survival, to the ever more severe damage we have inflicted on the environment around us. We must acknowledge and correct our grave mistakes in the past and present, if we want to keep on living and allow successive generations to flourish in the future.

Albert Street, G's local hub, is not smartly designed like some of the new holons, but it shows great historical flair – its Victorian buildings and other period features provide an insight into the past and demonstrate how much societies have changed over the decades and centuries. The street is colourful with diversity – people from all walks of life connect with each other and share through social technologies. It is a great space to learn about different cultures, professions, and languages. A sustainable fashion designer, a sound engineer for the film industry, and an orthopedist share one house. Next door, a citizenship teacher, a chef, a musician, and a tree surgeon live together.

G loves being a vital part of that eclectic mix. His partner currently lives 100 kilometres away, working on a special project. So, for now, G lives with his cat Chucky and has extra time for the unexpected. He enjoys having his own space, being a creative thinker, and periodically likes to explore different professional avenues. That requires time and focus, which is easier to achieve on your own.

G has had a colourful life. He grew up in Purpleshire where he had a rather unburdened and simple upbringing. After school he left to study cybernetics, but found it too theoretical and academic at that stage in his life. So he gave it up after only three months. Following his childhood dream, he later became a professional fireman, specialising in wildland fires and soon becoming a fire chief. He is a natural leader that everyone looked up to and had a few heroic moments that made him a favourite at the countless parties he attended in his heyday. After all, a brave man in uniform is always a hit with the ladies. Then, one spring day, a tragedy occurred during a ferocious fire: he and his partner got caught out while creating a control line. It was by sheer luck that G made it out of the fire in time. His colleague didn't; he died in the fire. G hadn't been keeping up with his fitness and was out drinking the night before. He still lives with the guilt that he might have been able to save his friend had he been fitter and faster on his feet.

After the incident, G was out of action for six months to recover from his injuries and trauma. He decided to shift his professional focus to human resources, specifically learning and development (L&D). He started by training new recruits within the fire brigade. Then, he devised physical and mental development plans for everyone in the unit, as a team is only as good as its weakest link. G enjoyed setting up and organising everything properly.

He soon realised that enhancements could be made by integrating different departments. However, this proved difficult, so he moved to a strategic unit within the fire brigade where he gained insight into performance measures and continuous improvement through fit-for-purpose technical solutions. He managed digital IoT projects within SOHOS [see p. 117 Green chapter] and soon worked on large-scale community-based integrations and benchmarking models. As a hands-on person, G led many projects directly, which often forced him to work late into the night and travel extensively. The solitude gave him time to think about what he really wanted, and it is at this point that he decided to come out about being gay.

Once he had his first serious relationship, he finally understood the importance of work-life balance. This all coincided with fire fighters taking on additional roles in society, which led G to move into a more facilitative role, bringing together people from other disciplines. He was able to draw on his organisational skills as a trainer and his ability to set objectives and break them down into goals to measure progress. He enjoyed being a facilitator, providing space for others to be creative, to flourish and take the lead when and where necessary; he increasingly managed the process rather than the content. This transition, in turn, helped him lead a more flexible life. Most of his projects exceeded expectations, but just when G thought he had it all, a new boss took over. This boss was a micromanager who wanted to know exactly what he was doing, when and where. G suddenly realised how much freedom his old boss had given him, how willingly she had shared information and flexed her muscles to support him from the top when he needed it. He quickly figured out the new dynamic wasn't going to work. What would the new boss require next, a timesheet?

Luckily, exactly at that time, one of his contacts from Platonopolis asked if he was interested in moving there. They were redesigning holonic structures and needed someone with his experience to take on a proactive role as a facilitator. Things worked a little bit differently there. As G felt it was time for a change in his life, he accepted the offer to broaden his horizon. Where better to be than a place where everyone is actively encouraged to take on different professional roles? This was a great stepping stone for him.

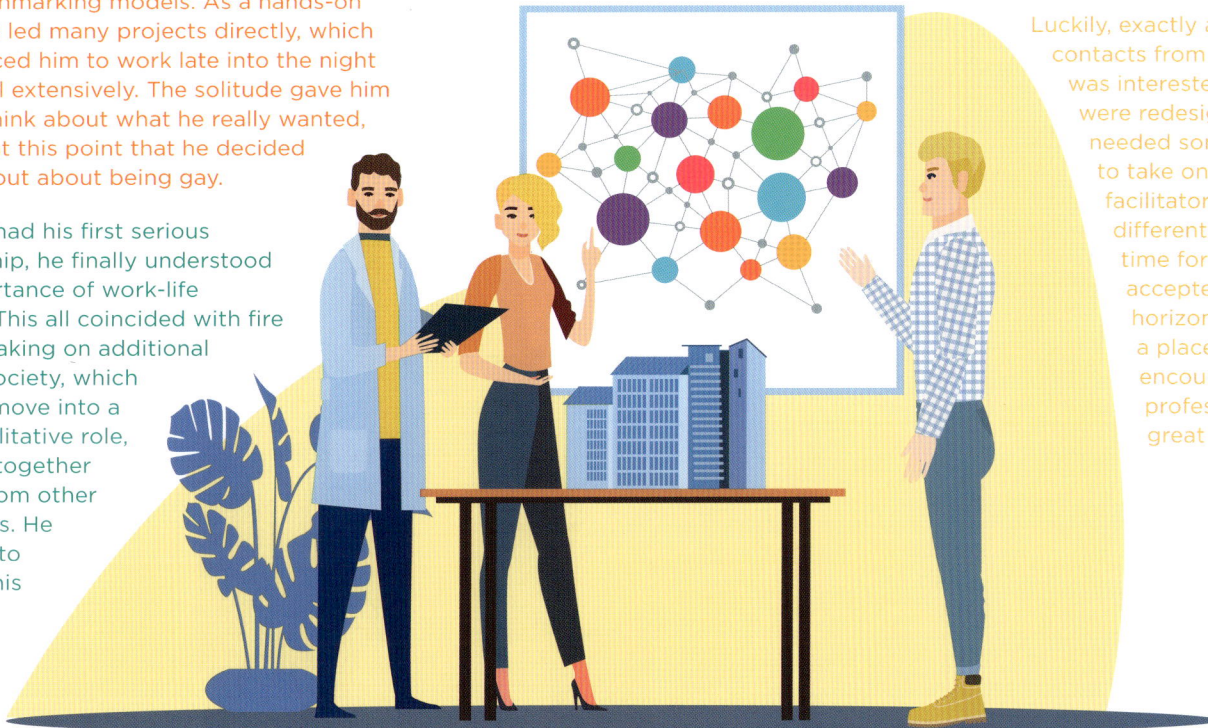

Settling in was very easy; the community provided him with all he needed. G enjoyed advising on the designs, because it required thinking about connections and interdependencies between different areas of life, and working through the entire web of players and possible outcomes. He worked with a variety of professionals and, for the first three years, was fully committed to this new job. Thinking through the wide range of scenarios that could result from his designs was mindboggling at times. When it came to finding solutions to specific problems, the focus wasn't on eradicating symptoms, but instead on identifying root causes. This is more easily done when following clear principles that entail listening to the people for whom you are creating the solution, having defined measurables in place, and identifying the right, rather than the perfect outcome.

G's dedication didn't go unnoticed; he was asked to stay on permanently via a formal decision process that required all of his colleagues and contacts to discuss and vote on whether he would fit into the community. Collective approval is an important aspect in this environment. Also, being a citizen in Platonopolis involves committing to lifelong learning and contributing to the community. G was asked to limit his main focus, facilitation, to 50% of his time and consider other roles he would want to take on. The objective is to gain insight into different areas of life and then integrate and cross-fertilise that learning. Consequently, only few people now work in large organisations; most join various professional networks instead.

G loves this. Over time, he has honed his facilitation skills and learnt what it means to let go of control. He enjoys facilitation so much that he wants to do more work in this area, and integrate different ideas and concepts he has come across over the years. He is thinking about initiating learning journeys where a group of people is provided with access and insight into other areas of work or life. In return, individuals are asked to work through a set of steps to share their viewpoints in such a way that everyone builds on each other's insight. This would open up a space for new, radical ideas and solutions.

G's second role is working in the local library, a popular place not only for gaining knowledge, but also for passionate people to share their stories, theories and big ideas.

The library's immersive technologies enable people to conceptualise and address complicated topics. This facilitates personal aha moments, interactions with other locals, and the identification of shared interests.

G also spends a small portion of his time advising Florence (our heroine from the Green chapter) and her colleague Eli on the best design for their performance app for fire fighters. Besides liking Florence and the company she works for, G has a personal motive to see this app thrive – it's a personal health innovation that people in Platonopolis could use and greatly benefit from.

Yellow society as a whole could be described as meshwork – a multi-layered, interwoven network made up of many smaller networks. It can appear chaotic, but the connections that humans establish through technology are as lively as those in our brain. Life has been localised as much as possible so that each level of society (e.g. hub, holon, or holarchy) self governs and people get involved in matters that pertain to them at the appropriate level. To be clear, a hub is equivalent to a neighbourhood in the old world, a holon to a village, a holarchy or SOHOS to a town, and a region to a small county. Holons handle holonic issues, regions handle regional issues, and so on.

In fact, localised governance has become a popular approach to improving the quality of life for all [See Green chapter, page 117] The idea is that, given we are all one species, sustained interactions between residents with different interests will better meet the needs of local areas and the world. People share new ideas and views, and create space for additional ones to emerge, which deepens relationships.

Advanced technology enables people to provide information and feedback on certain topics in real time. There are no more political powers or hierarchies; instead, networks of people come together temporarily to discuss relevant issues. For example, when a new bridge needs building, a network will come together to think through all that is involved. This means other networks receive a notification in the form of a pulse regarding elements pertaining to their expertise, such as natural resources, human labour, or waste management. In turn, these networks will send pulses to more specialised networks in the value chain, which provide feedback on their own areas of expertise until the initial network selects a suitable solution. Everyone involved has a specific role and simple, yet advanced technology solutions connect everyone together in an arrangement of intersecting vertical, diagonal and horizontal lines. Methods and tools adapt to individuals and skills-based networks. There are no bureaucratic processes at play. And as soon as the bridge is completed, the networks disperse again.

Data gathered throughout the project is analysed and made available to other networks to share the learning and outcomes. Transparency is essential to the betterment of society and has led to the creation of a huge knowledge bank so we can learn from failures, integrate information and develop it further. There is widespread acknowledgement that collective intelligence resulting from the collaboration and efforts of many will benefit everyone. All this builds on crowd intelligence and the wisdom of crowds, of which Wikipedia, Galaxy Zoo, and Waze were early success stories. As a consequence, citizens see themselves as part of an interconnected whole. Everyone is considered a resource that brings value to the network. Open and trusting relationships enable effective dialogue. Citizens share a purpose and vision focused on integrating all the knowledge and making it readily available to anyone at all times.

Furthermore, people have accepted natural ingenuity; they buy into nature's principles and follow its flow and forms when looking to solve difficult problems – biomimicry at its finest. G and the people around him truly appreciate nature's genius and work hard to integrate its greatest features into the fabric of society, even basing certain design elements on patterns or shapes found in nature. G is very grateful that what he

values most is not only discussed, but lived by individuals and society. He has always felt a deep connection to nature and feels so at home knowing that his community understands how beautifully interconnected the world around them is, and the value that knowledge brings to everyone.

This knowledge is taught in schools. From an early age, the following values are explored:

1. ALL LIFE ON EARTH AND BEYOND
2. INDIVIDUALITY
3. INDEPENDENCE
4. ACCOUNTABILITY
5. INTERDEPENDENCE
6. KNOWLEDGE
7. LIFELONG EXPLORING & LEARNING
8. OPEN-MINDEDNESS
9. COMPLEXITY & SIMPLICITY
10. TRUE DIVERSITY

+ Building on these values, people develop lots of strengths in Platonopolis:

- THEY ACKNOWLEDGE AND APPRECIATE DIVERSITY (INCLUDING ALL THAT THE GVS T1 LEVELS BRING);

- THEY ADHERE TO HIGH ETHICAL STANDARDS, WHICH CREATES SAFE ENVIRONMENTS FOR PEOPLE TO FLOURISH IN;

- THEY ARE ABLE TO INTEGRATE DIFFERENT INTERDISCIPLINARY LOGICS AND METHODS EFFECTIVELY;

- THEY ARE GOOD AT SEEING AND CONNECTING THE DOTS, UNDERSTANDING INTERDEPENDENCIES WHILE MAKING SENSE OF THE BIGGER PICTURE;

- THEY ARE CAPABLE OF FORECASTING THE POTENTIAL IMPACT OF CHANGES.

− That said, there's more than one side to everything and it is important to be aware of the weaknesses here too, which include:

- OBSESSIVE THIRST FOR INFORMATION IN THE QUEST FOR KNOWLEDGE;

- BEING TOO LOGICAL AND NOT COMPASSIONATE ENOUGH; BEING INTERESTED IN OTHER PERSPECTIVES, BUT NOT TRULY IN OTHER PEOPLE;

- GETTING CARRIED AWAY WITH SOMETHING NEW INSTEAD OF FINISHING WHAT HAS BEEN STARTED;

- BEING TOO RATIONAL AND DRIVEN BY THE MIND, STANDING IN THE WAY OF HAPPINESS;

- NOT ADHERING TO RULES OR CONVENTIONS WHEN THEY DON'T MAKE SENSE OR SEEM IRRELEVANT.

Characters like G can easily be misunderstood. He's a relatively self-aware guy who tends to approach topics with a completely open mind. A high level of self-confidence and independence can easily be mistaken for arrogance or lack of compassion. Hence, in the old word, people often misjudged him and misinterpreted what he said.

INDIVIDUALS

Before making the big move, G was a bit of an idealist participating in a lot of social protests and campaigns, which often turned out to be more about venting frustrations than concrete action. Over time he grew more perceptive of what is good or bad, and made a more conscious effort to seek out all sides of a story, recognising there is always more than one. However, it was only once he moved to Platonopolis that he was able to let go of prejudgment and adopt a completely new way of thinking. Now he understands that everyone has their own perspective and he truly believes they are all valid.

G is a colourful character in that he is able to rely on the experience gained in all the previous stages of his life, switching back and forth as needed to draw on skills acquired at each stage of his evolution. This helps him to develop constantly based on his ambitions. His career path is a good example of different mindsets building on top of each other. As a trainer, especially in the beginning, he learned to be very organised, plan a lot and pay attention to detail. When working as a consultant, he focused more on the clients. He was goal-driven and excessively dedicated at times. However, he wouldn't have been so successful had he not had a fair amount of organisational skills to start with.

> " IT'S DIFFICULT TO BELIEVE IN YOURSELF, BECAUSE THE IDEA OF SELF IS AN ARTIFICIAL CONSTRUCTION. YOU ARE, IN FACT, PART OF THE GLORIOUS ONENESS OF THE UNIVERSE. EVERYTHING BEAUTIFUL IN THE WORLD IS WITHIN YOU. NO ONE REALLY FEELS SELF-CONFIDENT DEEP DOWN, BECAUSE IT'S AN ARTIFICIAL IDEA. REALLY, PEOPLE AREN'T THAT WORRIED ABOUT WHAT YOU'RE DOING OR WHAT YOU'RE SAYING, SO YOU CAN DRIFT AROUND THE WORLD RELATIVELY ANONYMOUSLY: YOU MUST NOT FEEL PERSECUTED AND EXAMINED. LIBERATE YOURSELF FROM THAT IDEA THAT PEOPLE ARE WATCHING YOU. "

RUSSELL BRAND, BRITISH COMEDIAN

but we cannot grow if we ignore our previous abilities and perspectives. Instead, we need to leverage them, like a portfolio of skills to be drawn upon at opportune moments. The metaphor G uses is "selecting which arrow to shoot with your bow".

Along the way, G has developed a strong ethical core related to his experience and the way he values life, all life. He has strong opinions, but holds them loosely; he is principled, but not ideological. He even likes to have his mind changed and to broaden his outlook. He is not interested in distinguishing between right and wrong, but in finding instead as much of life's richness as possible.

Occasionally, G likes throwing himself into unknown situations to create learning opportunities. For example, he once volunteered at a sanctuary for chimpanzees because their DNA is 99% similar to ours. He wanted to experience firsthand the similarities and differences between us. He was astonished to see chimpanzees using plants as medicine, leaves as sponges, and exhibiting distinctive personalities. Spending time with our closest relatives deepened his understanding of our own humanity – for example, how we often complicate life unnecessarily.

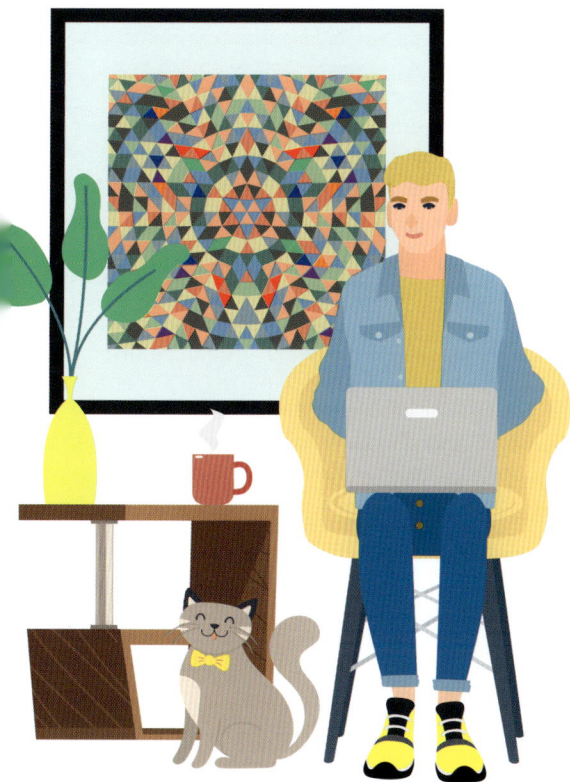

Today, he sees the world as a kaleidoscope – a colourful spectacle reflecting life's diversity. Over time, G has added new colours and perspectives to his viewpoints. He used to disregard his former opinions, feeling he had become better and his new views represented a more mature and evolved stance. Now he knows that previous mindsets are all still valid and have their place and time, in the past and in the future. We might progress functionally,

G sees every situation as a learning opportunity. He believes that you sometimes need to put yourself into very different situations, even engage with extreme logic or listen to radical perspectives. In nearly all cases there is something useful to add to one's understanding. In the worst case, the exception proves the rule.

G also likes paradoxes, and some level of ambiguity and unpredictability. To him, life is unpredictable and certainty is a subjective concept that simply cannot apply to it. His idea is to believe in self and navigate through life's uncertainty. He even enjoys humour that doesn't make sense. The more things are turned on their head, the better. He loves pioneers like Monty Python for creating so much hilarious nonsense. It is this endless curiosity that has added so much colour to his life. It is no longer about just staying alive, but living a "life of being".

On a personal level, G is driven by what psychologist Abraham Maslow called self-actualisation – essentially, the fulfilment of one's talents and potentials. If life has given us all capabilities, we surely have the duty to make the most of them, don't we? Why would we not want to?

Thus, G likes to look at the bigger picture. Ultimately, he wants to be a vital contributing part of the evolving universe. However small in the bigger scheme of things, his contribution has value and he doesn't want to be a waste of space. He believes this requires a process of constant give and take, and pushing ourselves to grow in a healthy direction.

This is a viewpoint he inherited from his parents. His mother was a tech futurist and his father taught chaos theory. They met working on a cybernetics project looking at a range of applications in anthropology, social sciences, and management. They fell in love over their shared fascination with Gregory Bateson, an English anthropologist, social scientist, linguist, visual anthropologist, semiotician, and cyberneticist whose work crisscrossed with those in other fields. Bateson was the inspiration for choosing Gregory as the name for their son.

G also has a son, who is trying to find his way in the world and grew distant from his father in his early years. However, as the boy developed, they started to share ideas and appreciate each other's viewpoints again. G loves seeing the world through his son's eyes. It is a very different generation.

His son is the only family G has left. So, he spends a lot of time with him and his partner Goto, who is originally from Japan. Goto helped G appreciate a minimalistic lifestyle, as well as reduce his consumption and waste. They share an open-minded approach and want to explore life together. During a walk through the nearby park, their discussions covered a wide range of topics: why leaves appear to be green; how to apply the different levels of the Graves Value System to customer loyalty; and why one can see the whole sun, but only half the moon at the same time.

G enjoys social happenings with his friends, a large, colourful network of people. They often provide him with inspiration, which generates new insight. Some friends come from his various professional networks, where he often meets new, like-minded individuals. In such a transparent society, trust comes easy. For starters, everyone supports the idea of creating change for the better. For starters they all support the idea of creating change for the better. With people like this, you establish an immediate connection and can afford to be more personal. Professional relationships often turn into friendships, and what better way to talk about life than over a glass of fermented grape juice?

When he gets a little carried away and has one glass too many, G knows he needs to make up for this to maintain some kind of equilibrium. So he goes to the gym – a place called Movin' – two to four times a week. They offer classes combining functional movements with high-intensity interval training. G likes the short bursts of all-out exercise alternated with slower recovery phases.

This helps him build and sculpt lean muscle that he uses in everyday life. He is in and out of that place within an hour. It does the trick for him.

In addition to the more functional approach of fitness, he loves surfing. Ever since watching the movie *Chasing Mavericks*, he has liked the idea of riding the waves. The inspirational true story excited him for he understood that riding some of the biggest waves on earth requires tapping into all four energy levels. [7-0]

Additionally, the waves seem to attract a wild range of individualists, so surfers are always interesting people to meet. The young main character in the movie was definitely a phenomenon in real life, but not necessarily one of G's heroes. His heroes are interdisciplinary thinkers, who can identify patterns from scattered ideas and events in life, and connect them to form a bigger purpose or lesson.

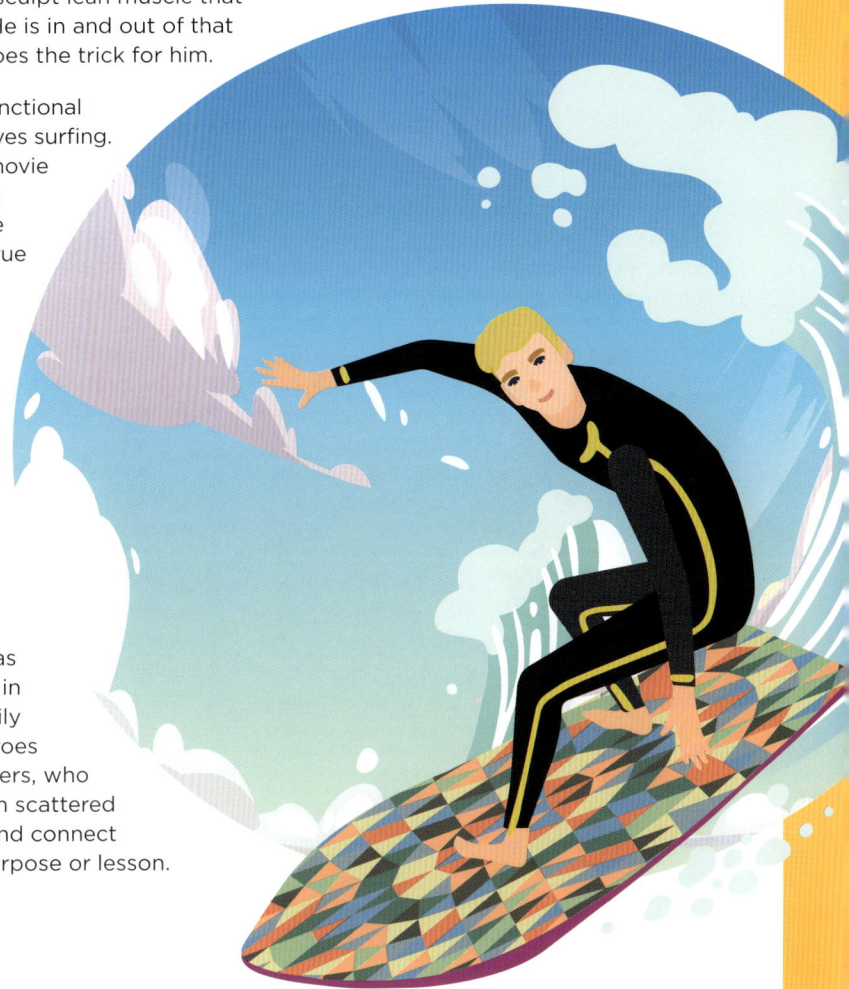

HERE ARE THREE PEOPLE THAT STAND OUT FOR HIM:

1

Ludwig von Bertalanffy, who was an Austrian biologist, widely recognised for his contributions to science as a systems theorist and known as one of the founders of the General Systems Theory (GST). Von Bertalanffy's thinking started in biology and extended into cybernetics, education, history, philosophy, psychiatry, psychology and sociology. His theories are still used today.

G believes that the GST will one day provide a conceptual framework for all these disciplines. For now, it remains a bridge for the interdisciplinary study of systems in the social sciences. [7-1]

2

Timothy Berners-Lee, aka TimBL, an English engineer and computer scientist best known for inventing the World Wide Web in 1989 (the famous "www" at the beginning of websites) while working at CERN. G is always amused thinking about ENQUIRE, the prototype from the 80s that "was a side project, done out of fun, to play a little bit with being able to store random associations." [7-2] "The web was originally conceived and developed to meet the demand for automated information-sharing between scientists in universities and institutes around the world"; basically a collaborative workspace for geeks. [7-3] It is thanks to subsequent developments, such as fibre optics, mobile abilities, blockchain, and eWallets, that the web has developed its full peer-to-peer potential. This man-made system has provided a platform from which many other systems further developed. Without it, there would be no cryptocurrencies or Internet of Things.

3

G's third hero is Clare W. Graves, because he began his research looking at and including various disciplines to understand human motivations. Furthermore, he created the Graves Value System (GVS) framework, which can be used as a starting point to make sense of other viewpoints, methods and models. G often uses a map as a metaphor. Imagine you had a group of people who wanted to go places. They would look for directions on a map. Graves' framework is similar in that it enables people to understand where they are in life, clarify where they want to go and what the general development path could look like. The framework itself, like a map, isn't all that exciting, but what you can do and where you can go with it is what it's all about. G believes there is a shared pathway and that orchestrated progress along the levels is the way to go.

A FEW THOUGHTS AROUND SYSTEMS THINKING

Before the 1940s, the terms 'system' and 'systems thinking' had been used by several scientists, but it was Bertalanffy's concepts of an open and general systems theory that established systems thinking as a major scientific movement. In the midst of the 20th century, von Bertalanffy was reacting to a growing belief in efficiency-driven management thinking. This was based on Taylorism and organisations where people functioned just like cogwheels in machines. Those of you who have watched Charlie Chaplin's movie *Modern Times (1936)* will have a good picture in mind. Von Bertalanffy believed people were very individualistic and unique, yet would easily slot in when provided with systematically organised environments – but it is not in our nature to be "institutionalised." [92] Ultimately, von Bertalanffy was emphasising holism over reductionism and organism over mechanism, while attempting to revive the unity of science.

Systems thinking in general concerns the study of systems by examining the linkages and interactions between their various elements. Most science is reductionist and tries to understand the world by studying individual aspects in isolation. However, exploring every item in a system doesn't reveal how whole systems work together. This is due to the sheer unpredictability of elements interacting with one another.

Systems thinking techniques provide a holistic inquiry of systems. [93] Interesting tools exist out there. [94,95]

There are two major kinds of systems: designed (or human-made) and natural ones. The latter range from subatomic to living systems of all kinds, natural micro-systems, our planet, the solar system, galactic ones, and even the universe. Complex, natural systems often have some inherent degree of unpredictability tied to the behaviour of key elements, players, or the structures of interactions. In designed systems like manufacturing, correcting defects and driving frictionless processes is worth pursuing. But most natural systems thrive on imperfection, randomness and noise.

At present, G is busy cross-referencing and integrating the GVS with work from other thinkers and practitioners, like psychologists Jane Loevinger, William Perry and Robert Selman. G believes Clare W. Graves, a ground-breaking professor of psychology, would be proud to see that his work has generated additional research and been applied in ways he might have never anticipated.

G likes exploring and mind travelling. He had an early fascination for the classical sci-fi series Star Trek. He still likes the idea of discovering far-away places without interfering with them, rather merely for the sake of understanding other life forms and their way of life. For G, too many sci-fi movies have a negative and often brutal theme. If there are other life forms so advanced that they can visit Earth, why would they want to harm us?

He thinks movies like *Contact* and *Arrival* offered a good illustration of humankind continuing to be its own worst enemy. Besides sci-fi, G and Goto also like travelling back in time. They enjoy watching period dramas to get a taste of bygone life. Sometimes they even go to the countryside to re-enact critical scenarios from history, using a technique called systemic constellation. Every participant gets into character by impersonating one of the historical figures.

Then, each person is positioned in the space as stand-ins and relationships are drawn to one another. In this way, the network of relationships between players can be visualised. It is a fascinating way to experience what certain crucial and often intimate events must have been like. G and Goto don't usually go very far, because of the energy and time that travelling consumes. They both own e-bikes and use public transport for trips further away. In addition, advanced Virtual Reality has become incredibly useful for "travelling" without physically going places.

Once every two years or so, G visits the old world by sailboat – cheaper than flying and less polluting. People like Eli (remember our hero from the Orange chapter?), whom he met a few times through Florence, try to make fun of him because the trip takes two to three weeks. Eli sees transport by sailboat as a rejection of technological progress. However, there is thinking behind the method. G usually brings various like-minded people with him on the sailing trip, to form a kind of think tank. Together they explore complex challenges in specific areas, using cybernetic processes to maximise information sharing and the development of ideas and solutions. Last time, G explored new avenues for engaging primary school children in the adoption of ethical practices. That was on the way to Chakran. On the way back, he worked on circular solutions for the medical industry.

Sometimes it is good to get insight into a completely different field. If not immediately apparent, we often learn at a later point what it was good for.

Generally, G and his fellow citizens love learning. They are motivated by:

G's love for learning is another reason he enjoys working at the library, where he can search the vast database for key words and concepts. His idea is to identify all the different references and schools of thought, then compare, integrate and synthesize them as necessary. It is a great place to be, even though G doesn't get along with his colleague Gideon, who is a bit of a lone wolf.
G thinks Gideon doesn't really fit into a holonic community enterprise. However, Gideon is very well read and has considerable insight into different topics, and how they relate to or crossover with each other. At times, he becomes obsessed with knowledge, seems to disappear in his thoughts and then doesn't have enough time to work on matters relating to the operation or organisation.

G and Gideon are both part of the steering network of their current project. Thinking ahead is great, but Gideon often thinks so far into the future that he dismisses short- and medium-term improvements that people in the community could at least enjoy during their lifetime. It is fascinating to implement long-term plans that will benefit children when they start working, but G thinks there needs to be a balance.

Gideon is a dualistic thinker who very often points out that every aspect of life is created from a balanced interaction of opposites or competing forces, such as good and evil, mind and body, ignorance and knowledge.

His reasoning can appear too black and white sometimes, so G thinks it best to keep engagements to a minimum and push back by putting some of Gideon's comments into perspective. After all, this is what a healthy system does – it balances itself out.

G's mindset is settled in systems thinking. As Aristotle stated, "The whole is more than the sum of its parts". In other words, a system must be understood as a whole and cannot be comprehended by examining its individual parts in isolation from each other.

G stumbled across systems theory during his L&D years at the fire brigade, when he became bored with training. He wanted to take learning and development to the next level.
He read *The Fifth Discipline* by MIT's Peter Senge, a 1990 best-seller defining how corporations can use systems thinking to become holistic, integrated "learning organisations." That is how G got into the topic and later became fascinated by Ludwig von Bertalanffy and his general systems theory (GST). The basic idea of the GST is that any set of distinct parts that interact form a complex whole. Being a surfer, G knows all too well that the weather is a good example of systems within a system. A few basic elements – like warm air, cold air and the earth's rotation – can create either beautiful or devastating spectacles, but always so complex that we can neither predict nor control them.

THE WAGGLE DANCE

Systems thinking promotes the importance of nonuniformity. A beehive can demonstrate this perfectly. When a worker bee becomes cold, it gathers with other bees and they all buzz their wings to generate heat. If a bee gets hot, it moves away and fans its wings to cool down. Worker bees manage the hive's temperature through these actions. If all bees were controlled by a thermostat with the same setting, too many of them would take the same actions at once, which would result in dangerous temperature swings. The hive benefits from having "heterogenous bees" with slightly different ideal temperatures. Hence, they are self-controlled.

Furthermore, a colony is a large superorganism. Individual bees move and act in relation to one another. The queen does not rule the colony top down. Instead, when they face major decisions – like finding a bigger place, bees make a choice from the bottom up. At the heart of any complex system lies a set of interacting key players. Bee scouts identify new potential homes and return to perform a waggle dance; the dance duration indicates how good the new site is. This recruits supporters who go and check it out. Multiple bees scout and waggle dance so that colony members visit and evaluate various sites. At some point, the largest number of bees waggling in harmony decides where to go. This is choice through persuasion and recruitment, not through any authoritative decision by the queen. [7-6]

LEADERSHIP

When G wakes up in the morning, he has a choice: go back to sleep, or get up and chase his dreams. He is a curious character and believes he only lives once, so he wants to make the most of life. He learned early on to be proactive and initiate things. He likes to dream big, knows that changes don't come easily, and that he is just one small player in a bigger set of systems. His latest dream project is to integrate all knowledge platforms in Platonopolis and beyond to create the ultimate knowledge network. First connecting and integrating libraries, schools, businesses and organisations, then individuals. Eventually, all this will lead to a peer-to-peer human intelligence network – something far bigger and more advanced than Wikipedia could ever be. He knows that, in order to embark and lead on a project of this magnitude, he needs to boost his resilience levels. It is such a long-term vision that even Gideon might be on board this time around. The first box has been ticked as he knows what it takes and can do the appropriate waggle dance.

In a second step, he needs to reach out to other possible key players or stakeholders, preferably some that share G's characteristics, objectives and values, and the ability to waggle dance too. He also needs to truly understand what their personal motivations are and appeal to their heart and mind, creating an environment of mutual trust. Promoting a shared vision is vital to the mission as he has no formal authority. It helps if G can identify gaps in his knowledge and recruit people who complement him. There is often a lot to learn.

This style of leadership focuses on the process of progression in all senses. G will have to clarify the next steps with all people involved, and will most likely use questioning techniques to do so effectively. He may also have to act as a sounding board to help others find a way forward. G knows he will only have to check in occasionally to see what is going on and keep the momentum going. He will create the space for possibilities and events to happen. This is best done by connecting key players, empowering them where necessary, and encouraging collective actions between them. [7-7]

Thirdly, G needs to get the key players to waggle dance to engage with their respective stakeholders and possibly revitalise their connections, given they belong to different communities and networks. Essentially, it is about repeating step two. G's continuous drive will help his team to figure out how to interest and motivate their connections while staying true to the overall vision. If they then go off and recruit other waggle dancers, G and the core team can ensure they all waggle in tune.

Next comes an exploration of how the interplay of these communities of libraries, schools and business associations influences the system at heart. For example, different businesses will be part of different industry bodies. These systems are complex, multi-layered, dynamic and unpredictable.

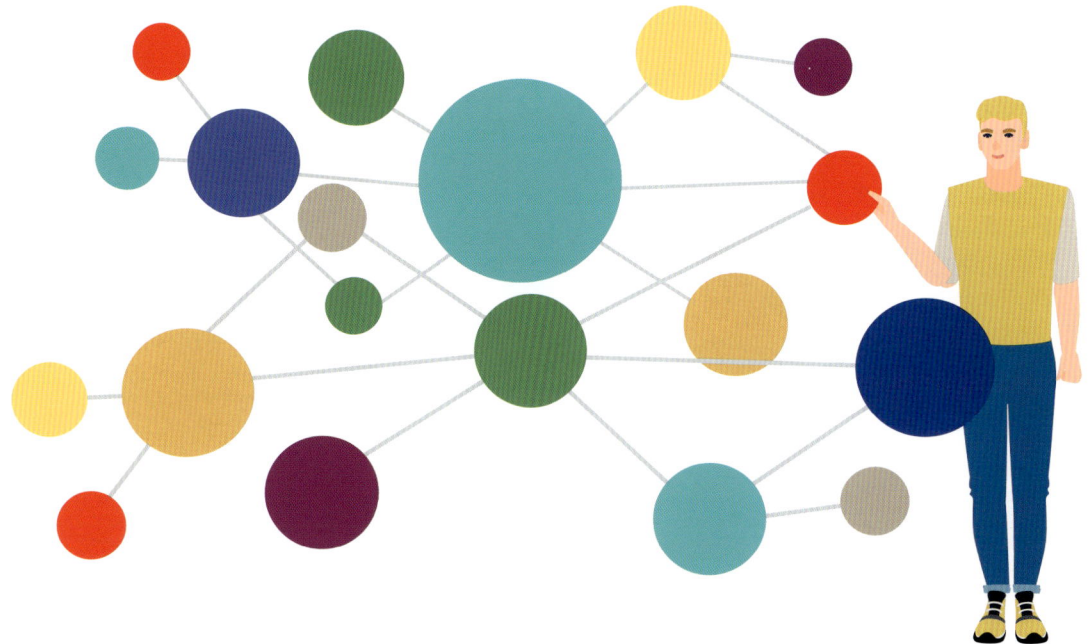

Last but not least, G needs to identify the meaningful signals amongst the overflow of information. This means being patient and allowing the system to self-organise and evolve. He will also have to develop metrics to gauge progress while avoiding excessive reliance on numbers as a guide to action. Embarking on an initiative like this is like sailing into the unknown. He wonders if he will ever reach any of the major milestones. Maybe it is too ambitious. Maybe his own attempt will fail, but planting the initial seed could spur someone else to run with the initiative at a later point and make it happen. They would at least benefit from G's input, without which such a venture could not be realised. He can't be sure at this point, but he is proactive, curious and resilient enough to give it a try right now.

According to Torbert's seven leadership styles, people at the 7th (Yellow) layer are closest to what he describes as the:

ALCHEMIST

Characteristics: Do not consider themselves more important than anyone else; high moral standards and an extraordinary capacity to handle many situations and different people simultaneously at multiple levels; ability to deal with immediate priorities without losing sight of long-term goals.

Strengths: Ability to generate social transformation by integrating material, transcendent, and societal transformations; can sense and use unique moments in their networks to initiate change for the better. This is often done by creating symbols and metaphors that speak to people's hearts and minds.

What sets Alchemists apart from Strategists is their genuine interest in the social conscience and future of the bigger whole (e.g. industry). They are willing to create meaningful relationships with other key players to rethink current relationships with clients and society as a whole.

TEAMS

As mentioned before, teams come together temporarily in a Yellow world. Citizens are engaged in many different jobs and roles, which means switching teams frequently.

G has software solutions to visualise his floating memberships to various networks and systems. He joins some out of personal interest, others because of his expertise, and yet others for further learning and development. The line between participating in and leading a team becomes blurred. Individuals usually lead for a short period of time because they care and have the skills. That is not the classical understanding of leadership. Here leaders are more like facilitators who collaboratively explore options, ensure responsibilities are clear, and then manage the way forward. A lot of the teamwork has to do with influencing skills because everyone is jamming, as in a jazz combo.

The key is to communicate without a personal agenda, judgement or force. This is especially important when dealing with people's anxieties, hopes and dreams. G often uses specific communication skills, like asking open-ended questions and listening actively to help others find answers for themselves. It is about trying to find the most ethical way of communicating.

> ## "
> SYSTEM LEADERSHIP CATALYSES COLLECTIVE LEADERSHIP IN OTHERS... SYSTEM LEADERS FOCUS ON CREATING THE CONDITIONS THAT CAN PRODUCE CHANGE AND THAT CAN EVENTUALLY CAUSE CHANGE TO BE SELF-SUSTAINING. "
>
> PETER SENGE, HAL HAMILTON & JOHN KANIA, THE DAWN OF SYSTEMS LEADERSHIP

This is crucial for healthy relationships and team dynamics, because everything we say or don't say, hear or overhear can consciously or unconsciously impact someone's feelings, behaviour, thoughts, and actions.

Communication skills are a main focus of development in the Yellow world, starting in primary school. The first step is to increase children's self-awareness with regard to intuition, personal values, beliefs and behaviours. Secondly, they learn about such things as empathy, observation, interpretation and filtering. Once children are clearer about themselves and where they stand in life, they learn skills like deep listening, questioning, timing, and logical reasoning.

The goal of all this is to maximise awareness and skills. Ultimately, this leads to a high level of understanding and openness between people, teams and citizens. People don't usually feel manipulated; the mutual ability to understand what the other person is doing fosters shared insight and trust.

AUTHOR'S COMMENT:
In tier 2 we can hardly differentiate between team members and team leaders. What we see is a type of collective leadership, where some members take the lead in areas they feel passionate or knowledgeable about.

Possible solutions are often explored collaboratively, with a 'leader' facilitating rather than directing. That made it difficult for me to distinguish the content of the two sub-chapters 'leadership' and 'team', which might therefore partly overlap.

PLANNING & STEERING

Paramount goals and total cost measures guide the overall governance of people and business networks, with serious consideration paid to the resources needed to deliver services and products. Systems are designed to take care of their own organisation and control. [7-8]

G remembers when people became serious about using an overall governance model. This happened some time ago and derived from the agenda for sustainable development that originally included 17 Sustainable Development Goals (SDGs) [7-9]. Building on the principle of "leaving no one behind", the agenda emphasised a holistic approach to achieving sustainable development for all.

The first step is to translate these goals into clear, measurable, achievable objectives. There are two main dilemmas in this step: one, it is difficult to prioritise the 17 goals when they are similarly important and urgent; two, an additional level of complexity is added by weighing off short, medium and long-term measurables and goals. For example, where there is a conflict between people and nature. Say, when the growing population in a desert starts putting too much strain on resources.

> " WE CANNOT IMPOSE OUR WILL ON A SYSTEM. WE CAN LISTEN TO WHAT THE SYSTEM TELLS US, AND DISCOVER HOW ITS PROPERTIES AND OUR VALUES CAN WORK TOGETHER TO BRING FORTH SOMETHING MUCH BETTER THAN COULD EVER BE PRODUCED BY OUR WILL ALONE. "
>
> **DONELLA MEADOWS, AMERICAN ENVIRONMENTAL SCIENTIST**

Yellow society people use tokens called TLCs (short for Total Lifecycle Cost) as currency. TLCs are calculated by evaluating the resources needed for products and services from cradle to grave. G likes the fact that people have to think through implications and interdependencies, which usually avoids costly short-term solutions – costly for stakeholders and the environment that is.

Furthermore, all network organisations are required to ensure that the facilities and processes needed to reuse or recycle their products are in place by their launch. None of this could happen without technology. G once saw the calculations that measure the value of natural resources, such as water. The TLC is dependent on reservoir levels, purification, distribution, and waste water management. These costs are measured continuously and updated in real time.

Everyone is interested in new ideas and innovation, as we all benefit if TLCs are reduced and SDGs reached. For example, when businesses consume water, they pay to have it cleaned again. This has led to the use of eco-friendly and natural detergents, washing powders and other cleaning products, which avoids the use of chemicals that kill all life in the process. This would be inconceivable in a Yellow world.

The planning and steering of networks is self-organised. All network members have the opportunity to contribute to new designs, products and services, and to important decisions. Networks analyse information and consider key principles to make decisions. People know there is often no right or wrong decision, but one that seems more aligned to the jointly agreed guidelines. It is all about learning and improving life.

ORGANISATIONS

G enjoys the organisation setups where he lives. No corporations and the like, just microbusinesses and temporary network organisations driven by people collaborating as individual, economic entities – much like freelancers used to. Tech has become the lubricant that enables and makes everything work.

G read a long time ago that the successful enterprises of tomorrow will be organised around building blocks of advanced computer and communication technology [7-10/11]. He is happy to see this has come to pass.

Indeed, the advent of sophisticated telecommunications equipment and high efficiency databases has created an ideal environment for the emergence of organizations capable of rapidly coupling to and decoupling from networks of other firms and individual knowledge workers. These network-based organizations may effectively combine teams which consist of empowered employees, consultants, suppliers, and even customers to solve one-time problems or take advantage of fleeting market opportunities. These advanced business entities possess three primary attributes: (1) structure is more important than strategy; (2) performance and knowledge trump credentials; and, (3) human resources are an organization's only sustainable advantage (Picot, 1999). [7-12]

> " NETWORKED ORGANIZATIONS ARE OPEN SYSTEMS OF ORGANIZATION THAT CONNECT PEOPLE DIRECTLY PEER TO PEER THROUGH INFORMAL NETWORKS OF COLLABORATION. "
>
> KEVAN HALL, FOUNDER & CEO, GLOBAL INTEGRATION

As individual economic entities, people earn TLCs by contributing to society and the health of the planet, and they redeem them by benefitting from society or the planet.

They are all clear about the core team's shared objectives and collaborate to realise the goals. It does help if a group comes together to pull this off to allow core players to focus on what they do best. It also lowers the costs as only needed resources are purchased. Team members can tap into other networks if they need additional resources, and partners can contribute value to the business idea if they see a real benefit.

These temporary network organisations remind G of how the production of films used to work, only with less ego or powerplays. From the conceptual idea for the film to the ongoing process during which different players come together – like producers, writers, the production crew, actors, film and sound editors, and many more – and dip in and out until the movie is released.

G is still looking forward to joining such a core initiative at some point. He would like to get involved in energy-generating solar art installations. In such a project, a core group first invests into a market-research network that feeds back on possible demand and expectations. After that, another group designs items according to customer needs, with an engineering network designing individual parts. You then look for networks and/or micro businesses willing to produce such items. Next, you need a network to deliver the parts for people to assemble. And finally, products can be delivered to sales locations or directly to end consumers who pay in tokens.

In this kind of initiative, the core team are like the film producers who see the idea through and make sure it comes to life. Along the way, network partners invest in the product if they think it is a good idea. They can ask for tokens in return, which is often the case with physical resources, such as when quartz is needed for solar surfaces. For services, people often invest because they genuinely enjoy collaborating and co-creating, rather than chasing financial returns.

One great side effect is that the players, networks and systems involved in the realisation of such products effectively manage demand, which gives a clear indication of the required supply. The more ground-breaking and useful a new product, the more people are willing to invest tokens, and the more products can be manufactured. At the same time, as transport consumes a lot of energy, localised production, assembly and delivery become particularly attractive.

MARKETS

G loves living in a market and society where everything is intertwined. Everyone can assume many different roles in a day. Therefore, access is more important than ownership. Technology is there to support human interactions and a self-regulating market produces less waste.

As we already know, G is part of many different networks. In some, he will provide input into certain products or services, contributing to market research in the same way members of the public are asked about their interest in solar-powered artwork. In his areas of expertise, he might help to co-create something. But he could also provide certain products or services, or consume in the traditional sense. This new economy emphasises interconnectivity. G is sometimes astonished to see the convenient and sustainable solutions people come up with. The packaging industry, for example, has been completely reinvented. As packaging is standardised so it can be reused, only higher grade, reusable plastics and, in many cases, compostable organic packaging make the cut.

G wonders if there will ever be an even more sustainable solution for toothbrushes. Then again, if we were to move away from the idea of a physical brush and think of it as cleaning teeth, we might be onto something. Never knock it until you try it. The systemised network of people has already achieved incredible things for the greater good

since its inception. The beauty is that, by constantly engaging with so many people, there is a lot of sense-checking going on.

Furthermore, there are no rich or poor people in G's society as there is no need to own a lot of things, which would just mean more wasted resources. Products like cars require an awful amount of tokens on account of their intense use of resources for production, maintenance, driving and recycling – not to mention the pollution. G doesn't understand why people ever owned cars individually only to drive them approximately 10% of the time (no more than 65 days per year). What a waste of everyone's resources with such devastating damage to the planet.

> " PRODUCTS WILL BECOME MORE AND MORE VIRTUALIZED AND DELIVERED AS A SERVICE WHICH AGAIN CAN BE AGGREGATED THROUGH NETWORKS ON DEMAND, IN A WORLD THAT IS CENTERED AROUND THE END USER. "
>
> MICHAEL MOSS, PHD, FREELANCE B2B CONTENT WRITER SPECIALIZING IN INFORMATION TECHNOLOGY

Nowadays, the world revolves around the access economy (formerly known as the sharing or services economy), which relies on the exchange of goods and services on the basis of access rather than ownership. G witnessed this development over the decades and finds it quite logical. Indeed, when access to a car, bike or tent becomes affordable, more convenient and reliable, then the necessity of owning one disappears. This clearly shows the impact of considering the TLC of products.

Advanced technology that constantly measures, monitors, connects and optimises makes all this possible. The information is processed by platforms that are interconnected in multiple ways. There is a growing interest in devices that can monitor and measure behaviour autonomously. G trusts that this is all done for the greater good. [7-13]

G sees the tech dimension as a separate world, but one that has nearly come to life by itself. The sheer amount of Artificial Intelligence, learning abilities and self-regulating mechanisms means that technology has become a real partner in making this world a better place. Technology mirrors human life in this part of the world. The constant engagement with people and the processing speed create continuous feedback loops that guarantee a high level of self-regulation in the market. As a consequence, waste is significantly reduced and put to good use in new networks, while we find out why and where things went wrong in the first place. This busy meshwork of people generates a lot of feedback, which encourages self-regulation. There is little space for bad apples.

AUTHOR'S COMMENT:

I am fully aware that the T2 society and markets described here sound a bit like utopia, but I believe that economies can create sustainable wellbeing for all.

There is no material wealth, dogmatism, or poverty. Equal distribution is possible, provided that we, as individuals, develop further and learn to balance our brighter and darker sides. We can see glimpses of that already and I, along with many other people within and outside my network, believe that we can reinvent ourselves.

However, this means we need to rethink politics, policy-making and money. We need to learn to let go of many of our unhealthy practices, however familiar they may feel. Change can be for the better. As the clever Albert Einstein once said "We cannot solve our problems with the same thinking we used when we created them." It is time to show we are not lemmings, that we can learn from our mistakes and improve by building on that learning. For example, the demise of the developed society as a consequence of deforestation on Easter Island, might just be a simplified precursor of what humankind is doing to its planetary island Earth. As the saying goes, history keeps repeating itself.

A practical tool to use for understanding and managing long-term changes is the Three Horizons framework by Bill Sharpe. Said Dawlabani's *MEMEnomics — The next-generation economic system* [0-15] is another insightful book to read with regard to future economic models.

LIMITATIONS AND GROWTH INTO NEXT LAYERS

The 1st (Beige) stage only trusts immediate family and simply tries to survive. On the 2nd (Purple) stage one can find a sense of belonging and trust in the tribe, traditions, and that elders will make the right decisions. People drawn to the 3rd (Red) stage count on themselves and their ability to win. On the 4th (Blue) stage, reliance on procedures and the system dominates, and rules are there to provide stability. By contrast, the 5th (Orange) stage puts its faith in technology, in its ability to measurably identify customer and market opportunities, and the power of ideas coming to life by aligning strategy with tactics, while continuously improving. People that feel drawn to the 6th (Green) stage believe in each other and the capabilities everyone brings to the table. They feel that the best person will lead when and where necessary. Individuals leaning towards the 7th (Yellow) layer believe in the intelligence of crowds and far-reaching, interconnected networks. Data captured and analysed with modern tech solutions provide useful insight. However, the ever-increasing amount of information feels overwhelming.

G shares his endless thirst for knowledge with many people, not just Gideon. However, cross-referencing and integrating knowledge on a global scale is a growing challenge. G too often tries to understand the world solely from an intellectual perspective. He feels that, with so many aspects in life, it is nearly impossible to grasp the whole picture. He wonders whether there is a natural and spiritual side that he and the Gideons of this world are missing out on. We simply cannot find happiness just in the mind.

Network organisations are self-organised and act sustainably through circular principles. The concept of the TLC currency ensures that everything is thought through. However, there is a big difference between considering nature and its resources on the one hand, and fully embracing the spiritual energies Mother Earth and the universe have to offer on the other. The logic of a human network is a powerful intellectual system, but it misses out on the bigger whole.

Yellow societies thrive by striking a balance between duties and autonomy. People can choose to use tokens or provide value to society. Wealth equality means greed or jealousy are virtually unheard of. Human networks regulate themselves; democratic and governance systems put the accent on dialogic and direct participation. Networks have managed to integrate head, heart and hands. However, it seems that true happiness can only be found when we fully immerse ourselves with our beautiful planet. Indeed, every molecule of our body comes from Mother Earth and will return to it at some point. If energy is never lost, what happens to the energy that our body holds? If it is part of the soul, where does it go after our physical departure?

The characteristics of 7th (Yellow) layer markets look as follows:

"EVERYONE IS A MULTI-FACETED PLAYER IN AN ENDLESS WEB OF MULTI-LAYERED MARKETS."

POLITICAL

- Individuals in different systems provide input and vote on topics that matter to them
- Networks at different layers of society (local, regional, or global) engage with each other
- Global networks collaborate on overcoming global challenges

ECONOMIC

- Every individual is an economic unit of their own
- Individuals earn and pay in tokens (TLCs)
- An access economy means people hardly own any material goods, but share them instead

SOCIAL

- Holding limited material wealth curbs jealousy and greed
- People provide value to society at various levels

TECHNOLOGICAL

- Tech is used to integrate the global wealth of information
- It plays an intrinsic part in daily life and is used for good

ENVIRONMENTAL

- There is a clear understanding of environmental costs and implications for all actions and products
- The total lifecycle cost (TLC) concept ensures sustainability
- Transport is resource-intensive and therefore people are encouraged to produce and sell as locally as possible

LEGAL

- Networks are self-organised and self-regulating
- Individuals who harm others and the greater good are punished not only by serving society in the area of personal failure, but also by learning and reflecting about the implications of their actions

8th LAYER

TURQUOISE: ALL IS ONE

INDIVIDUALS STRIVE FOR COMPLETE HARMONY WITH THEIR OWN SELF AND THE WORLD AROUND THEM. THEY ARE GLOBAL COLLECTIVISTS WHO ATTEMPT TO MANIFEST THEIR TRUE SELF FOR THE BENEFIT OF ALL LIFE. THEY EXPLORE THE BEAUTY IN SMALL THINGS, LIKE LEAVES, AS WELL AS THINGS AS GRAND AS THE UNIVERSE. THEY CONCEIVE THE ENTIRE UNIVERSE AS AN INTERCONNECTED LIVING CONSTRUCT OF KNOWLEDGE AND ENERGY, AND SEE THEMSELVES AS A LIVELY PART OF IT.

PEOPLE WORK TOGETHER IN MANY DIFFERENT WAYS. THE CONNECTIONS ARE ENDLESS AND CAN CHANGE DEPENDING ON NEED. THE MAIN FOCUS IS ON HEALTH AND WHOLENESS. PEOPLE ARE NOT PERFECT, BUT WITH A SHARED WILL THEY FIND A UNITED WAY FORWARD. TECHNOLOGY, DATA AND INTUITION GUIDE PEOPLE TOWARDS UNIVERSAL BALANCE AND HARMONY.

THE MARKETS ARE DOMINATED BY INDIVIDUALS AND SMALL COMPANIES. THEY FORM AN INTEGRAL PART OF THE SOCIAL FABRIC. SOCIETIES NO LONGER FOCUS ON CONSUMPTION OR MATERIALISM; LOTS OF TIME IS SPENT ON UNDERSTANDING LIFE BETTER, LEARNING AND DEVELOPMENT. IN MANY WAYS, LIFE IS LESS CONVENIENT BUT SIMPLER.

PEOPLE HAVE A WAY OF CONTRIBUTING TO THE PLANET'S HEALTH AND ENSURING MOTHER EARTH BENEFITS FROM THEIR ACTIONS AS MUCH AS POSSIBLE. THE COLLECTIVE IMPERATIVE BEATS INDIVIDUAL DESIRES. AS SOON AS THE RISING POPULATION STARTS TO STRAIN THE HABITAT, SOME PEOPLE MOVE ON. ALTHOUGH COMMUNITIES HAVE A LOCAL FEEL TO THEM, THERE EXIST MANY REGIONAL AND GLOBAL CONNECTIONS AND NETWORKS.

"

THE PROBLEMS YELLOW RECOGNISES...
CANNOT BE RESOLVED BY ISOLATED INDIVIDUALS,
NO MATTER HOW MUCH THEY KNOW OR LEARN.
THE HUGE AMOUNT OF RAW INFORMATION CALLS
FOR A RENEWAL OF ORDER AND COLLABORATIVE
SYNERGY IF IT IS GOING TO BE USEFUL. [8-0, PAGE 287]

"

TURQUOISE LIFE

Meet Hortense, who currently stands in her favourite place in the entire universe – her garden. She inherited the overgrown plot and run-down buildings on it from her great grandmother many years ago. She used to call her Mima and had a special connection with her. Hortense has never felt at home anywhere as much as she does here. The garden is special, not only through its design, but also because of the spring that runs into the north-flowing river close by. Some say Mima is buried in the garden, but somehow no one really knows if that's true. After all these years, who cares? We are all one anyway.

Hortense's place lies in the heart of a region known as Gaia, an unusual part of the world where you can experience the fullness of nature intermingling seamlessly with high-end technology. Tech is there for support when and where necessary – you'll notice high-speed magnetic trains silently swooshing by in the distance. Powered by solar energy panels fitted between the tracks four meters above ground, they allow wildlife to roam freely. Hortense observes the scene of human ingenuity from a distance. She particularly enjoys the spectacle at night, with those light beams shooting across the landscape. She calls it luminous moving art.

We have entered a place and time where humankind has started blending in with and is truly becoming a part of its habitat again.

Hortense's house is a good example, typical of this region. Most dwellings boast natural, sometimes live material. Clay makes up the outside walls, which are sometimes protected with bent willows to fit their rounded shape. Other parts are covered with creepers containing natural insect-repelling oils and fragrances. Hortense used hemp sheets to create the inside structures. This material is free of additives and chemicals, absorbs carbon dioxide and releases nitrogen back into the earth. An alternative is cedarwood for its lovely scent and ability to keep insects at bay. The roof is made from natural slate covered with a local moss that deflects the sun in summer and keeps in the warmth during the colder months. It might remind some of Hobbiton in Tolkien's Middle-earth.

> **ADJUST TO THE REALITY OF EXISTENCE, WHICH IS THAT YOU CAN ONLY BE, YOU CAN NEVER REALLY KNOW.**

Where products are human made – for example, for electricity and plumbing – they are designed and built to last. In the past, most people thought appliances would naturally break after a period of time. Little did they know that this was planned obsolescence; in other words, they were designed to break. If designed well, products can actually last surprisingly long. Once they do give up, people can dismantle them and reuse or compost the materials. This is continuous reuse and recycling in action.

Hortense lives in this nature-oriented holon (read more about the holonic structures in the Green chapter) with her husband Hermes. He gives her space when it comes to the living arrangements, and it works well for them. Hermes is amazed at Hortense's ability to grow their living spaces, literally speaking. When he needed a new study, they pushed through one part of the house and she grew the space for him using different plants. He then decorated the inside. Some of the materials and structures act as vents, and the design reproduces termite nests. The idea is that fluctuations in outside conditions create convection currents, which regulate room temperature. It works extremely well. For extra heat or to power their stove, they tap into the heat coming from the ground through underground reservoirs of steam and hot water. The entire community and its holons are built on top of this geothermal region. Specially designed boreholes and wells are located in specific areas to facilitate the release of the planet's internal pressure. The natural abundance of energy has attracted quite some local manufacturing, and it is a flourishing aspect of Gaia.

Hortense and Hermes love living here and feel integrated into the local community. The area boasts many small community businesses with purpose and soul, most of them designed and set up to solve societal needs. People work together in temporary projects to get things done, always with the health of Mother Earth in mind.

Professionals working in specific areas of expertise and skills organise in local guilds. These are professional associations of craftspeople or traders who oversee the research, knowledge management and practice of their craft or trade. They are organised locally, but collaborate globally. The idea of guilds dates back to Roman times. In the past, they were criticised for their rigid gradation of social rank, religious intolerance, and power plays, but they are nothing like that nowadays. They serve as collaborative hubs and networks for sharing ideas, knowledge and practices.

After all, carpenters in South America, Europe and Asia have more in common than separates them. This is also true for forest guardians and lumberjacks.

Today people understand that everything is interconnected. Children learn and explore this essential worldview at school. The environment still bears the sequels of many of the damages caused by previous generations and civilisations. However, Hortense recognises nature's ability to bounce back when given space and a little support.

The local currency, Universal Contribution (UC), was developed out of the TLCs (Total Lifecycle Costs; see Yellow chapter), but offers two main advantages.

First, each UC transaction generates a small surplus in Mother Earth's favour, similar to a value added tax (VAT). This 'tax' is re-invested in projects that foster life in harmony with

the planet. Thus, the more people take from the earth, the more they produce and trade, the more the planet benefits – a true win-win situation.

Second, in G's Yellow world, TLCs were needed to understand the real cost of products and services, and to get everyone on-board to get things done. The automation of TLC exchanges was barely noticeable as people still used up resources, or invested time and energy. Interactions were constantly monitored, measured and co-managed by predictive software solutions. In this world, people look out for each other within their local holon. They now rarely exchange UCs, but instead give and receive goods and services in a more natural mutual exchange manner.. Everyone is well aware of environmental implications of all actions and transactions – it's a subject well covered and discussed throughout the school curriculum – so there is no fear of the system being abused.

UCs tend to be reserved for jobs that garner little interest or far-reaching projects where the parties involved don't know each other. However, even this is slowly fading away as the understanding that the human race is a single organism increases. People will generally take on jobs that need doing once they understand the rationale and the collective benefit.

People in Gaia have a clear understanding of values and how to live authentically. Hortense learned these values in school and, while she might prioritise them differently, she can easily reel them off:

1. SELF-INQUIRY
2. GLOBAL COLLECTIVISM: CONSCIOUSNESS OF ALL
3. METAPHYSICAL TRUTHS
4. WISDOM OF NATURE
5. MYSTICISM & SPIRITUALITY
6. HOLISM & SYNTHESIS
7. RADICAL AUTHENTICITY
8. SPIRITUAL, EMOTIONAL AND PHYSICAL HEALING
9. SPONTANEITY
10. PLAYFULNESS (NO EGO)

Hortense feels lucky to have been born outside of Gaia, because it means she experienced other societies before coming here. This makes her value this environment and its people's strengths even more. People in Gaia possess:

- A NATURAL ABILITY TO TAP INTO AND LEVERAGE TRAITS INHERENT TO THE OTHER SEVEN LEVELS;
- SUPERNATURAL INTUITION AND INSPIRING LEVELS OF EMOTIONAL MASTERY;
- NON-JUDGEMENTAL THINKING;
- MENTAL AND BEHAVIOURAL FLEXIBILITY AND TOLERANCE;
- THE CAPABILITY TO INTEGRATE AND SYNTHESISE ANY INFORMATION THAT COMES THEIR WAY;
- TRUE BIG PICTURE THINKING WITH THE ABILITY TO EXPLORE DETAILS.

While nothing is perfect, Hortense understands that everything is meant to be the way it is. She knows there are areas of weakness to look out for among individuals in Gaia, who:

- CAN FIND IT DIFFICULT TO BE UNDERSTOOD;
- MUST WORK HARD TO CONNECT WITH PEOPLE CONCERNED WITH MATERIALISM AND EXISTENTIAL WORRIES (T1);
- MAY RETREAT AS THEY FIND THE APPROACH TO LIFE TOO MYSTICAL;
- MAY CONSIDER OTHERS PASSIVE AS THEY LET THINGS UNFOLD NATURALLY OR TRUST THINGS WILL EVOLVE BY THEMSELVES;
- STRUGGLE TO UNDERSTAND THE UNIVERSE AND ITS INFLUENCE ON US.

Furthermore, Hortense understands that all of Graves' layers have their merits and that we should strive to embody their healthier aspects, however challenging that might be. For example, Hortense is struggling to set and use Orange-stage measurable objectives. While adding performance-oriented analytics to her range of insights helps, it doesn't come naturally to her. She knows she needs to work on this, so she may join a few local learning and development groups.

INDIVIDUALS

Hortense's very colourful career started in Purpleshire. She spent her early years there and always had a special connection to her aunt Bo; everyone agreed they were kindred souls. Their connection remains intact even across time and space. They are both on the same wavelength.

Hortense moved away after school to start a career as an investigative journalist. She really did go undercover a few times and found most of the tough and uncertain situations thrilling. It felt like being on a quest for finding the truth and uncovering the culprits.

A few years in, Hortense investigated a corporation for ethical wrong-doing, but after identifying ruthless people operating in the supply chain, she ended up helping the company she was initially investigating.

She soon found out she was expecting and chose to keep out of harm's way by accepting another job in that same corporation. She took up a team leader role in the communications department and enjoyed a few years in a stable environment, which provided her with paid maternity leave and all the comforts of corporate employment. However, she missed the thrill of shaking things up like she used to. Once her little one was in pre-school, she applied for what she thought was a more challenging in-house role.

> " GAIA THEORY DIFFERS FROM MODERN ECOLOGY. MODERN ECOLOGY FOCUSES TOO MUCH ON HUMAN ECOLOGY AND THE STUDY OF MACRO-ORGANISMS AND HOW THEY INTERACT WITH THE WORLD. GAIA FOCUSES ON MICRO-ORGANISMS AND GEOLOGICAL FUNCTIONS.
>
> HUMANITY IS A SMALL SPECK IN GAIA'S LIFE. [6-7] "
>
> JAMES LOVELOCK, AUTHOR OF *GAIA*

Her company had acquired a similarly sized competitor and was heading for a merger. Hortense had a good relationship with the CEO by then and interviewed for the post of Head of Integration. During her pitch, she pointed out that she would only be interested if this integration was done in a purely performance-oriented approach, and not around political power plays. She suggested the Chicken Tikka Masala Way, which basically means combining the best of two worlds. The most popular dish in Britain is linked to the urban legend that a Pakistani chef added the very popular Campbell tomato soup to his curry to make the dish more palatable for the locals. As the company operated in a very competitive market, the CEO's upcoming bonus was linked to the integration's overall performance and his favourite dish was... well, you can guess. Hortense got the job, which turned out to be a bit more challenging than she had expected. Considering that approximately 80% of mergers don't deliver the expected financial returns within the first three years, she did a relatively good job and was praised on numerous occasions.

Nevertheless, politics eventually took over and everything seemed to become very mechanical. After the initial excitement wore off, her level of engagement faded. Financial targets and cost savings became the priority and her job lost all meaning for her.

Luckily she had invested in quite a bit of personal development for herself and her teams during that time. At a leadership development programme, she was introduced to working with horses and learned that all forms of leadership require good communication. Leaders can learn a great deal about observation, motivation, assertiveness, and body language from an animal weighing close to half a tonne. Soon after, Hortense left her corporate job and joined an equestrian team. The organisation worked organically with people helping and managing each other. This meant less pay, but there was much more meaning in what she was doing. Her professional career path and previous high-profile title clearly demonstrated that she understood and meant business. With the new job came a whole new world, in which she rekindled her love for animals and nature. Following turbulent changes,

a few of the horses developed several quirks. Hortense increased her focus on their mental wellbeing to try and identify the root causes. She uncovered a web of issues, ranging from traumatic experiences and malnutrition to underlying illnesses. Soon Hortense became quite an expert at understanding and treating complex health issues in multiple ways. For years she consumed books, researched papers and contributed to various studies looking at the animal's entire system. She had a knack for matching people with the right horses. She observed the animals, considered their breed, evaluated and adjusted their diet, and used a lot of herbs to cure certain illnesses and alter behaviours. For example, she boiled devil's claw for arthritis, mashed white cabbage for tendinitis, and used different kinds of microbes for anything from itchy skin to indigestion. She became a real expert in the medicinal and therapeutic uses of leaves, roots, and flowers.

This led to her re-discovering Mima's garden as she had always been a keen gardener. She started to read up on the garden's history and began to understand that there was more to the place than meets the eye. It is a natural and colourful plot where life abounds, but she quickly recognised there was some kind of magic at play as well.

FAMILY LIFE

At times Hermes feels like it is all going a bit too far. Energy vortexes, ley lines, electromagnetic fields, star constellations – what else do you want to throw into the mix? Hermes is a bit more Cartesian, being a professional surgeon who has gone through a traditional education. Half way through his career, he started combining alternative medicine practices and treatments with conventional medicine. Since then, he has been a proponent of integrative medicine,

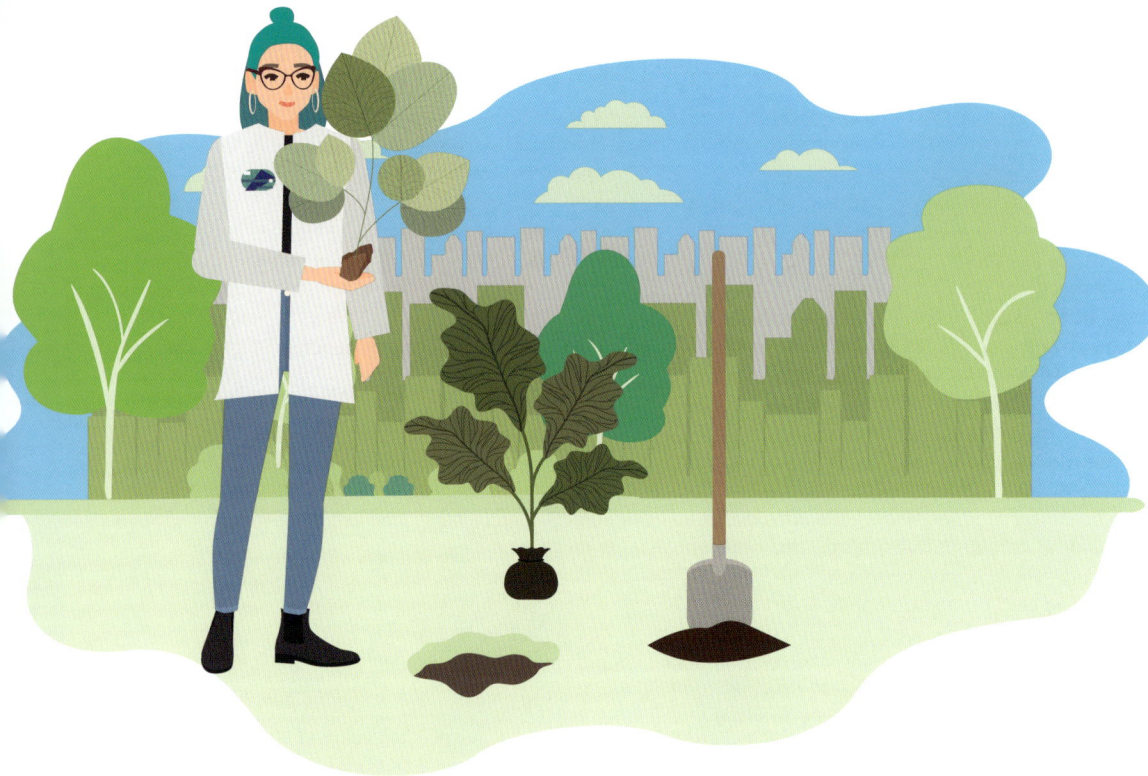

She started focussing on the wider ecosystem and reintroduced keystone species – animals and plants that have a disproportionately large effect on their natural environment relative to their abundance. The concept was introduced by zoologist Robert T. Paine in 1969.

Currently, Hortense works partly as a botanist and has found ways of bringing indigenous plants back to life, including many that can bring renewed energy and stimulate the body, heart, mind, and spirit.

She wouldn't go as far as calling herself a zoologist, but she also reintroduces all kinds of small animals. Hortense adopts a holistic perspective and considers a whole range of influences, including energy streams and vortexes – swirling centres of energy, containing higher-than-average earthly energy. Today's technologies can measure these vortexes, which most often appear at the intersections of ley lines or electromagnetic fields. [8-2] The energies seem to have different effects on people – something that Hortense seems to be able to identify, channel and match.

a healing-oriented approach that takes account of the whole person and all lifestyle aspects. This also considers the therapeutic relationship with his patients. Ultimately, he makes use of all appropriate therapies.

Hermes and Hortense met at a Heart awakening event, a concept originally pioneered by Raoult Bertrand. The idea is to first align the mind and the heart, and then to open one's heart through the combination of a range of meditations with modern technology, like the quantum healing system. [8-3]
Once everything is humming in harmony, we become empathetically connected to others

through energetic frequencies. This isn't too far-fetched for Hermes as Nikola Tesla already stated a hundred years ago: "If you want to find the secrets of the universe, think in terms of energy, frequency and vibration."

There are limits to what Hermes believes is possible. However, from time to time Hortense puzzles him when she makes the impossible happen. He had several patients over the years who seemingly didn't have long left to live. With a dozen or so of them he had tried every possible therapy, but nothing seemed to halt their decline. Hortense engaged with a few of them in a range of ways and somehow managed to cure them. She was very selective about the patients she chose. She never really shared her reasons and Hermes still wonders whether she even knows herself. It seems to have to do with levels of healthy influence certain individuals have on the world around them. It is a bit of a mystery.

Then again, Hermes often doesn't know why he takes to some people and not others. Living in a world without any material wealth or power helps, as the ego is less prominent. Artificial influences such as money or power have little impact on relationships or people, who can be themselves and make more of an effort. As for Hortense and Hermes, there doesn't seem to be any particular pattern for the people in their lives. Their close friends come from different walks of life.

They all highly value openness, tolerance, mindfulness, and curiosity, and share a love for nature. Their friend circles evolve over time, on either party's initiation, depending on where they are in space and life.

This applies to many things and is also true of their home and habitat. Their surroundings could be described as an open wild-life farm. They feel a deep connection to all the animals and each one has its own story. In fact, Hortense's constant companions are the double act Delilah and Toto. The latter is a Cairn Terrier that Hortense got as a puppy. Delilah is a house-trained KuneKune pig, and quite a chatty one. As different as these two are from one another, they never leave each other's side, particularly when one isn't well. Whoever said pigs and dogs can't be friends?

Everything in Hortense's life comes together in absolute harmony, as if divinely orchestrated. Everything seems to fall into place if she lets it. Even wildlife like newts, pine martens and fallow deer seem to have taken a natural liking to the place. Perhaps it's because the universe is actually one massive neural network, and once beings understand this to be true they live in greater harmony with each other. [8-4]

This insight was gained when humankind started solving the problem of quantum gravity by reconciling quantum mechanics and general relativity. Quantum mechanics suggests that time is universal and fixed, while general relativity states that time is relative, linked to the composition of space and time. Hortense believes another layer of people is needed to engage and tap into the neural network. For sure, that ability will provide more answers about the meaning of it all.

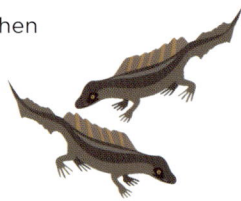

Hortense still had to intervene quite a lot in the beginning to counter the imbalances created by the previous occupants of Mima's garden. As mentioned, she re-introduced keystone species, such as specific solitary bees and hummingbirds.

Mima's records helped her identify which of the over 330 species of hummingbirds were native. Some only drink from certain plants. Their unique, elongated beaks can be used as keys to unlock or pollinate plants. To start with, Hortense planted specific flowers before attracting or releasing the needed hummingbirds, which are very picky when it comes to eating insects and spiders. Keystone species can return an entire area back to its biological origins. It took Hortense just over seven years to achieve her overall goal of bringing these biological microsystems back to life. She has benefited from the added diversity as much as her garden and environment have.

The setting makes for incredible scenery along Hortense and Hermes's walks. The two also regularly go running and cycling. The interesting thing is that being mindful allows you to pick up different patterns, whatever your mode of transport. Hiking or walking offer the advantage of easily accessing certain harder to reach areas. Hortense always takes time to observe her garden to see how plants interact and what insects they attract. The number and location of insects reveal the condition of the land. When you know what to look for, plant life isn't that mysterious after all.

THE GARDEN

After moving in, Hortense started to unwild the garden before rewilding it. She was convinced that the central pattern represented a five-lobed flower. Despite its fairly large size at about 30 metres in diameter, the pattern seemed obvious to her and the similar-shaped little pond with nymphoides in the centre provided a visual clue.

Now that everything has been arranged, the garden itself is clearly outlined with the surrounding hedge. Different bushes weave into one another, a mix of barberries, dogwoods, sea orachs, Cornelian cherry, and some elaeagnus. The latter is the most dominant and Hortense assumes that is because this species harbours nitrogen-fixing organisms in its roots. Nitrogen is a major component of chlorophyll, which allows plants to absorb energy from light and produce sugars from water and carbon dioxide. Hortense also keeps an eye on soil sulphur levels. All in all, she has become a bit of an alchemist over the years, but let's keep our eyes on the garden, which has more to reveal yet.

The other main features are the stones that originate from the land itself. Stone walls delineate the north and east sides. Paths are also made from stone and the main ones feature little walls of their own. All of these capture the warmth from the sun making the garden's atmosphere magical in the evenings – it is a space where nature flourishes, energises itself, and releases its healing powers.

Hortense seems to have the ability to combine numerous aspects to create an energetic system. Not only do information and resonances pass through the garden, but she has the gift to read them. She somehow understands the cyclical energies in motion.

It all started to make much more sense when a friend pointed out that the garden's pattern was the same as the pentagram of Venus. This was also the beginning of Hortense's interest in astrology. She believes the universe not to be mechanical, but rather a living being. This idea isn't new; Zeno, the philosophical founder of stoicism, already stated this around 300 BC.

Out of the box thinkers, like biologist Rupert Sheldrake, revived the idea at the beginning of the 21st century. It makes Hortense wonder how people could think of the universe in mechanical terms. After all, everything comes from one big bang, which is more akin to the emergence of life than switching on a machine.

Hortense is happy to reside in Gaia – people here don't live under the illusion that we are all separate beings in a purely mechanical universe, but try instead to bring the collective nature of consciousness to light. This consciousness is shared by humans and all things in the universe. [8-5]

AUTHOR'S COMMENT:
People like Hortense have naturally and intuitively created habits to live in harmony with the planet, understanding how beautifully interconnected the world is. They instinctively follow concepts that have emerged before (mainly on the 6th level then integrated in the 7th). The difference is that now they truly have come to life and become second nature. Here are a few examples of what we are talking about in the present day (2020s).

Biomimicry: The design and production of materials, structures, and systems that are modelled on biological entities and processes. It is about learning from nature by copying patterns, shapes and natural logics.

Biophilia: The biophilia hypothesis, also called BET, suggests that humans possess an innate tendency to seek connections with nature and other life forms. Edward O. Wilson introduced and popularised the hypothesis in his book, *Biophilia (1984)*. He defines biophilia as "the urge to affiliate with other forms of life".

Biomorphism: The modelling of artistic design elements on naturally occurring patterns or shapes reminiscent of nature and living organisms. Taken to its extreme, biomorphism attempts to force naturally occurring shapes onto functional devices.

When it comes to gardening and farming principles there are also the following two:

Permaculture: A combination of permanent and agriculture, this is an integrated system of ecological and environmental design. At the core lies a perennial and sustainable form of farming that works with, rather than against nature. For example, plants are grown in so called guilds — a mutually beneficial association that also fosters soil health. Permaculture is based on three ethics (earth care, people care, fair share) and 12 principles (including apply self-regulation and accept feedback, produce no waste, design from patterns to details, use edges, and value the marginal). These can also guide us towards a more conscious lifestyle for the greater good, not just in relation to growing food (read also about Bill Mollison, the thinking head behind this concept on the following pages).

Biodynamics: a form of alternative agriculture very similar to organic farming, but it includes various esoteric concepts drawn from the ideas of Rudolf Steiner. Initially developed in 1924, it was the first of the organic agriculture movements (read more about Rudolf Steiner on the following pages).

HORTENSE'S HEROES AND SCHOOL OF THOUGHT

Lady Eve Balfour and Jorian Jenks are two of Hortense's heroes. Not only were they leading figures in the development of the organic movement, but they also founded the Soil Association after WWII. Their mission was to deliver solutions that would ensure healthy, humane and sustainable food, farming and forestry, for everyone's benefit. [8-6]

Her aunt Bo is another hero of hers for the communal spirit that she, her family and friends have created in Purpleton and beyond. They might be a bit disconnected from the world, but they live in a beautiful community and look after everyone and everything in it.

Next is Serbian physicist, engineer and inventor Nikola Tesla. He was a truly passionate, imaginative, relentless, and creative thinker who sought to understand energy and push scientific boundaries. A real pioneer, idealist and genius, he wasn't interested in money, as the following incident shows. The Westinghouse Corporation wanted to use Tesla's technology and had agreed royalty fees. However, as usage of the technology and royalty fees shot up,

George Westinghouse begged Tesla to release the company of its obligations. He was heard to have stated "Your decision determines the fate of the Westinghouse Company." Tesla was grateful to the man who had always been straight with him and apparently tore up the contract and walked away from millions in royalties. He could have been one of the wealthiest men in the world, but instead ended up a poor man in a New York hotel room. [8-7]

Another person Hortense looks up to is Brazilian politician Jaime Lerner. He first worked as an urban planner and was then elected mayor of Curitiba, the eighth largest city in Brazil. Lerner is a rational and logical example of a man who simply took a different viewpoint to everyone else in Brazil at that time. "It was a change in the conception of the city. Working, moving, living leisure ... we planned for everything together. Most cities in South America separate urban functions – by income, by age. Curitiba was the first city that, in its first decisions, brought everything together." [8-8] Located near Paraguay and Argentina, Curitiba boasts world-leading characteristics, such as numerous recreational areas and relatively easy commuting thanks to an integrated transport network.

It was the first city to open a bus rapid transit (BRT) allowing passengers to step off a tube or train directly into a bus. This system has now been adopted by more than 300 cities worldwide. Hortense loves people like Lerner who take a fresh approach to life planning.

Another, arguably controversial, of her heroes is entrepreneur Jeff Bezos, who quit his day job in 1994 to establish his online bookstore Amazon from his garage. Hortense likes the fact that he challenged many outdated business models and even entire industries. Bezos was intent on creating a company that did more than just pay lip service to customer centricity. This new level of customer obsession, combined with measurability and continuous improvement, turned Amazon into a fierce competitor. It was a great catalyst for driving innovation, but also showed, in later years, how too much power can morph into ruthlessness and ultimately turn bad.

amazon

Hortense admires Martin Luther King Jr., a true leader who is undoubtedly one of the most recognised characters to have emerged out of the US Civil Rights Movement. His messages of love, cooperation, altruism, and justice are still referenced by people the world over. The way he led African Americans to the advancement of civil rights in a nonviolent way showed ingenuity. He was committed to achieving justice and equality for everyone. Hortense read one of his biographies and doubts she would have been able to handle the level of injustice and unfairness that he faced growing up. He had great role models, like his father and Mahatma Gandhi, but still... In his own words:

"I am now convinced that the simplest approach will prove to be the most effective – the solution to poverty is to abolish it directly by a now widely discussed matter: the guaranteed income... The curse of poverty has no justification in our age. It is socially as cruel and blind as the practice of cannibalism at the dawn of civilization, when men ate each other because they had not yet learned to take food from the soil or to consume the abundant animal life around them. The time has come for us to civilize ourselves by the total, direct and immediate abolition of poverty." [8-9]

He also wisely stated:

"We must recognize that we can't solve our problem now until there is a radical redistribution of economic and political power... this means a revolution of values and other things. We must see now that the evils of racism, economic exploitation and militarism are all tied together... you can't really get rid of one without getting rid of the others... the whole structure of American life must be changed. America is a hypocritical nation and [we] must put [our] own house in order." [8-10]

Hortense believes that, through the example of people like Martin Luther King Jr., humankind can progress to a place of greater unity.

Hortense will always have a special place for Bill Mollison in her heart. He is the Tasmanian guy who coined the term permaculture, an integrated system of ecological and environmental design that he co-developed with David Holmgren. Together, they envisioned a perennial and sustainable form of farming that works with, rather than against nature. [8-10] Bill Mollison went even beyond this by identifying local energy fields through the practice of rituals and a focus on the growth of particular plant functions. On the back of this, he set up a department called Environmental Psychology at the University of Tasmania in the 1970s.

Permaculture principles are practised in more than 130 countries, partly thanks to Mollison's extensive travelling. He has helped create a method that allows humankind to return to a more natural path. Three very simple ideas underpin this cultivation system:

- **EARTH CARE**

- **PEOPLE CARE**

- **FAIR SHARE**

Mollison was also influenced by one of Hortense's other heroes: Croatian-born Rudolf Steiner, who assumed many roles in his life. She first came across his ambitions to synthesise science and spirituality, and then of course discovered he was the founder of anthroposophy. However, it is what the Austrian intellectual did in 1924 that still amazes her today – he developed the idea of biodynamic agriculture.

This kind of farming allows a sustainable, "holistic approach which uses only organic, usually locally-sourced materials for fertilising and soil conditioning, views the farm as a closed, diversified ecosystem, and often bases farming activities on lunar cycles." [8-12] Also, "Steiner was one of the first public figures to warn that the widespread use of chemical fertilisers would lead to the decline of soil, plant and animal health and the subsequent devitalisation of food." [8-13] Here in Gaia everyone knows of the destructive nature of systemised farming and pesticide use. Hortense cannot help but wonder how people could have ever thought that deadly chemicals would be a sensible idea in a closed habitat.

Another person she is fond of is South-African statesman, military leader and philosopher Jan Smuts. He pioneered the concept of holism, which he defined as the "fundamental factor operative towards the creation of wholes in the universe." [8-14] It is hard to believe that he published this level of advanced insight in his 1926 book *Holism & Evolution*. [8-15] She finds it simply amazing to have the ability to truly understand holism and provide a body of work that is still insightful today. If only she could show him her garden!

WORK & FUN

Besides spending time in her garden, Hortense enjoys relaxing, doing nothing, or just having a laugh. She is quite minimalistic, but likes her gadgets. The one that makes her laugh the most is a singing and dancing Elmo. It is just amusingly silly. Her latest gimmick is a clock on the wall that has a repertoire of 144 sounds – a different one every hour on the hour. It's great for the imagination. The sounds range from animals to the body and the universe. She loves the sound of sun flares.

The most expensive gadget she owns is a modern, holographic play station that Hortense uses for attending virtual circles. These are groups of like-minded people from all over the world coming together in virtual sessions to share, synthesise and create ideas, systems, and services for the benefit of all. The holographic device is also great for watching classic movies. She likes things that make her laugh, think, or even change her viewpoint. Some of her all-time favourites are *The Man who Sued God, La Belle Verte (The Beautiful Green), Cloud Atlas, Avatar* and *OXV: The Manual* (aka as *Frequencies*), *Down to Earth* and *Kiss the Ground*.

Hortense's go-to info channel is Gaia.com, which covers a lot of her personal interests and offers further exciting topics for exploration. Inbuilt in this website are modern AI solutions that identify what else you might be interested in, clearly state why you might be interested in them, and how they relate to one another. The systems can identify and connect the dots of your personal interests, share calculated insights, and make credible suggestions.

Currently, Hortense watches a lot of programmes on astrology, energetic forces and quantum solutions. She has started exploring this wisdom for the benefit of the people constellations she holds in her garden. She schedules these therapeutic sessions to coincide with specific astrological formations. This proves to be a very powerful combination that often works well. Many people seem to experience physical and mental challenges, and sometimes overwhelm during certain astrological setups. Hortense is currently trying to figure out what needs adjusting. Her focus lies on the timings and increase of people's physical and mental tolerance levels. Maybe some of the ancient nightshades might soon prove useful.

In the meantime, she likes experimenting with energy fields for herself. She enjoys certain places in the garden at certain times – a great way of experiencing life through mind and spirit, to go beyond the range of regular human or physical experience and familiarise herself with what Buddha most likely called spiritual embodiment.

All her work is somehow related and ultimately all part of one. Some people know her as a healer, others as a herbalist or farmer. Anyway, these are just labels and it is often a question of perspective. A good example is the project she is working on with G (you might remember him from the Yellow chapter) and others. She liked G ever since they worked on a project to identify how best to site plants so as to block the spread of fires.

She admires his passion for seeking knowledge. At present, they are working on developing tinctures that strengthen physical and mental stress resistance. Hermes is involved too as it is about understanding the human body, including its pain and stress levels. Hortense also got Bo involved and these two just love exploring and talking about their plants.

Actually, Hortense also talks to her plants and has named them all. It is not unusual for people in Gaia to have

friendly relationships with other life forms. It is a bit different in Purpleton though, so Bo makes sure no one is around when she has a chat with her plants. One thing Bo has some doubts about is Hortense's claimed ability to reach a meditative state that allows her to sense the condition of specific plants. Having said that, Bo acknowledges that the world works in mystical ways and perhaps Hortense has discovered one of them, who knows?

Anyway, they both grow different plants in their respective gardens. Bo's interest in scientific research got them to work alongside each other. The first test results were promising, but show that some plants have higher variations than expected, and that properties also vary with the seasons and growth sites. It looks like some plants need to be bound to their indigenous habitat in order to develop their full range of powers.

Hortense sees this universe as an interconnected, living construct of matter, knowledge and energies. She wants to make a positive contribution, guided by her abilities and the needs of people and the planet. She loves life itself and is motivated by many different things:

The challenge in this world is the sheer abundance of knowledge, energy, ideas and possibilities. Hortense had to learn to stay true to herself to be able to prioritise and keep her focus.

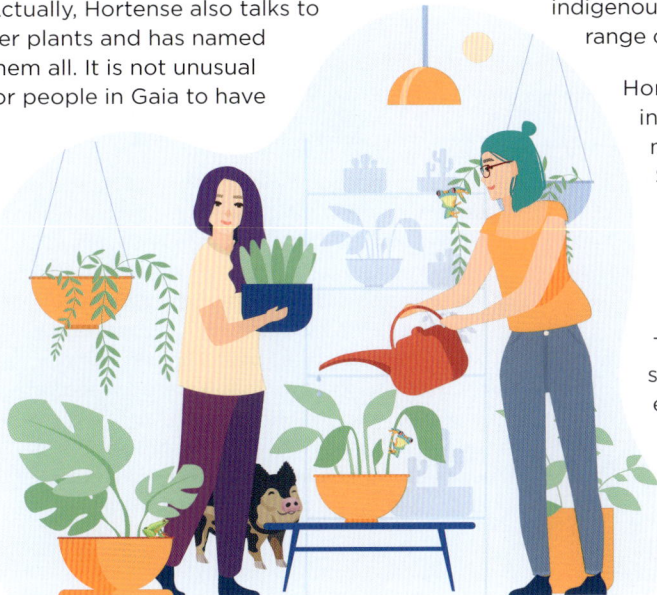

PURPOSE

Finding one's personal place in the world – where one contributes the most (duty > rights)

Contributing individual value to create global wellbeing

Being a healthy part of the world - ultimately for the progress of evolution

MASTERY

Great interest in understanding one's own intuition and energies

Dedication to constantly improving oneself and life

Ability to tap into natural and spiritual energies

Deep connection with other living beings

AUTONOMY

Being guided by higher spiritual forces

Total autonomy and absolute dependence in one

AN ANALOGY

If any kind of development captures this world best it has to be quantum thinking, which was the precursor of the Quantum Revolution. The insights of quantum physics, entanglement, computing, coherence, and so on led to a point where humankind was able to make a quantum leap. In natural terms, it was a metamorphosis.

It all happened when we accepted our scientific shortcomings and, instead of holding on to outdated dogmas, a younger generation of scientists rediscovered the childlike curiosity that had already driven passionate people like Nikola Tesla, Shen Kuo, Leonardo da Vinci, Albert Einstein, and others. It enabled people to move from:

EGO & FEAR	TO	HOLISM & LOVE
NEWTON'S THREE DIMENSIONS	TO	A 5-DIMENSIONAL WORLD
BINARY COMPUTING	TO	QUANTUM COMPUTING
DUALISM	TO	NON-DUALISM
A STATE OF SEPARATION	TO	WHOLENESS AND ONENESS
UNIVERSE	TO	A MULTIVERSE
AND SO ON...		

At that point we moved from an understanding of limited possibilities and scarcity to one of unlimited possibilities and abundance. For example, Hortense is no longer interested in products, let alone defined by them. She engages with information, frequencies, energies, spirituality and life. [8-16]

In Gaia, collaboration, awareness, togetherness and inter-dependencies represent the keys to an abundant world. Hortense hardly ever thinks "What is in it for me?"; instead she asks herself "How can I help and contribute?" This fundamental shift from the T1 world (stages 1 to 6) allows scarcity to be a thing of the past and the energy of abundance to take on a life of its own. Every day unlocks an unstoppable flow of abundance in life – all lives – and amplifies the give-and-receive cycle.

A subject that has always fascinated Hortense is the morphic field theory. Initial ideas go back to Charles Darwin who called it the unified consciousness, and Albert Einstein who referred to a unified field of intelligence in his book *The World As I See It*.

The terms morphic field theory and morphic resonance were first coined by biologist Rupert Sheldrake in 1973 (published in 1981). His idea is that memory is inherent in nature and that natural systems benefit from the collective memory of all previous things of their kind.[8-17] This also applies to all matter in the world. Based on this logic, Sheldrake proposed that this is also responsible for "telepathy-type interconnections between organisms." [8-18] It means our brains are more often receptors rather than creators of information.

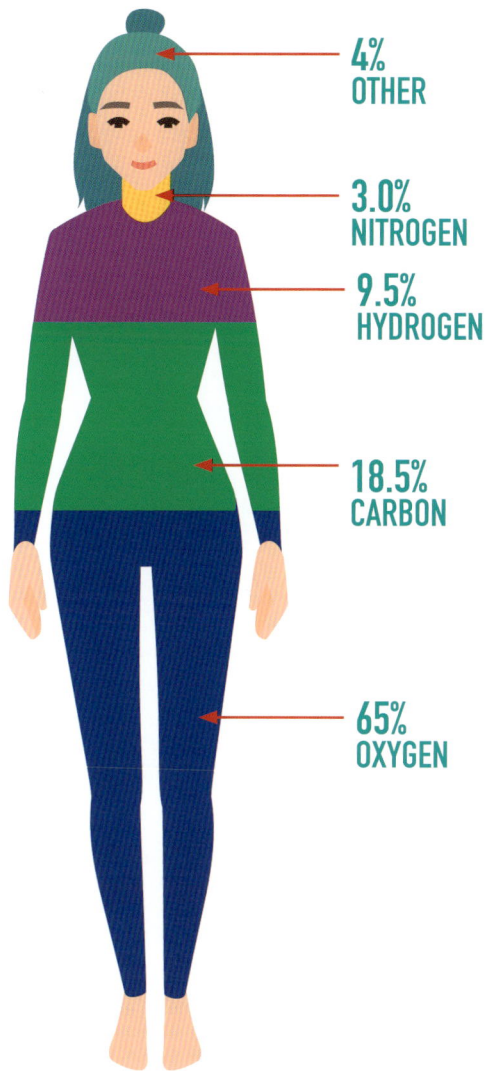

4%
OTHER

3.0%
NITROGEN

9.5%
HYDROGEN

18.5%
CARBON

65%
OXYGEN

This innovative thinking offered explanations to questions around inheritance, memory and the development of consciousness, and was crucial in rethinking our relationship with nature and the universe.

Hortense loves the idea of mental interconnections between organisms and collective memories within species. It brings to light the collective nature of consciousness – shared not only between humans, but all things in the universe. After all, we all stem from the same source. According to science, the ten most common elements in the universe, in decreasing order of abundance (mass), are hydrogen, helium, oxygen, carbon, neon, nitrogen, magnesium, silicon, iron, sulfur. More than 95% of our body mass is made up of four of those: oxygen, carbon, hydrogen, and nitrogen. The human body contains around 20 different elements, mostly issued from ancient stars.

This has been accepted as standard scientific thinking in Gaia and it continuously proves itself in the modern world of science. For example, the insights into subatomic particles revealed how these vibrating packages of energy pass on information to all things and beings. The latest research examines how the particles share information whilst beaming through one another. Hortense cannot wait to see what new opportunities come out of this.

It all makes perfect sense to her. All matter (every crystal, tree and so on) possesses some kind of consciousness and communicates via frequencies. We are relatively simple creatures in this universe and can therefore only pick up a fairly narrow bandwidth.

Hortense thinks this makes sense, because if matter had no consciousness, how would consciousness ever arise within us?

These new scientific ideas, spiritual experiences and additional skills weren't necessary during the first hundred thousand years of our existence, because, in biological terms, we were literally just trying to survive.

It is the survival of our species in T2 (layers 7 and above) that Hortense often discusses with her neighbour Hala. In the past, Hala accused Hortense of being overly critical of possible solutions for saving humankind from existential threats. Hala believes it is best to leave people and systems alone for they will work themselves out. Hortense tends to agree, but she feels that, with the aftermath of natural disasters and the unhealthy state of our planet due to past human actions, we need to be more proactive. Hortense thinks Hala can be aloof at times and tries to avoid critical points with statements such as "What will be, will be".

Hortense argues that humans have been reckless and neither truly aware nor disciplined enough to understand the responsibilities incumbent upon them, as a species with such influence on the planet. Hortense and Hala often want the same outcome, but disagree on how to get there.

AUTHOR'S COMMENT AND PLEA

Writing about the different levels turned into a bit of a personal journey for me. I appreciate the mission-critical importance that this 8th layer brings to humankind and how vital it is to have more Hortenses in the world. I, too, want to contribute.

I would start off with regenerating an old farm or piece of land in a bid to create a space for biodiversity of the mind and land — a step towards healing the Earth. I am with Dr Vandana Shiva (scientist, founder of the Earth University and a biodiversity conservation farm) on this:

"It's time to reclaim wilderness as a state of being in harmony, a state of being in peace with nature, a state of being healthy."

Thus, I wish to make a straightforward plea. I would like to get a few impact investors together to purchase an old farm or piece of land. After a period of time this venture should finance itself, be as self-sufficient as possible whilst also providing the investors with a natural place to come to, connect, regenerate and interact with one another.

My lady and I believe the time has come to organise and actively shape the health of our future. Are you in? If so, please reach out by email or on LinkedIn and we would be happy to connect and discuss this plan in detail.

The objectives come in a colourful range:

- Provide the right conditions for nature and the soil to regenerate themselves, which means diverse life can return to the land and environment around it

- Connect with the local community, bring traditions and indigenous plants and animals back to where they belong

- Create spaces for creative and innovative experimentation and thinking

- Align and comply with all relevant tax, legal, and health and safety standards

- Use modern technologies to utilise renewable energies and track all kinds of improvement in measurable terms

- Provide a space for social groups to connect and share; possibly work with organisations like the Positive Transformation Initiative to help people find their way back to nature and society

- Explore how the many lively dots are interrelated, how all life is part of a whole, and connect with similar initiatives across the world (e.g. Three Pools Farm in Wales, Knepp Castle Estate in Sussex, Tamera's Land in Portugal, and many others)

- Provide natural and creative spaces for 8th layer thinking and practices

LEADERSHIP

Holistic leadership is very much about providing creative spaces for life to emerge. It comes in various forms and practices that are all meant to facilitate healthy dynamics – allowing people to experience being part of something bigger and, in so doing, promoting human and universal growth.

The aim is to create a lively interplay between life on Earth and the universe. This is achieved through the dynamic cycles of the inner and outer worlds, through transcendent practices, which some call spiritual journeys. In many ways, this leads Gaia's inhabitants to reawaken again and again. Hortense loves these journeys for they enable her to reach the deepest levels of her consciousness. Sometimes, when everything is in the right place, she can get to a stage where she senses another state of being. She describes it as free consciousness – a place where she can sink into a field that is infinitely imaginative, infinitely resourceful, infinitely daring and able. From these flows of energy, she can create emergent cosmic psychological spaces for everyone and everything.

Gaia is such a spiritually advanced place that the range of transcendent practices is multi-faceted. Even children learn about, practise and experience these at school. The initial idea was to introduce human beings to these practices at an early stage in their childhood, but it turned out that some children already have natural unfiltered spiritual abilities. So these young individuals now collaborate with adults and act as spiritual scouts into worlds often unknown to adults. Yet another example of reverse mentoring that has proven key to the rediscovery of skills once forgotten by people in previous layers.

> ## " AS A LEADER, THE PERSON I NEED TO LEAD IS ME.
>
> ## THE FIRST PERSON THAT I SHOULD TRY TO CHANGE IS ME. "
>
> **JOHN C. MAXWELL, AMERICAN AUTHOR**

Hortense remains much attached to her garden. After all, as her name (Latin for gardener) suggests, maybe her destiny is here? It is also true that her mother loved Hortense Allart, a progressive 19th century Italian-French feminist writer and essayist. It was most likely these two and some other namesakes that influenced her mother.

Hortense conceives leadership as a combination of being herself and leading when and where necessary, to create nourishing energies and nurturing spaces. She believes her work isn't as much about leading as it is facilitating. She collaborates and co-creates with many others in local networks. In this way she both contributes and benefits. In fact, in a Turquoise environment it can be hard to decipher where the leading ends and the following begins.

That is similar to her gardening work where she designs spaces, creates the conditions for healthy soil, and engages with nature to learn what grows best where. Sometimes the plants themselves decide in which flower bed, from the 30 plus available, and in which companionship they want to grow. Nature always seems to find its way and, in the past, we humans have interfered with that process. Hortense merely facilitates and enjoys exploring as she goes along.

She applies the same non-directive, facilitative approach to the systemic constellations in her garden. This is a technique originally developed by German psychotherapist Bert Hellinger, who focused on family systems to disclose the deeper forces that subconsciously influence thoughts, behaviours and emotional experiences across multiple relationships and generations. [8-19] Hortense builds on this by adding another dimension: facilitating constellations at specific times, as determined by star constellations. In addition, participants go through sequences of yoga and meditations to broaden and deepen their senses.

Hortense is particularly keen to trial meditative sessions for large groups. This is a shared practice known in Gaia as collective spiritual leadership, which locals engage in once a day. The sessions address certain planetary and human needs, helps people focus on the topic at hand, channel energies, and allow everyone to experience being part of one organism. [8-20] This is Hortense's favourite part of the day.

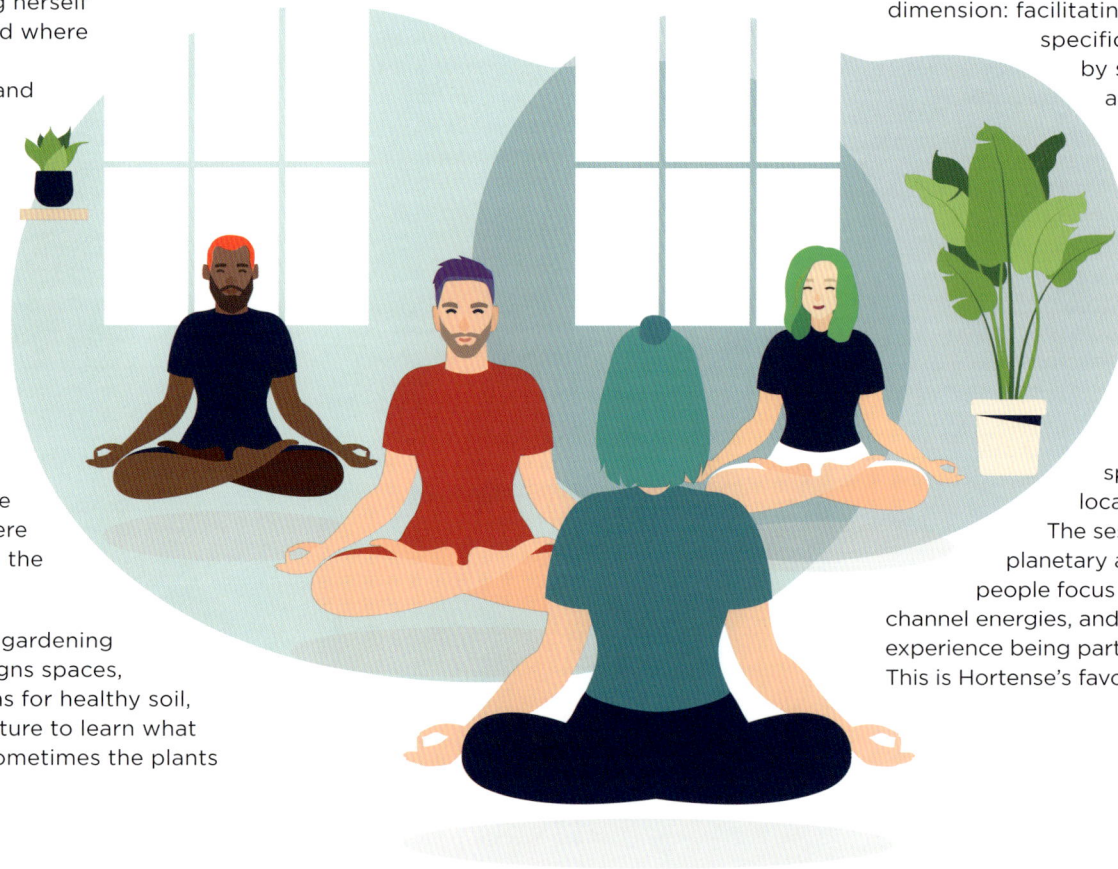

She starts by disconnecting from her outer environment, then her inner world expands and the magic happens when she floats into a bigger whole. In physical terms, this requires everyone shifting their brainwaves from low beta, to alpha, theta, and eventually delta. Once the collective reaches brainwaves of 0.5 to 4 cycles per second (delta), group members start to interact in synergy, like a hive. During these journeys, so-called "seers" can identify threats to life and channel energies for the greater good. Hortense introduced Bo to the sessions and, after a few years of practice, Bo is now able to fully join in.

These collective practices aim to bring people into the current realm of consciousness and everyone is welcome, whether or not they live in Gaia. This concept was already discussed by philosophers (like Confucius) thousands of years ago and has influenced many theories and schools of thought. Hortense often wonders what took people so long to rediscover wisdoms like stoicism or Ra (the law of one).

Her idea of leadership is ultimately to contribute positively to the evolutionary progress of humankind and the universe. She believes she is relatively insignificant on this journey and will not see the end of it, if there even will be one. However, she recognises that every living organism has a purpose. Take the example of a cell in a human body: it is just one of many in a temporary state of being. Yet, as we know, all cells have their part to play. They can be healthy and enable life, or grow out of control and become invasive, like cancer cells. An important difference is that healthy cells evolve into distinct cell types with specific functions, while cancer cells do not. Hortense sees a similarity here. Her life is determined by purpose and the meaning she brings to life. She measures this by the amount of love, smiles and happiness she creates.

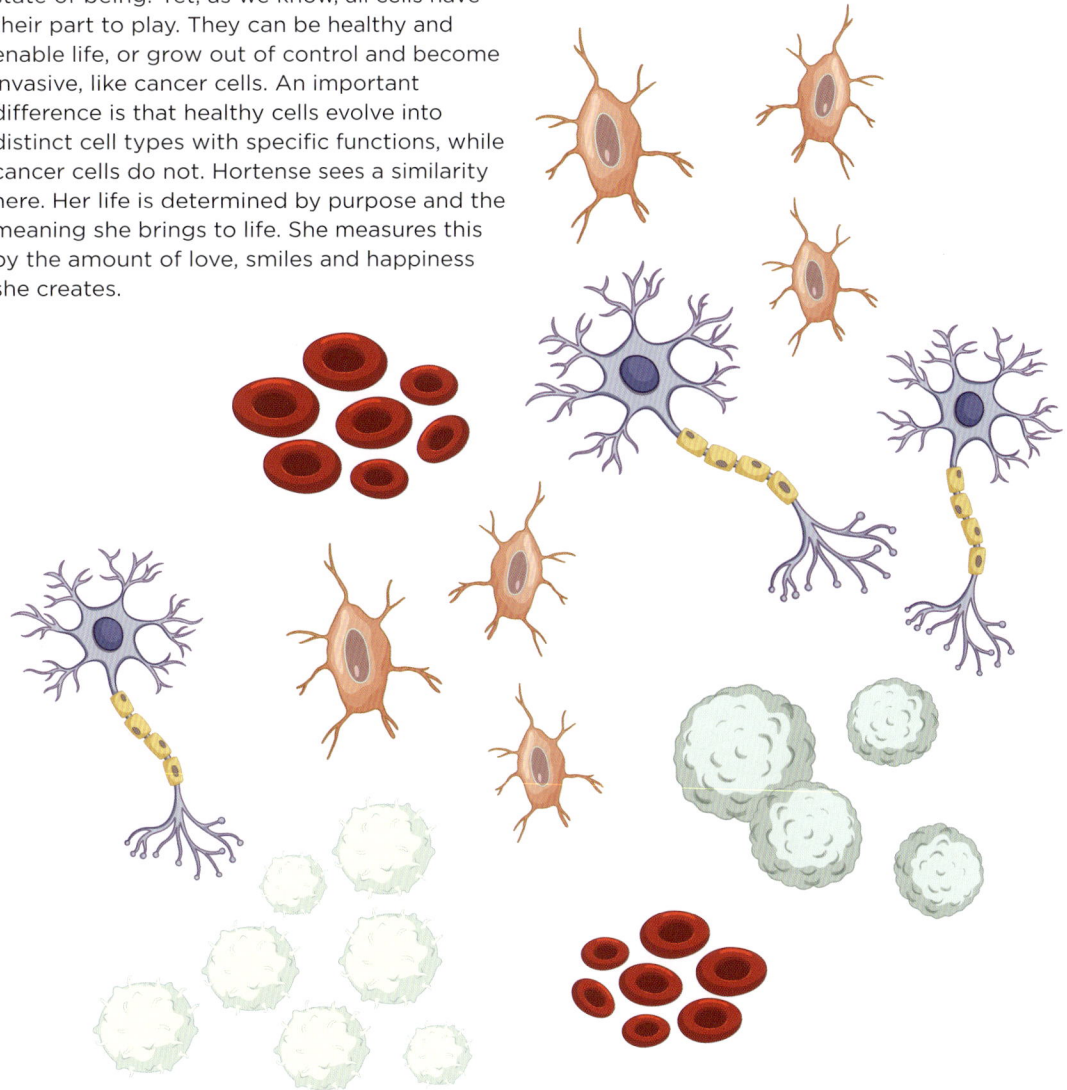

Over the years Hortense has been inspired by many people who are leaders in their own right. Here are a few names and references that are not necessarily purely 8th layer, but represent a good starting point for exploring ways of living that most current generations will never reach.

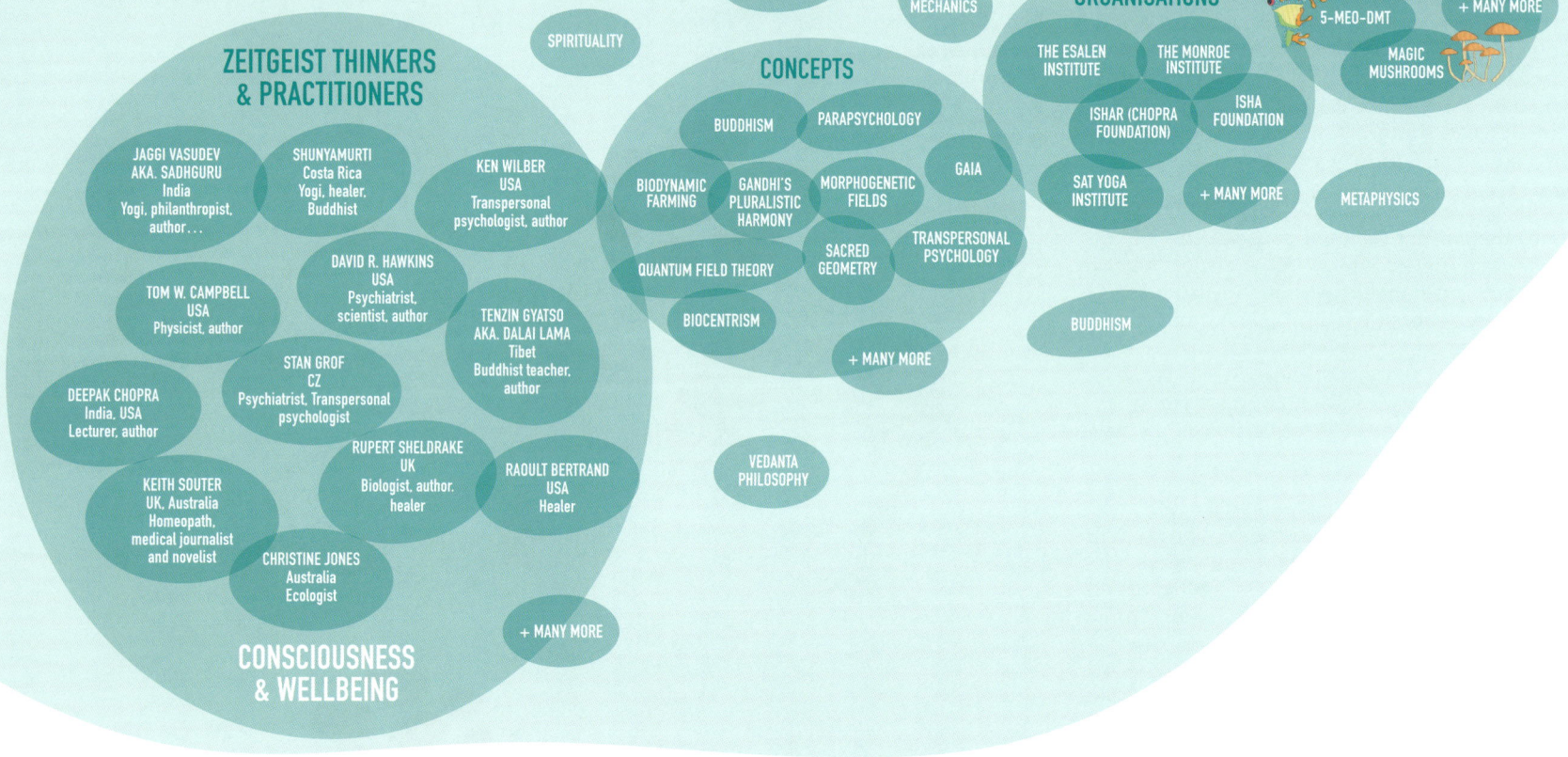

SELF-REALISATION

INTERFAITH DIALOGUE

QUANTUM MECHANICS

SPIRITUALITY

INDUCED SPIRITUAL JOURNEYS

5-MEO-DMT

+ MANY MORE

MAGIC MUSHROOMS

ORGANISATIONS

THE ESALEN INSTITUTE

THE MONROE INSTITUTE

ISHAR (CHOPRA FOUNDATION)

ISHA FOUNDATION

SAT YOGA INSTITUTE

+ MANY MORE

METAPHYSICS

CONCEPTS

BUDDHISM

PARAPSYCHOLOGY

GAIA

BIODYNAMIC FARMING

GANDHI'S PLURALISTIC HARMONY

MORPHOGENETIC FIELDS

TRANSPERSONAL PSYCHOLOGY

QUANTUM FIELD THEORY

SACRED GEOMETRY

BIOCENTRISM

BUDDHISM

+ MANY MORE

VEDANTA PHILOSOPHY

ZEITGEIST THINKERS & PRACTITIONERS

JAGGI VASUDEV AKA. SADHGURU
India
Yogi, philanthropist, author...

SHUNYAMURTI
Costa Rica
Yogi, healer, Buddhist

KEN WILBER
USA
Transpersonal psychologist, author

DAVID R. HAWKINS
USA
Psychiatrist, scientist, author

TOM W. CAMPBELL
USA
Physicist, author

TENZIN GYATSO AKA. DALAI LAMA
Tibet
Buddhist teacher, author

STAN GROF
CZ
Psychiatrist, Transpersonal psychologist

DEEPAK CHOPRA
India, USA
Lecturer, author

RUPERT SHELDRAKE
UK
Biologist, author, healer

RAOULT BERTRAND
USA
Healer

KEITH SOUTER
UK, Australia
Homeopath, medical journalist and novelist

CHRISTINE JONES
Australia
Ecologist

+ MANY MORE

CONSCIOUSNESS & WELLBEING

TEAMS

Hortense makes little distinction between leadership and team collaboration. She feels that it is important to have individuals championing specific topics in order to keep the momentum. For example, when she provides tinctures to other doctors and healers, she listens carefully to their requirements and they then seek a solution together. Being an expert in the field of botany as well as the history, distribution, and cultivation of psychoactive plants and their substances, she can be an insightful guide.

> ❝ OUR LIVES ARE NOT OUR OWN. FROM WOMB TO TOMB, WE ARE BOUND TO OTHERS.
>
> PAST AND PRESENT. AND BY EACH CRIME AND EVERY KINDNESS, WE BIRTH OUR FUTURE. ❞
>
> **SONMI-451 IN CLOUD ATLAS**

This mirrors the way she works with Bo and G on their project to find suitable natural substances to increase physical stamina. Reducing the carbon footprint is of prime importance in Gaia. Thus, Hortense advises Bo on how to grow specific plants in her area, closer to where the substances will be needed. Hortense always tries to look at the bigger picture. She knows Bo has a lot on her plate and that growing these plants will require time and focus.

That is why she suggested that Bo get some help with the project. Success is dependent on everyone involved sharing their values, interests and intentions. The rest is just about figuring things out together.

Some issues still need to be addressed, actively managed and improved in Gaia.

A good example is energy production and consumption. In the true spirit of teamwork, locals have started a community project with the aim of becoming completely self-sufficient. They run the project according to the U-Theory [7-7], which follows a very clear 5-step process:

1. They bring a wide range of people together – doctors, engineers, children, and so on. The more colourful the group, the better. As we all consume energy, everyone is concerned in one way or another. Co-initiation means agreeing first on the need for the project, getting an understanding of current energy consumption, current supplies, potential sources, expected developments, and so on. This is about opening the mind, connecting with others in the community and developing a shared intention.

2. Co-sensing is about observing what else is out there, in a non-judgemental way. Hortense is already planning to go on learning journeys to explore what others have done and the challenges they have overcome. This requires deep listening, connecting with others with the mind and heart wide open.

3. The presencing part of the process is the spiritual journey where everyone goes through a cleansing stage, letting go of previous beliefs and concepts. Individuals start sensing the future that wants to emerge through them. This is a time of intentional silences, for instance through meditation. [8-22]

4. Emergent themes and ideas crystallise into prototyping. Together, people co-create possible solutions, then go out and test them. They build connections, like roots, with each other. At least, that is how Hortense visualises it; no surprise there. It is about uniting will and motivations. For example, participants will sense into the kind of energy sources they are drawn to. Hortense knows of the old mining tunnels that collect geothermal heat. Will she be drawn to those?

Prototypes are used to learn, to sense check realities, and to identify the most suitable ways forward. At this point, core groups iterate different development processes individually and collectively. The aim is to coordinate mind, heart and hand to explore a new, better future.

5. Successful prototypes are turned into larger-scale solutions. It is about co-evolving, from the emerging whole, innovative and sustainable energy solutions that connect to create one. The last stage is about making things happen.

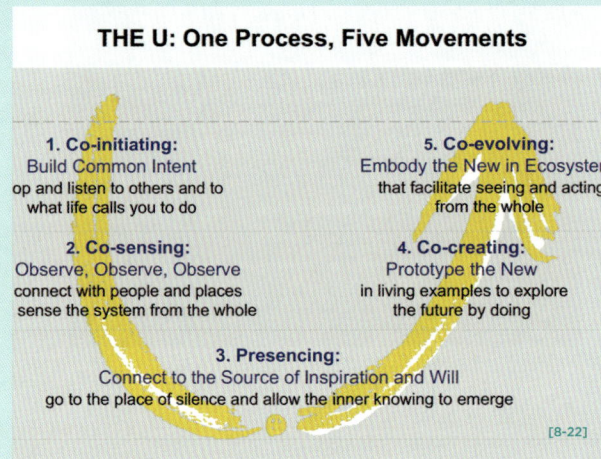

THE U: One Process, Five Movements

1. Co-initiating:
Build Common Intent
op and listen to others and to
what life calls you to do

5. Co-evolving:
Embody the New in Ecosystem
that facilitate seeing and acting
from the whole

2. Co-sensing:
Observe, Observe, Observe
connect with people and places
sense the system from the whole

4. Co-creating:
Prototype the New
in living examples to explore
the future by doing

3. Presencing:
Connect to the Source of Inspiration and Will
go to the place of silence and allow the inner knowing to emerge

[8-22]

Along the way, three grounding principles ensure a shared outcome:

• **Intention:** Always serve as an instrument for the whole

• **Relation:** Connect and communicate with the global social field

• **Authenticity:** Connect to your higher self to allow the future to emerge.

It will be one of many journeys that Hortense starts off on with others. She loves it and is eager to make her region even more self-sufficient.

She will meet a colourful range of new people along the way, connect with known acquaintances, witness the change in others and, ultimately, always be part of one.

PLANNING & STEERING

Gaia's inhabitants identify the region's priorities. Keeping the planet healthy and balancing out the universe are their ultimate aims.

The word 'health' in English is based on an Anglo-Saxon word 'hale' meaning 'whole': that is, to be healthy is to be whole.

Likewise the English 'holy' is based on the same root as 'whole'. All of this indicates that man has sensed always that wholeness or integrity is an absolute necessity to make life worth living." [8-20, p. 3-4]

Hortense couldn't agree more. She believes the way to go is to identify shared interests in reviving, preserving and regenerating healthy practices. Like everyone else, she is guided by a good balance of:

DETERMINATION	AND	**EMERGENT TACTICS**
NUMBERS	AND	**EMOTIONS**
OBJECTIVES	AND	**GUT FEELINGS**

She trusts in the wisdom of people in the future and believes that other ecosystems will self-regulate even more. Nature has brought us here, and now that we are reconnected, all we have to do is to allow ourselves to be guided towards oneness.

> **" THE WILL TO BECOME IS THE DRIVING FORCE AT THE HEART OF EVERY LIVING BEING. THERE IS SOMETHING IN THIS WORLD YOU WERE PUT HERE TO DO THAT ONLY YOU CAN DO. "**
>
> **ANDREW DENNIS, BIODYNAMIC FARMER, UK**

ORGANISATIONS

Two main purposes drive Gaia's organisations: promoting a healthy life; helping people find meaning in their life by realising their potential. They achieve this by offering jobs that match people's interests with regions' identified priorities.

There are numerous businesses run by craftspeople and specialists in Gaia; most of them count fewer than 20 employees and specialise in certain products and services. These small entities connect with and learn from each other, exchanging ideas through a global web. Hortense has been collaborating

> ## " TURQUOISE CAN DETECT THE HARMONIC FORCES WHICH GOVERN ORGANIZATIONS. "
>
> ### LEO GURA, FOUNDER @ ACTUALIZED.ORG

with a few of those companies over the years. It always fascinates her to see how such closely knit local teams manage to engage with huge global networks through virtual research centres and the likes.

The overall setup reminds her of Peter Kropotkin's thinking. He might have been born to a privileged family in mid-19th century Russia, but he did believe in a fair society. He fought the early stages of capitalism, arguing that cooperation is more natural and beneficial than competition as a basis for all societies. In 1902, he also coined the term 'mutual aid', meaning the voluntary, reciprocal exchange of resources and services for a shared benefit. He advocated that people care for one another and that they change living conditions for the better.

He promoted the "idea of replacing global trade with local production and a global exchange of knowledge". [8-21] In practice, this thinking means local production and services leading to urban and regional self-sufficiency. This results in what some termed the '20-minute neighbourhood' where

people can meet most of their daily needs by obtaining all goods and services within less than half an hour from their home, whether on foot, by bicycle or public transport.

A number of small community hubs complement the shortened supply and transport chains. All of the holonic structures offer staple products and day-to-day services. Companies are connected through a three-dimensional web along and across their value chains. [8-23]

MARKETS

Gaia feels like a living mesh of people, organised in healthily spread-out groups; humankind here is in natural balance with Mother Earth.

People abandoned materialism a long time ago. It is incredible to see how few products and goods we need once we remind ourselves that life is about living. Hortense appreciates the fact that products are manufactured with a modular approach. For example, her mobile device has one main backbone and she can plug whatever else she wants into it. She documents all of her gardening work diligently to monitor how certain plants change over time. Therefore, she always wants to use the latest photo lens available. When she gets an update for her device, she simply trades in the previous one or exchanges it with someone else, who then only needs to plug it into their own device to sync it up and use it in their own way.

Gaia has completely minimised waste in this way, because everyone understands that resources are taken from Mother Earth. If not reused, individual parts and accessories are dismantled into their elementary building blocks. Here, the core idea of the circular economy incorporates a large and growing percentage of natural solutions. It simply means following nature's lead because nature knows no waste.

Hortense remembers the time of transition. Once people realised how little they needed, everyone started living in abundance. This existence refers to life in its abounding fullness of joy, continuous growth, and strength of mind, body, and soul.

> " IN THE DEEPEST MYSTICAL SENSE, NATURE IS HUNGRY FOR OUR PRAYERS. HUMANS ARE LIKE A WINDOW OF THE HOUSE OF NATURE THROUGH WHICH THE LIGHT AND AIR OF THE SPIRITUAL WORLD PENETRATE INTO THE NATURAL WORLD. "
>
> SEYYED HOSSEIN NASR, IRANIAN, PROFESSOR EMERITUS AT GEORGE WASHINGTON UNIVERSITY

This mindset also finds its way into workplaces. Companies form an integral part of the world here, and cooperation thrives within and beyond company boundaries. Cooperation, trust and respect are a given as everyone strives for health and wholeness. However, a healthy level of competition is maintained and managed through the UC currency. When an organisation has been outcompeted by others over a long period of time, it may disperse or evolve into something else. Nothing lasts forever and so natural transformations are not only possible, but happen with the planet in mind. Everyone understands that:

Individual < Collective < Planet < Universe

Gaia's society is very peaceful; there is very little if anything to fear. This world has evolved and benefited from a complete fusion of eastern and western philosophies. The integration of different aspects of science, tech, nature, medicine, mysticism, and spirituality has led to a kind of tranquillity. Hortense enjoys the creative tension from debating viewpoints, but there is always a strong sense of belonging, everyone's ultimate goal, and a shared interest in self, humankind, Mother Earth, and our universe. Hortense sees society as a living organism that needs to be nourished. We might not have understood the purpose of it all, but that doesn't mean there isn't one. Everyone here is committed to contributing a little puzzle piece during their lifetime, and helping upcoming generations discover the overall picture at some point.

LIMITATIONS AND GROWTH INTO NEXT LAYERS

Our journey on the road to a Turquoise world (*The Turquoise Brick Road*) has been a long one and we have met many characters along the way.

Amon sees himself as a living part of nature, but is unaware of what nature really is, because life is about survival.

Bo has chosen a communal life in harmony with nature. She appreciates what the earth has to offer and lives in balance. She makes sense of the world through natural gods, superstitions, and a reverence for the supernatural.

Conan believes in human power gods. Nature is tough and, when you launch into the unknown, Mother Earth creates serious challenges for you. So, bring it on! Charlie wants to dominate and take advantage of nature; Earth's fruits and resources are there for the taking.

Doc disconnects herself from nature, because she only believes in intellectual activity. She values the systematic study of the structures and behaviours found in the physical world, and does this through observation and experiments. Given humankind's limited ability to understand complexity, this partly results in limiting beliefs and dogmas.

In the meantime, the mass mobilisation of natural resources satisfies a growing hunger for mass consumption.

Eli recognises the advantages technology affords and leverages them to maximise profits. Natural resources can be optimised and exploited in measurable terms, if nothing gets in the way.

Florence believes in relationships between people and nature. She recognises the short-sighted and endless greed of 3rd level capitalism, the 4th level belief in separation, and damage caused by the masses. She sees people burnt out and resources exhausted by 5th level goal-getters driving performance to excess and rewarding themselves with status symbols. Who needs a $300,000 chocolate truffle, a $1 million pooch, or a $70 million Ferrari when nine million people die of hunger every year and endless habitats disappear along the way?

G appreciates Florence's viewpoint, because he too suffers the consequences of previous environmental mistakes and societal unfairness. He not only connects the dots better than all the others put together, but also grasps the interdependencies. He understands that all knowledge needs to be integrated into one to create a kind of status quo and a base from which to move forward.

Like Bo, Hortense lives in harmony with Mother Earth. Her thinking goes a bit further by seeing herself and humankind as one with Mother Earth and the entire universe. While Bo believes in God, Hortense believes in the zero point energy field, assuming they are one and the same, just called by different names.

In many ways there is no more separation between life forms, there is just oneness and a healthy wholeness to be nurtured. Surely, human evolution cannot end here, can it?

The characteristics of 8th (Turquoise) layer markets look as follows:

"BUSINESS AND GOVERNANCE ARE A NATURAL PART OF LIFE AND GLOBAL GOVERNANCE"

POLITICAL

Making use of collective intelligence and intuition

Decisions are made, whenever possible, in the circles where they matter most

Glocal setup: manage local, regional or global-specific networks

ECONOMIC

This layer benefits from tech infrastructure and knowledge platforms put in place by previous levels

Most trade is carried out locally

There is a strong regional network of holons and SOHOS where additional goods are exchanged

Trade routes provide resources that cannot be created or grown locally

Success is measured in new ways: Joy of Existence (main metric), vitality, harmony, happiness

The currency is based on levels of Universal Contribution (UC)

SOCIAL

Personal freedom (no social stratification)

People spend a lot of time in their local communities

Opportunity to move according to personal interests, changes in life circumstances, and the needs of the whole (to ensure the biggest impact)

A more natural life, without status-driven materialism

TECHNOLOGICAL

Tech is used as much as necessary (vs possible)

Provides bio feedback to enhance human awareness

Technology is used less than before and replaced with natural solutions (e.g. cancer dogs)

Powered exclusively by renewable resources

Generally a mix of tech and alternative techniques [which were often seen as incompatible in the past]

ENVIRONMENTAL

No more separation between people and their habitat: it is all seen as part of the whole.

We live in a higher 'spiritual' level of relationship

Rediscovery and improved understanding of purple habits and rituals

LEGAL

Networks of self-regulation and self-control

Constellations are used to solve critical cases

Rehabilitation through learning, reflective interventions, and making up for the damage done

IN THE MEANTIME, LIFE GOES ON...

With Hortense's support Bo is able to also consider the astrological patterns and appropriating plants at the suitable stages. Every plant goes through various natural phases and timing is important to ensure specific properties.

Amon is happy to spend all day in the garden looking after the plants. He feels very pleased with himself for having the opportunity to talk to Hortense and G. The two men, especially, seem to have clicked instantly and get on very well.

Bo has rediscovered her great grandfather's small hunting lodge in the nearby woods. It is very run down, but the plan is that Amon will do it up and then move in. Bo has nothing but praise for him, and believes the only reason he has been marginalised is because he isn't from here. Furthermore, he lives a simple lifestyle and, unfortunately, some people are very suspicious and overly protective. The way a man treats his dog says a lot about him though; similarly, Bo is yet to meet a bad person who is kind to plants. Bo is accepted by all, even by Brishna, and is already considered one of the elders. She is convinced, as are Hortense and G, that Amon will soon be accepted by the locals.

She even has the funny feeling that he will be good at shin kicking. If that is the case, Amon might soon help them to win, which would give him a free admission ticket into the wider community. Life goes on. It is a never ending quest.

AUTHOR'S COMMENT:
I assume you are as interested as I am to understand what the journey beyond looks like. If we follow Clare W. Graves' logic, then the 9th (Coral) layer is generated out of the shortcomings of Hortense's layer. However, I am not even sure what it might look like.

My best guess is that our habitat's lifespan is limited and Mother Earth seems to renew itself in regular cycles, so becoming too comfortable might not work for the time we have available to move on. Maybe it is like a game where you only have a limited time to complete the first round (T1) on this spinning nucleus of matter?

We might need transcendent wonderers and wanderers to explore new spheres in the universe and make it off this hub before everything starts all over again. Maybe we are wise enough to halt the destructive cycle of the world in time, or to find a way to live with the new realities. I don't know and most likely never will; but my daughter's generation might.

In case you are interested in the 2nd tier, I recommend you look at Ken Wilber's integral work, or Don Beck's insight @ www.humanemergence.org.

What I do know is that we need to get our act together if we want future generations to discover the purpose of our evolution. For sure, human evolution should not end with our current generations, should it?

9th LAYER

CORAL: A TRANSPERSONAL BEING

As pointed out in the first chapter, this framework is open-ended. It would be too arrogant to believe we are the pinnacle of evolution. Watch the news this evening if you have any doubts.

AUTHOR'S COMMENT:

If Graves' logic still applies, then this 9th layer bears similarities to Conan's 3rd level. We know that the 3rd level arises in children around the age of three. This is when they develop their ego, their self-awareness, and want to explore the world. Humankind started to evolve to this degree of consciousness around 8–10,000 years ago, which led to individuals leaving the tribes behind to seek new adventures.

In our current times, these are the radical thinkers and young entrepreneurs who go out and accomplish things. We know the 3rd level is an incredibly powerful one and if there are any parallels with the 9th layer, then this will accelerate our growth in unseen ways.

The 3rd level comes with the danger of allowing ego and fear to drive us. The 9th layer, however, will not have such a destructive side, nor will it derail people or entire societies. Being in Tier 2, the 9th layer aspires to holism and unity. In any case we can rest assured it is going to take us to new heights.

It doesn't end here, but why bother talking about what might be if we cannot first prepare the healthy and necessary groundwork?

CHAPTER 10

"TO WHOM MUCH IS GIVEN, MUCH IS EXPECTED. "

DON E. BECK

10.1 WHO WAS THE MAN CREATING THIS GROUNDBREAKING WORK?

To better understand the man behind the Graves Value System and his motivations, I want to take you back to the 1950s and the atmosphere in the US at that time.

After WWII, when Harry S. Truman was president (1945-1953) and the long-lasting effects of the Russian Revolution were ongoing, a sense of hyper-nationalism prevailed in many countries. The fear of a communist revolution in the US became the overriding justification for challenging social order, even with such largely unrelated events as incidents of interracial violence. [10-1] It was also the era of McCarthyism whereby accusations of subversion or treason without due regard for evidence were made. Named after US senator Joseph McCarthy, who produced a series of investigations and hearings in an effort to expose supposed communist infiltration of the US government, this practice had its origins in the Second Red Scare, which lasted from the late 1940s through to the 1950s. [10-2]

> ## "OK, SO WHICH ONE WAS RIGHT?" [0-1, P. IV]

At the time, Clare W. Graves (1914–1986) was a psychology professor at Union College in New York where he had graduated in 1940. In addition, he was teaching at two other schools, and providing golf consultancy and coaching services (because he could). During that time, he witnessed all around him injustices created by some people believing they were better than others, and he "became sick of it all". As Graves noted "All in all, conflict and confusion, contradiction and controversy lie everywhere in the world of adult humans". [C-1, p.15]

When one of his students asked him which one of the many scholars (Jung, Loevinger, Watson, or Maslow) was right, no one was aware of the amount of energy this question would unleash. [C-1, p.6] It was at a time when Graves didn't seem to be very inspired by his own academic work. So in the early autumn of 1952, he set off to study the best of human nature. [10-3] He wanted to find out "what people conceive to be the mature human personality in operation." [C2, p. 42]

He started by researching what was out there with regard to the stages of human development. Whilst others would have looked at it from a perspective of psychology, sociology or anthropology, Graves took a broader and more inclusive view. He asked students to state their idea of a healthy, mature personality and exchange viewpoints before writing a defence or modification of their original statement.

After that, the students were asked to carry out secondary research by looking at what other leading authorities had to say on the matter. Again, they had to defend or

modify their opinion in written format. [C-2, P.16] Graves repeated this with eight cohorts over eight years. Each year, he tasked a panel of independent judges [C-2, p.17] with reviewing the findings and providing a level of scrutiny.

Up to this point, Graves was still trying to validate the work of his contemporary, American psychologist Abraham Maslow [10-4], with whom he occasionally worked. It was in one of Maslow's lectures that Graves witnessed

him being unfairly scrutinised by his peers. [C-1, p. iv] This appears to have been a rather traumatising experience leading Graves to be very careful about presenting his own work from then on.

In 1960 Graves held over 1000 data sets, the conceptualisation of which did not match any existing models. In his words, "The data stopped me cold for a while. I didn't know what to do with it." [10-5]

To our benefit, he found the data too intriguing to let go and persisted with his analysis. Eventually, he saw a pattern emerge that led him to identify two distinctive clusters: [C-2, p.19]:

1. A group-oriented cluster believing in denying and sacrificing oneself;

2. A self-interested cluster believing in expressing and promoting oneself.

In 1962, following further international analysis and research, Graves discovered that these two main tendencies each translate into three subsets of their own that alternate in a predictable order as follows [C-2, p.20ff.]:

- **Express self at any cost [self]**

- **Deny self now for later reward [group]**

- **Express self for self-gain by engaging with others [self]**

- **Deny self to get acceptance from others now [group]**

- **Express self, but not at the expense of others [self]**

- **Deny self to conform to existential realities [group]**

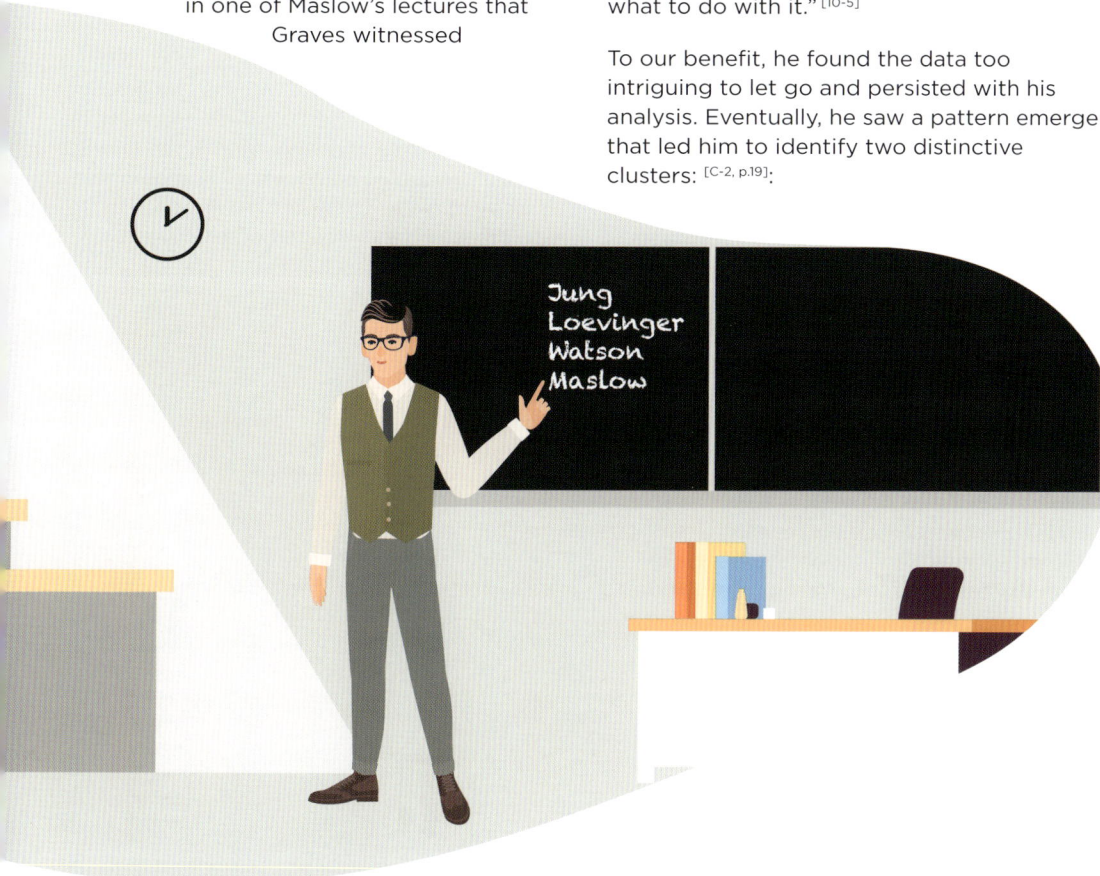

Jung
Loevinger
Watson
Maslow

Shortly after, he looked beyond his typical target groups and identified two more levels that come before the ones listed above. It gave him great satisfaction to see that they even follow the same pattern as the others, alternating between expressing or denying oneself and between an individual or group mentality. [10-6] Hence, the eight levels of human development as we now know them were revealed. At that point, Graves realised that his findings went beyond those of Maslow's levels and that this was truly groundbreaking work.

Later that year, he established a set of key principles relating to his framework:

• A mature person emerges over time

• There is a universal growth path that all humans follow

• People on different levels are motivated by different values

• Growth follows a cyclical pattern

• There is no end state, rather infinite room for growth and evolution.

He continued to research and validate his work. In 1969, he identified two additional key principles:

• The levels "of the psychological development of the human being arise as the result of the interaction of two determining forces." [C-2, p. 51] The framework was illustrated by a double spiral helix with two strands that represent the interplay between an individual and their environment.

• People are born with the capacity to progress as much as necessary. This means that, when a person from one level faces existential challenges, s/he is physically equipped to rise to the challenge by the brain activating a new part. Thus our coping tactics evolve with individual, societal and organisational development. However, this only happens as required. It might also answer one of the questions Charles Darwin struggled with: "Why do we humans have such big brains?" [0-20] We have the potential within us to grow far beyond our current state. In many ways, the seventh Yellow layer is just a new beginning – the tip of the iceberg in terms of our potential and capability.

In 1971 Graves presented his research, methods and findings in 'A Seminar on the Levels of Human Existence' to the Washington School of Psychiatry. He stated: "What I am proposing is that the psychology of the mature human being is an unfolding, emergent, oscillating spiral process marked by progressive subordination of older, lower-order behaviour systems to newer, higher-order systems as man's existential problems change." [10-7]

He developed a theory that he hoped would reconcile the various approaches to human nature and questions about psychological levels of maturity. He called this theory, amongst other titles, 'The Emergent Cyclical Levels of Existence Theory' [ECLET]. [10-8]

Graves continued to work with his two protégés, Christopher Cowan and Don Beck. However, he began to struggle with his health in the mid-80s and died before he could organise and finalise his body of work. This is the main reason he hasn't received the recognition he deserves.

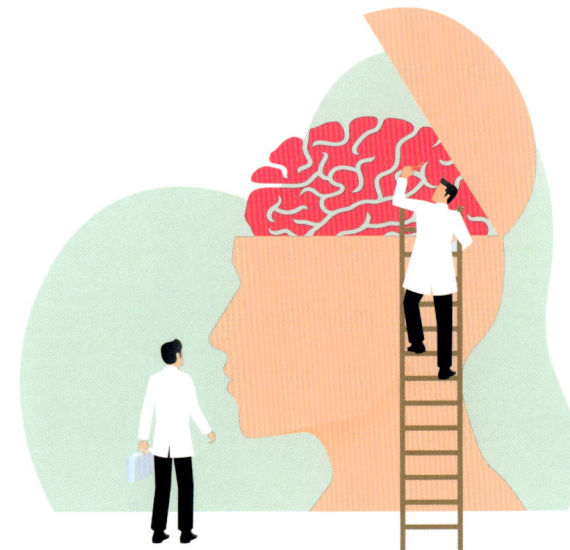

The Graves Value System with its interdisciplinary, integrative open-ended approach sets Graves' work apart from that of many of his contemporaries who sought a final state of human development. His inclusion of the bio, psycho, social and systems theories as vital co-elements helped develop one of the most systemic concepts that is still evolving today and hopefully into the future.

Graves managed to capture all of the stages of human consciousness that have developed to date, that is the ongoing "ping pong game of life", as he called it, between an individual and their life conditions. His achievement can be defined thus "The values systems framework is a hierarchically ordered, always open to change set of values, morals, ethics, beliefs, and preferences that come together in a self-organising principle to define an individual, a group or a culture." [10-9] If it sounds complicated, that's because it is in many ways. However, it aptly reflects the complexity and dynamism of people and the world around us. The beauty of Graves' work is that, despite the complexity, it is easily applicable to individuals, groups and cultures.

As Albert Einstein stated, it is desirable to keep even complex matters like the human development stages of consciousness as simple as they can be, but some things cannot be reduced to anything simpler as they would lose vital elements. This is why the Graves Value System cannot be simplified any further.

One could say that the framework enables us to come to terms with ourselves and our lives and, hopefully, to ensure humankind's continuous evolution.

Should you be interested in more information about the mastermind himself, please go to www.clarewgraves.com or read the book *Clare W. Graves: His life and his work* [10-10].

The following three chapters explore the application of the Graves Value System: personal, organisational and large-scale societal change. The real power of the framework comes into play when examining how these three perspectives relate and influence one another on the map of life.

10.2 HOW CAN THIS FRAMEWORK HELP YOU PERSONALLY?

Do you sometimes find yourself in situations where you try to sort out simple things with someone – take, for instance, a discussion about recycling with your neighbour – but it feels like you two speak different languages? Do you have trouble following your friends' logic in conversations and feel that your worldviews are at odds?

Well, these are just two mundane situations where stepping back and identifying the dominating stages of each person involved can prove helpful. Doing that might help you find the right language to build common ground with others and is a healthy starting point for all conversations.

You'll find more examples of how this framework can help you personally in the two initial chapters, 'What you can expect out of this book' and 'Why did I write this book?'

Again, the GVS is like a map for human development and human personality types in that it helps you to identify where in the development spectrum you and others around you are, based on prevailing characteristics and, hence, how to interact with and respond to others accordingly. Most research shows that self-awareness is essential in life and acts as a catalyst for progression. Therefore, the framework also helps you to assess where you want to go based on your personal and professional goals and what to expect along the way as you evolve and develop new traits.

As parents, we are ultimately responsible for our lives as much as we are for raising our children. So I hope this book provides a conscious starting point for your continued growth and a more harmonious world.

The following mind map is merely there to provide food for thought.

PERSONAL GROWTH

RAISING CHILDREN

The first 4 levels apply to nearly all humans in their early stages of life. For parents, understanding their child's growth stages can make life a lot easier for all. They will better understand their child's priorities, motivations and immediate desires.

BEIGE: 0-18 MONTHS

PURPLE: 18 MONTHS–THREE YEARS

RED: 3+ YEARS

BLUE: SCHOOL AGE

UNDERSTANDING ONE'S PAST

We have all had experiences for which we didn't really understand the underlying drivers and causes. Often, revisiting them with the levels in mind helps clarify matters and provide a greater level of understanding that can in turn help our personal development. Life must be lived forwards, but it can often only be understood in retrospect. Hindsight is 20/20 after all!

SETTING AND ACHIEVING GOALS

You can use the framework to consciously plan your career path. Remember G and Hortense's professional journeys? That doesn't mean that transitions will be any easier. However, the why, what, how and so what will be clearer for you.

SELF-AWARENESS

Get some insight into what is important to you, what motivates you, and how you can grow based on these factors, if you so choose. Understanding where you are now in your development can help you better prepare for the road ahead and even reach your goals more easily.

AUTHENTICITY

What people say rarely matches their true motivations. Try to figure out the level someone is gravitating towards based on their actions, not just their words. Asking 'why' two to three times will reveal their true colour(s).

RELATIONSHIPS

The framework starts off by considering who in your life exhibits mainly healthy character traits. Next, it helps you understand what level they desire and how that relates to you, who is possibly holding you back and who is helping you grow.

UNDERSTANDING OTHERS BETTER

Become more empathetic, understanding and able to predict others' interests and behaviours. When someone complains about someone else, listen to what that says about both parties.

HEALTHY PROGRESSION

As the saying goes, you are the company you keep. If you want to progress along the levels and ultimately reach or at least get close to Turquoise, join a group of people seeking to become more attuned to themselves, to others and to Mother Earth.

COMPANY CULTURE FIT

Culture is to an organisation what personality is to an employee. After working out your preferences, you will more easily identify a company at a stage that is the right fit for you.

AUTHOR'S COMMENT:
I would like to encourage everyone to build on the stories and vision of this book. Take action! Together we can make this world a better place.

The team behind this book has so many ideas on what to do, whom to reach out to, and how to apply the framework for the greater good. We welcome people to get in touch with us to ask questions, brainstorm further ideas and even partner with us on existing or future projects.

I, for one, am reaching out to schools and universities, particularly business schools, to integrate this framework into their lectures. I would like to see people applying the levels to subjects such as history, philosophy, finance, music, arts, and technology to see how these map out on the evolutionary stages.

There are so many ways this framework can be applied to help humankind evolve to its greatest potential. Below are a few examples:

1. **Universities** and **business schools** could make this practical framework part of their introductory curriculum so students can better understand themselves as well as varying forms of business, economics and politics. They could also encourage more research into and applications of the framework, create greater understanding of different approaches, how all things relate to one another, and find innovative ways forward that respect nature and all life.

2. A colourful Cirque du Soleil show could travel through the different levels visually, artistically and musically sharing the insight from each development stage with a global audience.

3. A TV programme could bring together a historian (e.g. Linda Colley), a biologist (e.g. Rupert Sheldrake) and a scientist (e.g. Brian Cox) detailing when and how humanity has entered the various development stages.

In fact, the characters in each level of this book lend themselves to an engaging style of storytelling around change management and transformation. For example, one could say "We need more performance-driven Elis in politics and integrative Florences in society".

Craig is interested in pursuing the use of characters and personification to bring change management business stories to life in a more compelling and captivating way for the average audience to relate to.

Valentina wants to engage with the Conduit Club in London to bring this insight into thoughtful and constructive conversations about social and environmental impact and theatrical performances to inspire further action.

Séverine is interested in exploring the use of the framework in inclusion and conflict management work to better resolve cultural, socio-economic, religious and political differences that continuously arise and create division around the world.

Kerstin wants to engage with people open to applying this framework to regenerative farming. As a B Leader (www.bleaders.uk) she wants to use this to support individuals and organisations to strive for the UN Sustainable Development Goals.

Understanding that evolution is a journey, we would all like to encourage Western political leaders to aspire to the Orange and Green stages by instilling true engagement with communities, making their objectives transparent and measurable, making better use of modern technologies, giving leaders the mandate to deliver, measuring progress, and holding politicians and business leaders to account. It isn't about blame or pointing the finger, but continuous improvement. There is room for growth in all spheres and on all sides. We need to find a way out of this self-perpetuating vicious cycle of corruption, devastation, wars, and destruction if we want future generations to stand a chance of living in a more peaceful environment.

We have endless ideas to share. Please don't be restricted by our limited imagination. There is so much more we can achieve together; especially when the right colourful mix of self-aware people comes together, respects one another, uses this map as a navigation tool, and identifies the mountains they want to move. This is exactly what this framework enables us to do. It is time to rock as one global team!

Please get in touch! Let's chat over a cup of whatever you fancy, explore possibilities further and inspire each other to grow together.

WOULD YOU LIKE TO FIND OUT MORE ABOUT YOURSELF?

Below is a link to a free online test that can give you a better idea about yourself. It is important to answer the questions based on what you really feel and think, and not how you would like to be. Be self-critical if you want this to work for you!

- https://www.pathfinder.management/personal-freemium-en/

If you are interested in using and/or co-developing these diagnostic tools further, or want to implement them for social causes, please get in touch.

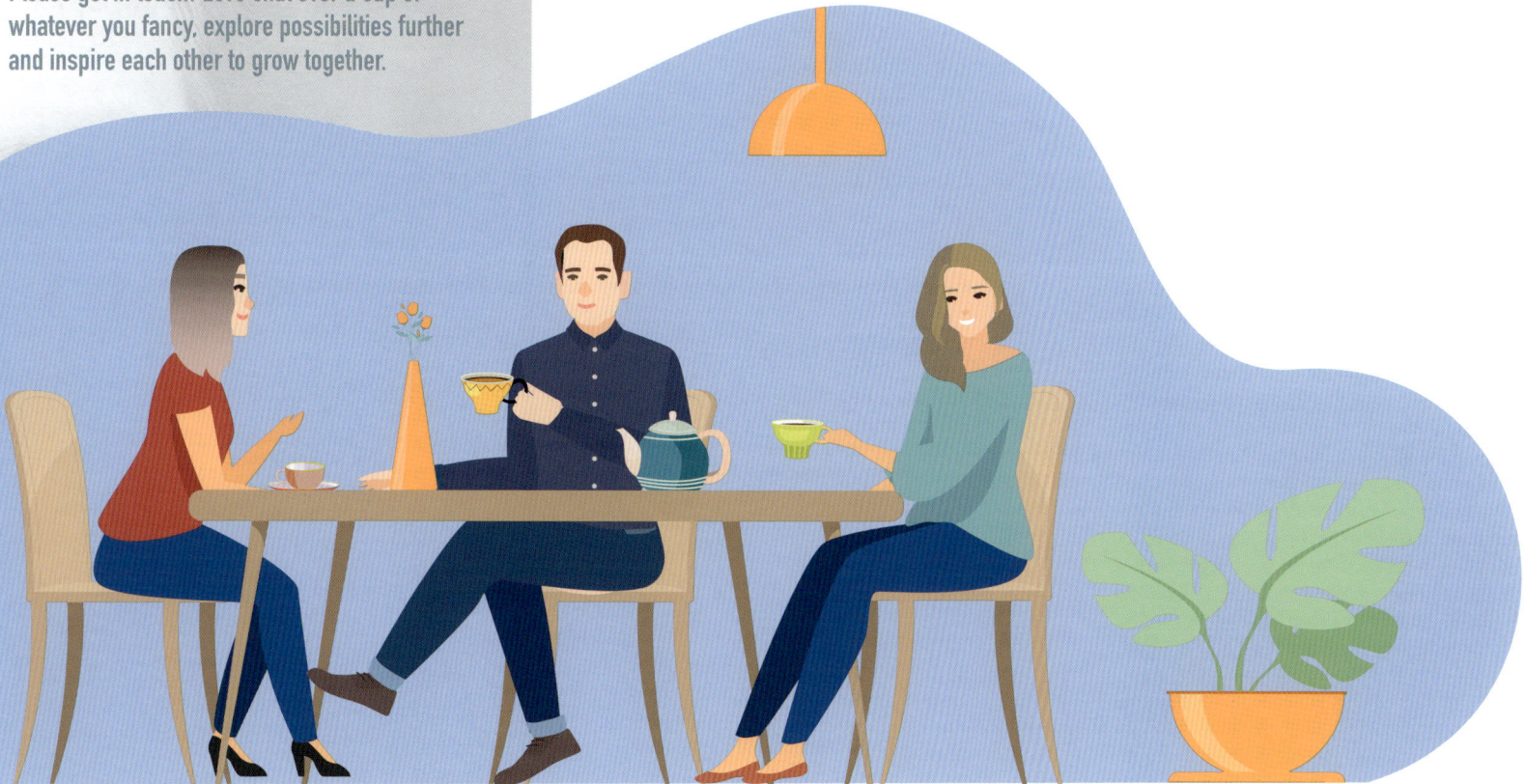

10.3 HOW CAN THIS FRAMEWORK HELP YOU PROFESSIONALLY?

Imagine you're trying to sell a social learning platform – built on principles of collaboration, self-determined learning with no inbuilt control tools – to a risk-averse, controlling corporation. You believe it's ingenious, but you can't get the decision-makers to buy in. The questions from potential buyers drive you mad:

• How can managers track individual learning progress?

• How can they rate the success of participants?

• How does the platform fit in with the corporation's existing IT system?

• Do you have detailed specifications and documentation?

This is a good example of a self-determined learning provider meeting a systemised corporation.

Identifying the natural colour fit of your product or service and that of your target group can be a good starting point and make a difference in sales. Also, mapping all stakeholders according to their preferences can be beneficial in multi-stakeholder settings. By highlighting the different interests, values and priorities, this enables

you to tailor communication and find a more suitable way forward. In short, it helps to understand others before seeking to be understood.

Applications abound in the business world. If, for example, you take two dimensions from our individual vs. group perspective and in-house business vs. external market, you end up with four quadrants that fit various examples.

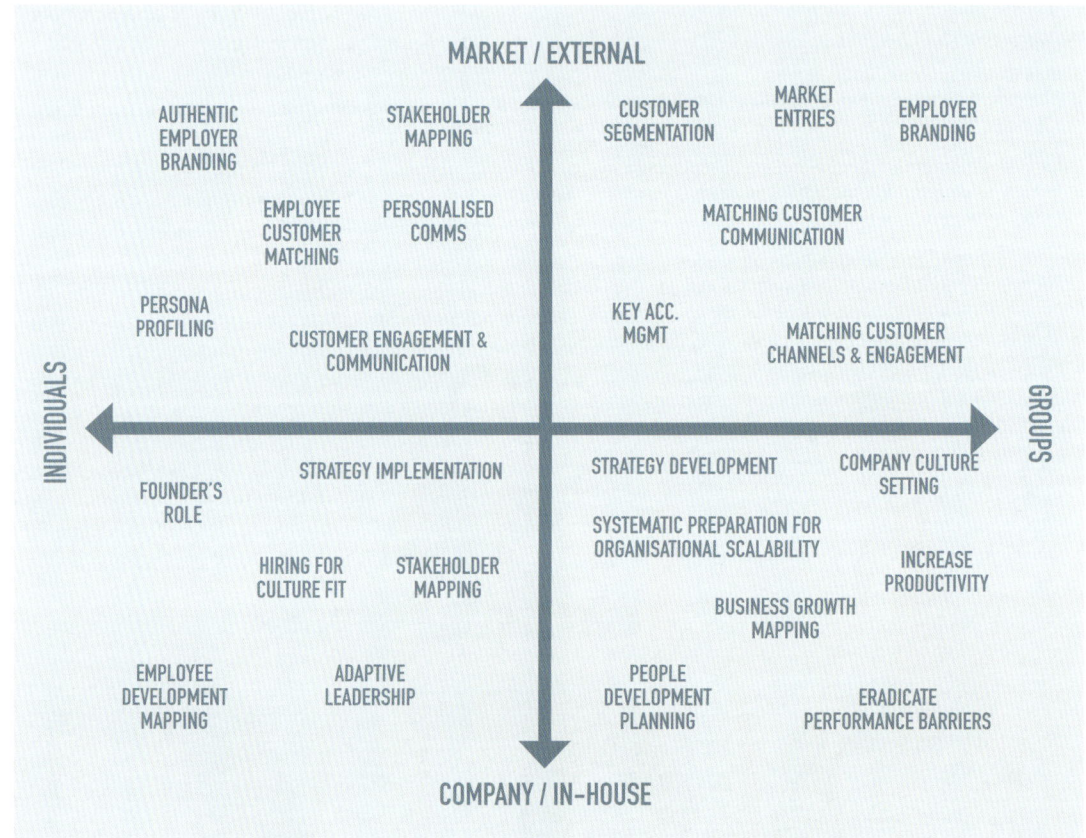

MARKET / EXTERNAL

AUTHENTIC EMPLOYER BRANDING

STAKEHOLDER MAPPING

CUSTOMER SEGMENTATION

MARKET ENTRIES

EMPLOYER BRANDING

EMPLOYEE CUSTOMER MATCHING

PERSONALISED COMMS

MATCHING CUSTOMER COMMUNICATION

PERSONA PROFILING

CUSTOMER ENGAGEMENT & COMMUNICATION

KEY ACC. MGMT

MATCHING CUSTOMER CHANNELS & ENGAGEMENT

INDIVIDUALS

GROUPS

STRATEGY IMPLEMENTATION

STRATEGY DEVELOPMENT

COMPANY CULTURE SETTING

FOUNDER'S ROLE

SYSTEMATIC PREPARATION FOR ORGANISATIONAL SCALABILITY

HIRING FOR CULTURE FIT

STAKEHOLDER MAPPING

INCREASE PRODUCTIVITY

BUSINESS GROWTH MAPPING

EMPLOYEE DEVELOPMENT MAPPING

ADAPTIVE LEADERSHIP

PEOPLE DEVELOPMENT PLANNING

ERADICATE PERFORMANCE BARRIERS

COMPANY / IN-HOUSE

Below are examples from each quadrant above to further illustrate the usefulness of the GVS:

MARKET ENTRIES [MARKET/GROUPS]

A market entry strategy is the planned distribution of goods or services to a new target industry or territory. It entails the origination, formation and management of contracts in a foreign territory where the import and export of services is concerned. Quite often companies enter new markets based on the intuition, personal preferences and relationships of their executives. It would be much more effective for leaders to identify the colour sweet spot of their product or service and figure out the best fit in relation to the Graves levels. For example, imagine a bunch of people wanting to buy an energy drink: Red Bull would sell best to Conan; a science-backed energy drink to Doc; an exclusive high-end brand to Eli; and an organic smoothie with seeds, turmeric and wheatgrass to Florence.

Now, consider how your home market compares to your potential new markets. For example, a 3rd-level Red market or industry has few regulations, but many unpredictable variables. On the other hand, a 4th-level Blue market is often saturated and heavily regulated, making it difficult for a product that needs to pass a lot of tests and standards (e.g. food).

Every market has its unique characteristics and many of the fundamental ones can be identified according to their maturity stage. The PESTEL overviews for each stage provide food for thought here.

STRATEGY DEVELOPMENT [COMPANY/GROUPS]

This is an organisation's strategic planning or game plan. It starts by setting specific medium and long-term goals and objectives, which will often need adjusting along the way in response to competitor moves and shifting market dynamics.

It helps to understand that strategy development and implementation differ fundamentally at every maturity stage.

Below is an example of how strategy development is arrived at in each of the four most common levels.

You can see how just one aspect of managing a business is fundamentally different at every stage. This also has an impact on the tools and methods that best suit a company. Tools are more useful to the levels at which they were developed. For example, design thinking for strategy development is a natural fit for the 5th (Orange) stage. Hence, the framework is great for sense-checking investments.

STARTUP / MICRO-BUSINESS	SCALEUP / CORPORATION	DATA-DRIVEN ENTERPRISE	AGILE BUSINESS
By the boss and their confidants; often intuitively reactive and ad hoc.	Top down, starting with the executive floor; internal experts and/or external strategy experts.	With consideration of market and competitor data, identifying opportunities with knowledgeable employees and possibly suitable strategy consultants and/or industry experts.	By all employees interested in strategy, with any required support from partners and external consultants with market perspective.

HIRING FOR CULTURE FIT [COMPANY/INDIVIDUALS]

Clarifying which level a hiring unit operates from can be a good starting point to understand which characteristics and soft skills a potential new employee should bring to the table. On the other hand, hiring for non-fit might be more advisable in certain circumstances, such as a unit in the transition process from one level to another.

Let's say, an efficient, cost-driven IT hardware seller is trying to become a customer-oriented IT consulting and installation firm. In this case, management might do well to hire for culture non-fit as it is important to hire people already experienced in consulting, solution selling and cost-benefit calculations. This means recruiters need to update the profiles and skill sets they are looking for.

Similarly, job seekers should check if a potential new employer promotes any demotivating or unhealthy practices. In this instance, how and why questions are particularly helpful to ask. The trick lies in translating management practices and procedures into values.

The chapter with the growth values is also a good way of checking how much a future employer might be able to grow with you [see page 31].

When looking for a job, it is important to look out for firms with a positive culture. Where a company scores on the above comparison chart is what you should uncover during your next interview. Don't just take any job; look for one with a company that helps you thrive.

DESTRUCTIVE / UNHEALTHY		CONSTRUCTIVE / HEALTHY
STATUS QUO & SUPERSTITION	BEFORE	CHANGE & ADAPTATION
EGO & FEAR	BEFORE	EMPLOYEES & BUSINESS IDEAS
SYSTEM & RULES	BEFORE	EMPLOYEES & CHANGE
TARGETS	BEFORE	PEOPLE
CONFORMITY	BEFORE	DIVERSITY

PERSONA PROFILING (MARKETING) [MARKET/INDIVIDUALS]

Personas are fictional characters representing different customer groups. Besides the usual grey criteria and characteristics commonly used by marketing experts, we recommend adding colour(s). This helps when trying to identify specific target groups. Using the right words, knowing where and how to approach potential customers can put the odds in your favour. For example, a Red Bull ad is best placed before an upcoming, action-packed super hero movie.

The general slogans below illustrate the different personas exhibited across the four main levels:

CONAN	DOC	ELI	FLORENCE
"CUT-THROAT DEALS! YOU ARE BETTER OFF WITH US" "WE DO WHATEVER IT TAKES"	"WITH US YOU RECEIVE CLEARLY CALCULATED ADVANTAGES. WE HAVE TRIED & TESTED METHODS." "WE ARE ACCREDITED BY..."	"WE USE STATE-OF-THE-ART TECHNOLOGY. WE ARE COMPETITIVE, PERFORMANCE-DRIVEN AND DELIVER MEASURABLE RESULTS." "WITH US YOU WILL ACHIEVE MORE."	"BY BEING PART OF OUR COMMUNITY YOU CAN SHARE YOUR BENEFITS WITH OTHERS THROUGH YOUR ACHIEVEMENTS."

AUTHOR'S COMMENT:

Over the years, with the support of many other coaches, facilitators, trainers and consultants, my team have put theory into practice and gained a great deal of experience. This framework has proved useful in many situations and with many different clients and companies. [10-11] For example, I used this with the director of one of the leading F1 teams to not only colour code his stakeholder map, but to more easily develop his influencer map and action plans. He loved it, because the insight made him a much better influencer.

I have also used it with a leading wealth management bank. We redefined and reorganised all their customers into five new segments (red, blue, orange, green, yellow/turquoise). They tailored the communications, features, advantages and benefits to their clients. They even went beyond that by matching them with authentic advisors (e.g. Conan with Conans, Doc with Docs).

We support startups and scaleups through their colourful growth stages. [10-12] I am currently working with Consilience Ventures, a startup with a Yellow spirit and the ability to significantly influence venture capitalism for the better. I cannot wait to see the organisation develop to its full potential.

We also recently worked with two organisations in automotive and personal development. Our remit entailed helping them to reshape their organisations by applying permaculture and circular economy principles to their business model.

These are just a few examples to give you an idea of the broad range of ways to apply the GVS to business. I encourage you to get in touch if you are looking for a contact or wish to explore these or other concepts further.

WOULD YOU LIKE TO FIND OUT MORE ABOUT YOUR BUSINESS?

As said before, personality is to an individual what culture is to a group. Therefore, if self-awareness is essential to personal growth, then awareness of the company culture is vital to employees' motivation and to the continuous growth of the business; not in size but in maturity. We spend a lot of time in the workplace and deserve it to be a happy place.

Here is a free online test you can do to gain some insight about your company.

• Organisational Test @ www.pathfinder.management/scaleup-freemium-en

Please note the Pathfinder assessment tools [10-13] are a combination of specific Graves levels with the McKinsey 7S Framework developed by Tom Peters and Robert Waterman. [10-14] It is a practical example of how useful the framework becomes when combined with other logic and models. The full version assesses a company against 35 business drivers – five for each of the seven key internal elements of a firm's organisational design: strategy, structure, systems, shared values, style, staff and skills. It unpicks possible misalignment and confusion, and provides a shared understanding of where people are in the organisation. It also clarifies where employees want to take the company (culture) and clearly outlines the steps needed to get there. In essence, it works just like a map.

Again, if you are interested in co-developing these diagnostic tools further or want to use them for social causes, please get in touch.

HOW ABOUT LARGE-SCALE SOCIETAL CHANGES?

Why do we say that history keeps repeating itself? How many wars are there currently and why are there so many? Is there a way of orchestrating larger changes collectively?

Applying the Graves framework to large-scale societal changes can be very powerful. As Graves and his scholar Dr Don Beck proved many times, this is where the GVS comes into its own. In times of climate emergency, pandemics and increasing social inequalities, a tool that can help facilitate multi-stakeholder projects and movements is needed more than ever. The psychology behind the levels is an accurate reflection of the motivations and concerns of larger groups – a starting point for bringing divided groups together.

Graves himself embarked on this journey with Beck in the 1980s. In **South Africa**, they designed parts of the transition away from the apartheid system. Beck worked closely with F.W. de Klerk and Nelson Mandela, while the latter was still in prison, on preparing the country for the transition of power. Beck's advice on how to build national cohesion was summarised in the movie *Invictus*, in which the coach of the Springboks – the South African national rugby team – received advice on developing the winning strategy that brought the country together. In 2005, Beck was recognised "for his invaluable contributions toward the peaceful creation of a democratic South Africa." [10-15]

Beck continued on this path and formed a network of non-profit think tanks under the Center for Human Emergence (CHE) in collaboration with a handful of global change agents who had trained with him for years. The centres still dot the globe from Canada and Mexico to the Netherlands, the United Kingdom and South Africa.

They aren't just think tanks, but rather think-and-do-tanks making conscious change visible in their respective communities and regions.

In the **Netherlands**, with support from the local CHE head Peter Merry, Beck introduced a new organising principle to help Dutch society open up to new immigrants. They called it Societal Mesh Works, and it created a new tapestry that overarched the entire society and the mutual sharing of accountability and responsibility.

In 2005, with Said E. Dawlabani and his wife Elza Maalouf, Beck created The Center for Human Emergence **Middle East** (CHE-ME), driving an initiative that sought to break the stalemate of failed negotiations and bloody violence.

There is so much to say about the Middle East initiative. I will let Said explain this in his own words later in this chapter.

WHAT NOW?

I believe there is a way out of the current crises. Societal and environmental changes are closely interconnected and will be even more so in the future. Climate Change, with all its implications, hits the poor and disadvantaged hardest. Social change is not sustainable without environmental change, and vice versa. The human race needs a big mindset shift and I can see it is underway in pockets, but it is not a cohesive or consciously collective act. If we could come together – for the first time – to act as one, we might stand a chance of turning things around. At this point, I believe the framework will be crucial in identifying a suitable way forward that is acceptable and accessible to many. The overall objective of this book is to make as many people as possible aware of this framework, to strengthen our understanding by building on it and make it available to all as a map to manoeuvre ourselves out of this self-made mess.

I would be thrilled if you, valued reader, would reach out to one of the CHEs. Rest assured, you will be met by open-minded people with their hearts and minds in the right place. By coming together and talking, ideas will flourish and projects might even emerge. Together, we can make a real difference.

MIDDLE EAST – AN INSIGHT REPORT

Said E. Dawlabani created the Center for Human Emergence Middle East (CHE-ME) with Don Beck and Elza Maalouf. So far, I have only met Said Dawlabani online, but I am humbled by his kindness, his decade-long drive for positive change and his efforts to show how Graves' framework can be a powerful force in creating positive change.

The following is an excerpt of a recent interview with him. It is a good example of the power of the framework.

By 2005 the Middle East had become resigned to a predictable future of failed peace treaties and continued violence. In preparation for this new adventure, Dr Beck, Elza, and I formed the Center for Human Emergence Middle East (CHE-ME). I agreed to handle all the Center's needs and administrative tasks in the United States, while Elza and Dr Beck did the work on the ground.

By the time our work in the Middle East began, Dr Beck had garnered the attention of many global leaders, including George Bush and Tony Blair. He had worked with President Bush from the time he was the governor of Texas and had advised Tony Blair's policy unit. In the Middle East, however, he was mostly known for his work in helping dismantle the Apartheid system in South Africa. Several intellectuals on both the Israeli and the Palestinian sides had known about Dr Beck's work with Nelson Mandela and F. W. de Klerk and were looking forward to being part of an initiative that sought to break the stalemate of failed negotiations and bloody violence. Hopes were high that the same thinking that helped dismantle Apartheid would be spread in the Middle East to help resolve a conflict of historic proportions.

From their first visit, Dr Beck and Elza hit the ground running. They met with stakeholders on both sides. They made presentations to the intellectual elites at Israeli and Palestinian universities. They recruited leaders from both sides who knew the two local cultures well, but were hungry for a fresh approach to solve the conflict. They trained them on how to become experts in the value-systems methodologies and its applications to nations. There were brilliant engineers and successful entrepreneurs on the Israeli side who cared about both the Israelis and the Palestinians equally. There were Palestinian intellectuals who had spent time in Israeli jails and were transformed by the experience, and after leaving prison decided to dedicate the rest of their lives to the pursuit of peace.

In her book *Emerge* [10-15], Elza chronicles the applications and developments on the ground between the years 2005 and 2008. By the start of the second year of work, we had gathered enough data from both cultures to determine the causes of failure of past peace treaties. Our research had uncovered that there were vast developmental gaps between Israel and Palestine. This was at the core of the failure of all the past peace treaties. It was an asymmetry in institutional capacities that unfairly prevented the Palestinians from meeting the conditions for peace. These findings compelled the CHE-ME and our Palestinian and Israeli partners to begin work in helping the Palestinians build the needed capacities that would eventually lead them to have an independent and resilient state. Our mission became known as the Build Palestine Initiative.

Like a wildfire being fanned by the media, the goal of our mission spread quickly. It represented both the hunger for something new and the excitement of peaceful coexistence. There were meetings with governors and Knesset members and university professors working on the science and anatomy of peace. No stakeholder on either side was left out. Members of the Third Generation Fatah movement as well as the radical Hamas movement were trained in seeing the conflict through different eyes. There were powerful Israeli and Palestinian business leaders who saw the wisdom of peace through commerce and committed to hiring Palestinians in their factories. By the third year, every town and hamlet in the Palestinian territories had heard of the work that was being done. They called our Palestinian partners and us the 'people of the spiral'. Officials in the Israeli government took notice as well. There were more meetings with Knesset members and at the Israeli Ministry of Defense. The office of the president of Israel had taken notice and had given us the nod of approval.

By the beginning of 2008, the movement had reached critical mass, and no one was happier than Elza. In February of that year, along with our Palestinian partners, we organized a Nation Building Conference where over seven hundred community leaders came from every part of the West Bank to engage in a first-of-a-kind exercise to design a future state informed by the new and powerful paradigm of value systems. Most of the attendees identified as members of the Third Generation Fatah party made up of young, college-educated professionals who held the greatest promise for a resilient and peaceful future. As Elza describes this critical event in her book, before taking to the stage at that conference she had asked herself if the grassroots, collaborative work that was being done might become a template that could transform the region.

After the financial crisis of 2008, Dr Beck and Elza shifted their focus to influence powerbrokers in Washington. The Build Palestine Initiative became a case study they presented to all who would listen. At the State Department they met with the Office of the Assistant Secretary of State for the region, which subsequently sent personnel to train in Spiral Dynamics. At the Washington Institute, they met with President Clinton's past envoy to the Middle East, Dennis Ross, who had heard about our work and wanted to know more about the merits of our approach. Elza offered edits to Mr Ross's book, *Statecraft*, about Sharia Law and cultural misconceptions about Arabs in general and Palestinians in particular. They presented their case to the United Nations through its Values Caucus. They submitted a proposal to the American Psychological Association (APA) to create a new branch of psychology that Dr Beck named Psychology at the Large Scale. The three of us worked together on the proposal that sought to bring together the work of three prominent psychologists: Muzafer Sherif, the father of social psychology and Dr Beck's PhD advisor; Clare Graves, Dr Beck's associate and the brilliant developmental psychologist behind the academic work on value systems; and Dr Beck himself, focusing on his own work in developing the Spiral Dynamics framework and the Sherif-Graves hybrid models he created and applied in South Africa and through the Middle East. The proposal was accepted, and all it needed was enough signatures from APA members to become official. But as we began that work, the global economy was plunged into the worst economic crisis since the Great Depression, forcing us to put the plan on hold.

Elza wrote a book named *Emerge* about the Middle East experience and how she was changing the Middle East through the applications of Spiral Dynamics and Integral Theory in major Middle East businesses.

10.4 WHO ARE SOME OF THE FELLOW GRAVESIANS?

The previous pages have clearly shown how versatile the framework is. Naturally, more and more people are working with it and one of the two colour codes. Many people use it in personal development, others for professional or organisational development, and hopefully more will follow in Beck's footsteps by applying it to large-scale social change to bring more peace to the world. It is a tried and tested model!

That said, there are currently a number of communities applying this model, but no overarching body. After decades of misunderstandings, distrust and petty disputes, it is clear that many people talk about a 2nd tier more than they live it. Ironically, the framework is brilliant for checking people's level of authenticity. The objective of this chapter is to highlight some of the trusted key players you can reach out to and to encourage everyone to find a shared way forward.

Bill Lee and the **'Values Group'** were fascinated by Graves' work and did us all a great deal of service by capturing, organising and sharing a lot of the original material. Much of the original work can be discovered at www.ClareWGraves.com

Don Beck and **Christopher Cowan** were instrumental in ensuring continuation of the work. They later added colours to the levels, developed the framework further and published their book *Spiral Dynamics* in 1996. After Cowan passed away in 2015, **Natasha Todorovic-Cowan** continued the work under NVC Consulting and is one of the few people left who knows how Clare W. Graves liked his coffee.

As mentioned, **Don Beck** leads the Center for Human Emergence (CHE), which functions as a global facilitator of the conscious evolution of the human species. See www.humanemergence.org. We all wish him the energy and health needed to continue doing more of what he does best – social change for the betterment of people.

Now for the 3rd Generation of Gravesians.

There is a sizable CHE group in the Netherlands offering training and consultancy in Dutch - www.humanemergence.nl/. The women to look out for are **Anne-Marie Voorhoeve** and **Anita Floris** at The Hague Centre, whom you can read about at http://www.thehaguecenter.org/.

Teddy Larsen, with **Don Beck's** support, founded the first Center for Human Emergence in Denmark in May 2004. Larsen has comprehensive practical experience spanning over 20 years with the application of Spiral Dynamics in small, medium and large organisations. He is the co-author of the 2018 book *Spiral Dynamics in Action – Humanity's Master Code* written with **Don Beck, Rica Viljoen, Thomas Johns** and **Sergey Solonin**.

Said E. Dawlabani has also worked closely with **Don Beck**. In my interview with Said, he divided his engagement and commitment to the Graves framework into four phases:

1. His engagement with **Elza Maalouf** and Don at the Center for Human Emergence Middle East;

2. His own advancement of the framework through his socioeconomic applications known as MEMEnomics; [0-15]

3. His own personal reflections on the power of the framework and what triggered him to write his upcoming book, The Light of Ishtar, and his renewed commitment to interpret climate change through the Graves model;

4. His ambitious future plans to do what no one since Graves has been able to achieve: bring back the Graves/Spiral Dynamics model to a US-based academic institution that can act as a legacy and global clearinghouse to embody humanity's never-ending quest based on Graves' principles.

One person who picked up on Graves' work early on is **Ken Wilber**. He developed the integral theory, a systematic philosophy and framework highlighting the agency and characteristic of each domain of science and research, thereby showing how they complement, inform and influence one another. This can be helpful as a tool to see where interventions might have the most impact. It is a beautiful example of Yellow's ability to bring complicated themes together and integrate them. Wilber combined the levels with two dimensions (individual/collective and interior/exterior), giving it more practicality. Wilber's rainbow colours differ from those of Spiral Dynamics. His All Quadrants All Levels (AQAL) framework honours all quadrants, levels, lines, states, and types. He designed a system that could function as a tape measure, empty of all content, so the different developmental models could be compared to one another. His integral theory grew out of his early work, combining Western psychology and Eastern philosophy.

This links directly to www.integrallife.com which is likely the largest and most comprehensive Integral community out there. It is managed by **Corey DeVos**, who is a passionate individual highly involved in the Integral movement. The site provides a mix of information, practice and connections to people in the integral space.

There is also The **Integral European Conference** (IEC), which has become the leading event in the international integral community.

Founded by **Bence Ganti**, it is not only a huge social catalyst where international integral collaborations begin, enabling our human capital to grow, they also have a mission based on integral principles. The conferences cover findings, applications, research and experiential processes. All in all, it is a great achievement and you can read more about it at https://integraleuropeanconference.com

Jeff Salzman offers a post-progressive look at politics and culture through his lively page www.dailyevolver.com. It is about interpreting emerging politics and culture through a lens of consciousness evolution.

Frédéric Laloux, who came across Spiral Dynamics through **Jenny Wade**, published *Reinventing Organizations: A Guide to Creating Organizations Inspired by the Next Stage in Human Consciousness*, which coined the term 'teal organisations'. He uses **Ken Wilber's** colours. Find out more at www.reinventingorganizations.com and the wiki based on the book: https://reinventingorganizationswiki.com.

Those mentioned above are just a few of the people that have built on Ken Wilber's insight. There are more mentioned on Wikipedia and it is well worth surfing the net to read about their work.

Christopher and Sheila Cooke offer the application of a holistically informed agricultural practice, across the whole food and fibre supply ecology for the UK and Ireland, through 3LM (Land and Livestock Management for Life). 3LM is a hub in the global Savory Network, www.3lm.network, and a division within a much broader 'multi-sector' education and advisory service based upon the Spiral Dynamics integral lineage. This comprehensive approach is offered through 5 Deep Limited. www.5Deep.net

Jon Freeman is a leading master practitioner and trainer whose work can be found through the website www.spiralfutures.com. Jon works in organisational development and in mentoring and coaching. With Auke van Nimwegen (www.valuematch.net), Jon offers the only online Spiral Dynamics Fundamentals certification training authorised by Beck.

Jon is a passionate advocate for and developer of the Graves and Spiral Dynamics integral (SDi) inheritance. His book, *The Science of Possibility*, links the Gravesian dynamics (individual/collective and growth of ecological complexity) to fundamentals of patterns in scientific perspectives. It is widely regarded as the science of the Turquoise values level. He has applied the four-quadrant model and both interior and exterior perspectives to economics and our approach to money in *Reinventing Capitalism*. Coming soon is also a simple manual for raising children, *Seven-stage Parenting*, which can be viewed and obtained as an eBook through www.spiralworld.net.

Michiel Doorn came to Spiral Dynamics and Integral Theory after a successful career as a sustainability and climate change engineer, realizing that people's values and meaning-making systems are the real actors of change. He has now incorporated personal and organisational coaching to offer a fully integrated approach, which you can learn more about at www.the2nd.life.

Another practitioner is Nicholas Beecroft, who has applied the framework to Western civilisation, analysing the group psychology of the West, its pathologies, strengths and features. He has integrated Spiral Dynamics into the analysis of his books *Analyze West: A Psychiatrist Takes Western Civilization on a Journey of Transformation* and *The Future of Western Civilization*. His latest one, New Magna Carta, is a bold vision and strategy to rejuvenate Western civilisation. On the 800th anniversary of the original 'Great Charter', Nicholas proposes a clear vision of who we are, what we believe and value, where we want to get to, and the necessary steps to get there. Find out more at www.newmagnacarta.org

In an interview with Robin Lincoln Wood [bit.ly/robinwoodauthor], author of various books in which the thinking of Spiral Dynamics is embedded, for example, "*A Momentous Leap – Thriveable Transformation in the 21st Century*", pointed out several leading practitioners in the field:

Paul van Schaik [www.integralmentors.org] published a series of books on Thriveable Cities. Bjarni Jonsson who has insights into major social transformations based

on the Icelandic experience. J. Kim Wright and Luemara Wagner who understand the value systems and how they relate to legal systems, law, justice, rights and peace. If you are interested in spirituality, communities Jim Lockard is your man.

Terry Patten looks at our global tipping point, and a radical integral ecology. He explores how the momentous gap be used to trigger momentous leaps, mind- and worldshifts. Michiel Doorn looks at emerging technologies through the lens of Spiral Dynamics. Keith Rice explores 'A 2nd Tier Approach to a 1st Tier World'. Nicholas Beecroft examines what is needed to facilitate the emergence of a Thriving Global Civilization.

Anne-Marie Verhoeve tells the story of the Hague Center for Global Governance as a second tier organization. Teddy Hebo-Larsen takes a look at the future of democracy and the "Beta-Condition" – The Scandinavian Experience. Teddy also offers Spiral Dynamics accreditation training authorised by Beck

For more information and papers, please go the page of the event [10-17].

Below are some additional players in the field that I have come across, including several that I have worked with directly in London (e.g. Keith Rice www.integratedsociopsychology. net, Kerstin van Eckert www.pathfinder. management) and in Germany (e.g. Hartmut Wiehle www.v4ch.de, Rainer Krumm www.9levels.de, Petra Gregory www.authentica-coaching.de/, Robert Siegers www.profiledynamics.com).

A GLOBAL DIRECTORY – A SHARED INITIATIVE?

I know some people out there are also on a mission to create "an international network promoting integral consciousness, holistic and integrative action, developing integral theories and practices." [10-18]

It is time to create a pragmatic and non-commercial global directory – with the objective to provide the broader community of integral thinkers around the world with a platform that can serve as a community builder outside of social media. This is meant for all kinds of integral thinkers, metamodernists, Wilberians, Gravesians, Spiral Dynamics practitioners.

Firstly, it should be a place where players who work with any form of Graves' work to be able to list themselves; to list their area of expertise, interest and possible interest in collaborative research.

Secondly, a directory where people who look for experienced players in the field are able to identify them according to expertise, location and possible interest in collaborative research. Additionally, if you are interested in working with someone who uses some form of the Graves Value System, are looking for a qualification, want to carry out or build on existing research or help develop new applications, and/or want to meet like-minded people, please go to:

If you are genuinely interested in co-creating or have an idea on how to make this happen, please get in touch with the author.

Ultimately, I would like to encourage people to explore further research into Gravesian applications, to verify and extend his work whilst staying true to his original framework and levels. There is a lot of work to be done. We need to consider the other half of the double helix referring to existential reality. That is the world around us and, as all change agents know, the system is nearly always stronger than the individual.

We are well advised to change our businesses and societies for the better if we want for people to progress to a more holistic world of love, togetherness and abundance. Ultimately, we are all in this together – for better or worse.

It is time for us all to come together if we want to prepare ourselves for the social and environmental challenges ahead of us.

10.5 WHO ARE THE CREATORS OF THE TURQUOISE BRICK ROAD?

RHYS MARC PHOTIS – AUTHOR

Rhys wrote the book, because he believes that with the speed with which we are destroying our habitat we are quickly running ourselves into a very unpleasant, intractable situation. Mother Earth will prevail and some of us will live on, but a Mad Max scenario is not what Rhys has in mind for his young daughter. His mission is to make Clare W. Graves's work more widely known and applied by building on it and using it as a key to getting us out of this self-inflicted chaos.

Of German, English and Cypriot heritage, Rhys is fluent in both English and German, has lived in ten countries, and loves the multicultural dynamic of his birthplace and current home in Camden, London. Influenced by entrepreneurial family members, he understood early on that having lots of money comes at a cost and how it feels to lose it all at once. Rhys used to start and scale companies in emerging markets but soon reverted to more purposeful work. Nowadays, he is a thought-provoking speaker, MC, coach, facilitator and advisor, using the Graves logic to support individuals and organisations to become more self-aware and clearer about their path to success.

To him business is all about people. He believes that multiple techniques are required to enable people and organisations to change for the better, and that workplaces should be both challenging and fulfilling to foster individual and collective growth.

Rhys has a bit of a marmite effect on people. He strongly believes in continuous improvement and sees this as an uncomfortable, but vital part of life. He challenges himself and others too much at times and is known for frowning when he's thinking, but he means well; after all, he is just a man.

Rhys is passionate about nature, organic ingredients and cooking fresh food. In his world, the seasons determine the menu. He loves trees, dogs, horses and all of nature's diverse richness. He is critical of the wasteful world we have created and wants to catalyse a return to a healthy way of life. To him, a journey along the Turquoise Brick Road entails a positive contribution to evolution by enabling mankind to live up to its potential and purpose.

KERSTIN VAN ECKERT – WINGWOMAN

Kerstin got involved in the book because she wants to live in a Turquoise world and believes that, by spreading the word about a possible pathway, more people will want to join in and start the journey. She accompanied Rhys on his mission from budding idea to published book. This included endless brainstorming sessions, review cycles, long philosophical walks, challenging discussions, insights into mind-blowing concepts, scientific discoveries, setbacks and successes. In short, an emotional rollercoaster and wonderful learning experience. Kerstin is a multilingual mediator, coach and facilitator.

After a typical career in various industries, living and working in six different countries, she now focuses on supporting SMEs to become more sustainable and grow healthily. She specialises on culture and organisational development, using permaculture principles, circular economy tools and the Graves Value System for designing healthy, inclusive and successful businesses. Kerstin also acts as a BLeader – an ambassador and consultant for the BCorp movement – and facilitator with social enterprise She Leads Change. She runs the latter's flagship programme "Leading from Within" and co-created their "Leading for Collective Impact" programme. Kerstin's aim is to increase our awareness and expand our consciousness to live more creative, inspired and balanced lives. Additionally, she founded Amaroq Organic, a sustainable pet food business, with the aim of bridging regenerative agriculture, animal welfare and climate change.

Kerstin is kind and can have a calming effect on people, but also quite the opposite. She is a good listener and people love telling her their stories.

When she gets impatient (which happens quite quickly if people violate her core values), it is best to let her venture off on a long walk with her dog.

Kerstin is passionate about people and our planet, and believes that everyone and everything is interconnected. She loves all of nature's creations – yes, even spiders and creepy crawlies – and feels we have a short window of opportunity to turn around the climate emergency and avert the destruction of Mother Earth. She is an advocate for collaboration and community-building to create a better world for future generations. To her, a journey along the Turquoise Brick Road entails getting involved in regenerating land and the bond that keeps us all together.

VALENTINA – EDITOR

Valentina jumped at the chance to help bring this book to life, because it represents everything she has built the last 20 years of her life and career on: marrying her personal passion to resolve social and environmental issues with her business acumen to develop practical, efficient and sustainable solutions. Her mission is to promote ways of living that benefit all life on Earth — people, animals and plants — and to shift the mindsets of people who are both knowingly and unknowingly destroying this planet for short-term personal gain.

A dual US-Italian citizen who was born in Italy and raised across Europe and the US, Valentina learned from a young age that a wide range of experiences breed greater understanding, acceptance of diversity and creative thinking that can transform lives for the better. Her own experience includes living in eight countries, working across six sectors, learning six languages and travelling around five continents. She works to leverage this background and the extensive contacts she has built along the way to help individuals and companies, especially social enterprises, build and scale strategies that provide effective solutions to social and environmental problems.

She is known for her bleeding heart, a vivacious character, workaholism (for the things she is passionate about) and an unfortunate tendency to be late for just about everything, mainly because she tries to do too much. She generally balks at meaningless small talk and prefers fruitful conversations that lead to profound discoveries or some kind of evolution.

Valentina believes that insecurity — in terms of a real or misperceived threat at either an individual or collective, national level — is the main underlying driver of most major problems in this world. After decades of working in both the public and private sectors, she feels that too few philanthropists truly understand the root causes of the issues they claim to want to resolve and too many nonprofits lack the resources and innovation to carry out sustainable solutions. Her mission is to encourage greater research into and collaboration between them.

To her, a journey along the Turquoise Brick Road is about getting to the root of human desire, understanding the psychology behind it and showing people of all backgrounds and personality types that there are ways to live in harmony with this planet while still leading deeply fulfilling lives.

SÉVERINE SEALES – PROOFREADER

Séverine didn't think twice about getting involved with the book because she believes in the power of story-telling, and this story is about every and any human out there. Whilst there are examples of great applications of Graves' work, bringing the levels to life through a story is a first. This medium allows readers to truly appreciate the message as they travel along the Turquoise Brick Road – they will recognise their own journey thus far and imagine the road ahead.

Born and bred within a mix of cultures and languages, Séverine has always sought variety throughout her life. This has included using or playing with eight languages, practising yoga and capoeira, dancing and horse riding, baking and meditating, moving home (12 times so far) and engaging with an eclectic circle of friends. Séverine has enjoyed a varied career, from supporting Erasmus students at university through to teaching French and German in a secondary school, assisting CEOs in various third sector SMEs and the NHS, teaching ESOL in further education, advising the public and training volunteers within a Citizens Advice Bureau. She currently offers linguistic and administrative services in a freelance capacity.

Known for her kindness, warmth, dry sense of humour, and for keeping a cool head in a crisis, Séverine lives for service and social justice. Her values of integrity, compassion and courage guide her life choices.

She meets life's creatures and experiences with a smile and an open heart.

Séverine's passion for and fascination with diversity in all its forms developed very early on. As did the ability to accept, value, and sometimes seek difference around her, recognising the great potential for learning within that exposure. She loves life within and around her, and seizes every opportunity to connect with it. To her, a journey along the Turquoise Brick Road is a fun route to self-realisation.

CRAIG CORNOCK – DESIGNER

Craig designed the book because it's always a bonus for a designer to work on a project that they believe can make a difference to our lives. He first met Rhys and Kerstin at their mutual friend Jon's birthday party in Primrose Hill, London. Jon mentioned that Rhys was writing a book and needed a designer who understood their vision. Craig was impressed by their enthusiasm and passion and the rest, as they say, is history...

Craig grew up in Malaysia and Singapore until the age of seven, his family then travelled back to the UK due to his father's job.

When his parents went back to Singapore three years later, Craig remained in the UK so he could have a stable education. Craig's interests lay in the sciences but it became apparent that he had a talent for art. One of his teachers urged him to take art as an extra subject and he excelled at it. This paved his way for a career as a designer and, after studying in Birmingham, he found employment in London with companies that variously specialised in publishing, branding, advertising and retail design. Craig started his own design business in 2015. He lives in North West London with his wife, son and Labradoodle.

Craig is an eternal optimist and always tries to see the best in people and situations. Perhaps that is why he's perceived as a relaxed and convivial character who rarely gets anxious. The only subjects that agitate him are pollution, human rights, animal welfare, and that he's too old to skateboard anymore.

Craig is an ardent fan of music, art, food and travel. He recently visited Japan, which satisfied many of his passions, and he also had the luck to watch England thrash New Zealand during the Rugby World Cup semi-finals in Tokyo. To him, a journey along the Turquoise Brick Road can bring a change for good in how we all live and work. It's time for corporations to give back and do good rather than chase profits.

10.6 WHERE CAN I FIND ADDITIONAL INFORMATION AND REFERENCES?

PICTURES of Clare W. Graves

Courtesy of Special Collections, Picture File, Schaffer Library, Union College [Confirmed 5 Aug. 2020].

CORE MATERIALS

[C-1] Cowan, Christopher & Todorovic, Natasha (2005). The Never Ending Quest: Dr Clare W. Graves Explores Human Nature: A Treatise On An Emergent Cyclica. Santa Barbara, Ca: ECLET Pub. [best procured via https://spiraldynamics.org/resources/books/].

[C-2] Graves, Clare & Lee, W.R. (2002). Graves: Levels of human existence: transcription of a seminar at the Washington School of Psychiatry, October 16, 1971. Santa Barbara, Ca: ECLET Pub. [best procured via https://spiraldynamics.org/resources/books/].

[C-3] Pink, Dan (2018). DRIVE : the surprising truth about what motivates us. S.L.: Canongate Books Ltd.

[C-4] Harvard Business Review. (2015). Seven Transformations of Leadership. [online] Available at: https://hbr.org/2005/04/seven-transformations-of-leadership.

PREFIX

[P-1] Baum, Frank Lyman (1994). The wizard of Oz. London, Hamstead: Parragon, Cop.

[P-2] www.clarewgraves.com. (n.d.). Dr Clare W. Graves. [online] Available at: https://www.clarewgraves.com/theory.html

INTRODUCTION

[0-0] Visual adapted from Dawlabani, Said E. (2019). Clare W. Graves Emergent Cyclical Double-helix Model of Adult Bio-Psycho-Social Systems Development.

[0-1] Beck, Don & Cowan, Christopher (1996). Spiral dynamics : mastering values, leadership, and change. Cambridge, Mass: Blackwell Business.

[0-2] Wilber, Ken & Wachowski, L. (2017). A brief history of everything. Boulder, Colorado: Shambhala Publications, Inc.

[0-3] Graves Value System - Pathfinder. (n.d.). Pathfinder. [online] Available at: https://www.pathfinder.management/graves-value-system/.

[0-4] Reference to Purpose, Mastery, Autonomy: The RSA (2010). RSA ANIMATE: Drive: The surprising truth about what motivates us. YouTube. Available at: https://www.youtube.com/watch?v=u6XAPnuFjJc.

[0-5] William R. Lee (2001). The Implications to Management of Systems-Ethical Theory. Dr Clare W. Graves (1962). [online] Available at: https://www.clarewgraves.com/articles.html [Accessed 8 Mar. 2020].

[0-6] William R. L. (2001). An Emergent Theory of Ethical Behavior Based upon an Epigenetic Model. Dr Clare W. Graves (1959). [online] Available at: https://www.clarewgraves.com/articles.html [Accessed 20 Aug. 2020]

[0-7] McDonald, Ian (2010). Introduction to Spiral Dynamics. Cheshire: Hot Snow Books, UK

[0-8] Jeffrey, S. (n.d.). How to Use Spiral Dynamics for Psychological and Leadership Development - The Origins of Spiral Dynamics. [online] Available at: https://scottjeffrey.com/wp-content/uploads/2019/04/Spiral.pdf [Accessed 28 Jun. 2019].

[0-9] Wilber, K. (2007). Integral spirituality : a startling new role for religion in the modern and postmodern world. Boston, Mass.: Integral Books.

[0-10] Cowan, Chris (1981). Summary Statement: The Emergent, Cyclical, Double-Helix Model Of The Adult Human Biopsychosocial Systems (Handout prepared by Chris Cowan for Dr Graves' presentation in Boston, Mass.) [online] Available at: http://www.clarewgraves.com/articles.html [Accessed 6 Mar. 2020].

[0-11] Howard, L. (2005). Introducing Ken Wilber : concepts for an evolving world. Bloomington, Ind.: Authorhouse.

[0-12] William R. Lee (2001). Value Systems and their Relation to Managerial Controls and Organizational Viability. Dr Clare W. Graves (1965). [online] Available at: https://www.clarewgraves.com/articles.html [Accessed 18 Mar. 2020].

[0-13] Dobbelstein, Prof. Thomas & Krumm, Rainer (2012). 9 Levels for Value Systems Development of A Scale for Level-measurement. Market Research Institute Customer Research 42. Journal of Applied Leadership & Management, DE.

[0-14] Bär, Martina, Krumm, Rainer & Wiehle, Hartmut (2015). Unternehmen verstehen, gestalten, verändern das Graves-Value-System in der Praxis. Wiesbaden Springer Gabler, DE.

[0-15] Dawlabani, Said (2013). MEMEnomics : the next-generation economic system. New York: Selectbooks, Inc.

[0-16] Book Alexander, Charles N., & Langer, Ellen J. (1990). Higher stages of human development: Perspectives on adult growth. Oxford University Press.

[0-17] Photis, R. (2018). An Entrepreneurs Journey. [online] Vimeo. Available at: https://vimeo.com/253213927 [Accessed 6 Aug. 2020].

[0-18] Wikipedia Contributors (2019). Gross National Happiness. [online] Wikipedia. Available at: https://en.wikipedia.org/wiki/Gross_National_Happiness.

[0-19] Bidadanure, J.U. (2019). The Political Theory of Universal Basic Income. Annual Review of Political Science, 22(1), pp.481–501.

[0-20] William R. Lee & Cornish, E. (1974). Human Nature Prepares for a Momentous Leap. [online] Available at: http://www.clarewgraves.com/articles.html [Accessed 18 Mar. 2020].

[0-21] Graves Value System - Pathfinder. (n.d.). Pathfinder. [online] Available at: https://www.pathfinder.management/graves-value-system/ [Accessed 19 Jun. 2020].

[0-22] Cowan, Chris (1982). Unpublished Seminar Handout (Used by Dr Graves in his presentations sponsored by The National Values Centre; prepared by Chris Cowan). [online] Available at: http://www.clarewgraves.com/articles.html [Accessed 18 Mar. 2020].

[0-23] Sørensen, Kenneth (2017) Psychosynthesis and the seven types. Psychosynthesis: Dimensions of Growth, by Firman and Vargiu. [online] Available at: https://kennethsorensen.dk/en/transpersonal-dimensions-of-growth/ [Accessed 30 Mar. 2020].

[0-24] Hofstede, Geert (2001). Culture's consequences : comparing values, behaviors, institutions, and organizations across nations. Thousand Oaks, Calif.: Sage.

[0-25] Johnson, S. (2007). Who moved my cheese? : an amazing way to deal with change in your work and in your life. London: Vermilion.

[0-26] Kotter, J. (2016). Our Iceberg Is Melting. Pan Books.

[0-27] Kegan, Robert & Lahey, Lisa (2009). Immunity to change : how to overcome it and unlock potential in yourself and your organization. Boston: Harvard Business School, Cop.

[0-28] Maslow, Abraham (1993). The farther reaches of human nature. New York: Penguin Compass.

[0-29] Assagioli, Roberto (2007). The act of will : a guide to self-actualisation and self-realisation. London: Psychosynthesis & Education Trust.

AMON'S EXISTENCE

([1-1] (n.d.). https://storymaps.esri.com/stories/2016/refugee-camps/.

[1-2] (n.d.). https://borgenproject.org/facts-about-refugee-camps/.

[1-3] Mayer, M. (2001). The Fed : the inside story of how the world's most powerful financial institution drives the markets. New York: Plume.

[1-4] Bernstein, P.L., Volcker, P.A. and Wiley (2008). A primer on money, banking, and gold. Hoboken, N.J .: Wiley.

[1-5] Interview with Nick & Pascal (2 Aug. 2020). Living in Regent's Park (London).

[1-6] Wikipedia Contributors (2019). Human. [online] Wikipedia. Available at: https://en.wikipedia.org/wiki/Human.

BO'S PURPLESHIRE

[2-1] Valéry, P. (1970). Analects. Princeton, N.J.: Princeton University Press.

[2-2] Rošker, J. (2014). Epistemology in Chinese Philosophy (Stanford Encyclopedia of Philosophy). [online] Stanford.edu. Available at: https://plato.stanford.edu/entries/chinese-epistemology/.

CONAN'S ARENA

[3-1] Interview with Busch, Jan-Peter (23 Sep. 2019). Sifu Wing Tsun & Muay Thai practitioner https://cma-academy.de

[3-2] Miller, D. (1992). The Icarus paradox : how exceptional companies bring about their own downfall. New York: Harper Business.

[3-3] Probst, G. and Raisch, S. (2005). Organizational crisis: The logic of failure. Academy of Management Perspectives, 19(1), p. 104.

DOC'S ENVIRONMENT

[4-1] Meadows, Donella & Randers, Jørgen (2012). Limits to growth : the 30-year update. London: Earthscan.

[4-2] Cem Nizamoglu (2019). Al-Kindi, Cryptography, Code Breaking and Ciphers « Muslim Heritage. [online] Muslimheritage.com. Available at: https://muslimheritage.com/al-kindi-cryptography/ [Accessed 12 Nov. 2019].

[4-3] Wikipedia Contributors (2019). Ada Lovelace. [online] Wikipedia. Available at: https://en.wikipedia.org/wiki/Ada_Lovelace.

[4-4] 14:00-17:00 (n.d.). ISO 30408:2016. [online] ISO. Available at: https://www.iso.org/standard/63492.html [Accessed 18 Nov. 2019].

[4-5] Pontefract, D. (2018). Flat Army : creating a connected and engaged organization. Vancouver ; Berkeley: Figure.1.

[4-6] Cortez Subsea | Subsea Inspection & Pipelay - Aberdeen & Asia. (2015). The Principles of Scientific Management | Cortez Subsea | Subsea Inspection & Pipelay - Aberdeen & Asia. [online] Available at: https://www.cortezsubsea.com/blog/the-principles-of-scientific-management/.

[4-7] Rostow, W.W. (1971). Stages of economic growth. Cambridge University Press.

[4-8] Leitner, Sabine (2020) Eastern & Western Philosophies. 16-week course. www.newacropolisuk.org, Week 8

[4-9] Farrar, Siobhan (2020) Eastern & Western Philosophies. 16-week course. www.newacropolisuk.org, Week 12

ELI'S SPHERE

[5 -1] Are You Good or Evil?, (2018). BBC Horizon. 7 Aug.

[5 -2] T.W.B.U. (n.d.). Anatomy of an OKR: How to set your OKRs – Gtmhub team blog. [online] Available at: https://gtmhub.com/blog/anatomy-of-an-okr-how-to-set-your-okrs/ [Accessed 2 Feb. 2020].

[5 -3] Kaplin, Robert & Norton, David (1996). The balanced scorecard. Harvard: HBS Press.

[5 -4] Waterman, R.H., Peters, T.J. and Phillips, J.R. (1980). Structure is not organization. Business Horizons, 23(3), pp.14–26.

[5 -5] agilemanifesto.org. (n.d.). Manifesto for Agile Software Development. [online] Available at: https://agilemanifesto.org.

[5 -6] Jeff Bezos & family. (2019). Forbes. [online] Available at: https://www.forbes.com/profile/jeff-bezos/.

FLORENCE'S WORLD

[6–1] Tiimiakatemia. (n.d.). Business school without teachers, lectures or exams. [online] Available at: https://www.tiimiakatemia.fi/english [Accessed 5 Mar. 2020].

[6–2] Holons www.panarchy.org. (n.d.). Arthur Koestler, Some general properties of self-regulating open hierarchic order (1969). [online] Available at: http://www.panarchy.org/koestler/holon.1969.html [Accessed 20 Mar. 2020].

[6–3] Sven Erik Jørgensen and Müller, F. (2000). Handbook of ecosystem theories and management. Boca Raton, Fla.: Lewis Publishers.

[6–4] Hutchins, Giles & Storm, L. (2019). Regenerative leadership : the DNA of life-affirming 21st century organizations. S.L.: Wordzworth Publishing.

[6–5] Kay, J. (2000). Ecosystems as Self-organizing Holarchic Open Systems : Narratives and the Second Law of Thermodynamics.

[6–6] Correspondent, J.H.E. (2020). Finnish basic income pilot improved wellbeing, study finds. The Guardian. [online] 7 Mar. Available at: https://www.theguardian.com/society/2020/may/07/finnish-basic-income-pilot-improved-wellbeing-study-finds-coronavirus.

[6–7] Ashitha Nagesh (2019). Finland basic income trial left people "happier but jobless." BBC News. [online] 7 Mar. Available at: https://www.bbc.co.uk/news/world-europe-47169549.

[6-8] Macionis, J.J. and Plummer, K. (2012). Sociology : a global introduction. Harlow, England ; New York: Pearson/Prentice Hall.

[6–9] The School of Life (2016). SOCIOLOGY - Auguste Comte. YouTube. Available at: https://www.youtube.com/watch?v=OhVamhT4Q3s&t=11s [Accessed 9 Mar. 2020].

[6–10] Higher Logic. (2018). What Burning Man's 10 Principles Can Teach You About Building Community. [online] Available at: https://www.higherlogic.com/blog/what-burning-mans-10-principles-can-teach-you-about-building-community/ [Accessed 6 Oct. 2020].

[6–11] She Leads Change. [online] Available at: https://www.SheLeadsChange.org [Accessed 10 Mar. 2020].

[6–12] Sen, S. (2018). The Next Generation Organizations. [online] Medium. Available at: https://medium.com/beyond-thinking/the-next-generation-organizations-60688e8b34e2 [Accessed 21 Mar. 2020].

[6–13] Cho, A. (2010). The jazz process : collaboration, innovation, and agility. Upper Saddle River, Nj: Addison-Wesley.

[6–14] Kahn, A. (n.d.). Miles Davis and Bill Evans: Miles and Bill in Black & White. [online] JazzTimes. Available at: https://jazztimes.com/archives/miles-davis-and-bill-evans-miles-and-bill-in-black-white/.

[6–15] who-knows.imtqy.com. (n.d.). Summary of The Jazz Process. [online] Available at: https://who-knows.imtqy.com/books/14664/index.html [Accessed 6 Oct. 2020].

[6–16] Chavrik (2011). George Clabin interviews Bill Evans about Scott LaFaro in 1966. YouTube. Available at: https://www.youtube.com/watch?v=IIzbINNrqcQ [Accessed 13 Mar. 2020].

[6–17] Gould, J. (2012). Josef Skvorecky on the Nazis' Control-Freak Jazz Hatred. [online] The Atlantic. Available at: https://www.theatlantic.com/entertainment/archive/2012/01/josef-skvorecky-nazis-jazz/250837/.

[6–18] Laloux, F. (2014). Reinventing organizations : a guide to creating organizations inspired by the next stage of human consciousness. Brussels: Nelson Parker.

[6–19] Wikipedia Contributors (2020). Dunbar's number. [online] Wikipedia. Available at: https://en.wikipedia.org/wiki/Dunbar%27s_number [Accessed 20 Mar. 2020]. Page 19

[6–20] Ro, C. (2019). Dunbar's number: Why we can only maintain 150 relationships. [online] Bbc.com. Available at: https://www.bbc.com/future/article/20191001-dunbars-number-why-we-can-only-maintain-150-relationships.

[6–21] Harter, J. (2018). Employee Engagement on the Rise in the US [online] Gallup.com. Available at: https://news.gallup.com/poll/241649/employee-engagement-rise.aspx.

[6–22] Editor (n.d.). 3 Benefits of Consistent and Thoughtful Experimentation. – Like Minds. [online] Available at: https://wearelikeminds.com/3-benefits-of-consistent-and-thoughtful-experimentation/ [Accessed 19 Mar. 2020].

[6–23] Bcorporation.net. (2018). About B Corps | Certified B Corporation. [online] Available at: https://bcorporation.net/about-b-corps.

[6–24] (n.d.). [online] Competing in the Cognitive Age Competing. Available at: https://www.protiviti.com/sites/default/files/united_states/insights/ai-ml-global-study-protiviti.pdf. [Accessed 14 Mar. 2020]

[6–25] www.ideo.com. (n.d.). Tools by IDEO. [online] Available at: https://www.ideo.com/tools.

[6–26] Flow Cherry, K. (2011). "Flow" Can Help You Achieve Goals. [online] Verywell Mind. Available at: https://www.verywellmind.com/what-is-flow-2794768. Page 28.

[6–27] Harari, Yuval N. (2020). Yuval Noah Harari: the world after coronavirus|[online] www.ft.com. Available at: https://www.ft.com/content/19d90308-6858-11ea-a3c9-1fe6fedcca75 [Accessed 31 Mar. 2020].

TRANSITION CHAPTER

[M–1] Wilber, Ken (2007). Integral spirituality : a startling new role for religion in the modern and postmodern world. Boston, Mass.: Integral Books. Page 84.

[M–2] Editors, T. (2018). 10 Beneficial Insects That Will Actually Help Your Plants. [online] Good Housekeeping. Available at: https://www.goodhousekeeping.com/home/gardening/a20705937/beneficial-insects/ [Accessed 12 Apr. 2020].

[M–3] Lockard, Jim (2015). WHAT IS 2ND TIER AND WHY DO I WANT TO GO THERE? [online] New Thought Evolutionary. Available at: https://newthoughtevolutionary.wordpress.com/2015/10/06/what-is-2nd-tier-and-why-do-i-want-to-go-there/ [Accessed 11 Apr. 2020].

[M–4] Editors, T. (2020). 26 Plants You Should Always Grow Side-By-Side. [online] Good Housekeeping. Available at: https://www.goodhousekeeping.com/home/gardening/a20706481/companion-garden-planting/ [Accessed 15 Apr. 2020].

G'S MESHWORK

[7-0] Loehr, J.E. and Schwartz, T. (2008). The power of full engagement. Gurgaon: Shubhi.

[7-1] Wikipedia Contributors (2019). Ludwig von Bertalanffy. [online] Wikipedia. Available at: https://en.wikipedia.org/wiki/Ludwig_von_Bertalanffy.

[7-2] Academy of Achievement. (n.d.). Sir Tim Berners-Lee. [online] Available at: https://achievement.org/achiever/sir-timothy-berners-lee/#interview [Accessed 1 Jul. 2020].

[7-3] Home.cern. (2019). The birth of the Web | CERN. [online] Available at: https://home.cern/science/computing/birth-web.

[7-4] Miller, J.H. (2015). A crude look at the whole : the science of complex systems in business, life, and society. New York: Basic Books, A Member Of The Perseus Books Group.

[7-5] The Academy for Systems Change. (2015). Systems Thinking Resources. [online] Available at: http://donellameadows.org/systems-thinking-resources/.

[7-6] Sherwood, D. (2002). Seeing the forest for the trees : a manager's guide to applying systems thinking. London: Nicholas Brealey.

[7-7] Dreier, L., Nabarro, D. and Nelson, J. (2019). What is systems leadership, and how can it change the world? [online] World Economic Forum. Available at: https://www.weforum.org/agenda/2019/09/systems-leadership-can-change-the-world-but-what-does-it-mean/.

[7-8] Claus Otto Scharmer (2009). Theory U : learning from the futures as it emerges. San Francisco, Calif.: Berrett-Koehler ; London.

[7-9] Un.org. (2015). #Envision2030: 17 goals to transform the world for persons with disabilities | United Nations Enable. [online] Available at: https://www.un.org/development/desa/disabilities/envision2030.html.

[7-10] Advergize Business. (2020). Network Organizational Structure: Examples, Definition, Advantages & Disadvantages [online] Available at: https://advergize.com/business/network-organizational-structure-examples-definition-advantages-disadvantages/. [Accessed 12 Jul. 2020].

[7-11] Jarvenpaa, S.L. and Ives, B. (1994). The Global Network Organization of the Future: Information Management Opportunities and Challenges. Journal of Management Information Systems, 10(4), pp.25–57.

[7-12] The Rise of Network Organizations, Michael Moss, P. (n.d.). The Rise of Network Organizations. www.academia.edu. [online] Available at: https://www.academia.edu/2776404/The_Rise_of_Network_Organizations [Accessed 21 Jul. 2020].

[7-13] Innovation, S. (2016). Network Organizations. [online] Systems Innovation. Available at: http://www.systemsinnovation.io/post/network-organizations [Accessed 13 Aug. 2020].

ADDITIONAL READING:

Davenport, Thomas H. (2019). THE AI ADVANTAGE : how to put the artificial intelligence revolution to work. S.L.: Mlt Press.

Harari, Y.N., Purcell, J. and Haim Watzman (2018). Sapiens : a brief history of humankind. New York: Harper Perennial.

Senge, P.M. (2010). The necessary revolution : how individuals and organizations are working together to create a sustainable world. London: Nicholas Brealey.

Kaku, M. (2012). Physics of the future : how science will shape human destiny and our daily lives by the year 2100. New York: Anchor Books.

Rees, M.J. (2018). On the future : prospects for humanity. Princeton, New Jersey: Princeton University Press.

Kaku, M. (2019). FUTURE OF HUMANITY : terraforming mars, interstellar travel, immortality, and our ... destiny beyond.

HORTENSE'S UNIVERSE

[8-1] Lovelock, J.E. (2016). Gaia a new look at life on earth. Oxford, United Kingdom Oxford University Press.

[8-2] How Stuff Works. (2015). What are ley lines? [online] Available at: https://science.howstuffworks.com/science-vs-myth/unexplained-phenomena/ley-lines.htm [Accessed 3 Jul. 2020].

[8-3] New Acropolis UK. (n.d.). Introduction to Eastern and Western Wisdom. [online] Available at: http://www.newacropolisuk.org/events.php [Accessed 3 Jul. 2020].

[8-4] Sheldrake, R. (2020). Science Delusion. Hodderstoughton.

[8-5] Gaia.com. (n.d.). Morphic Fields and the Universal Mind with Rupert Sheldrake. [online] Available at: https://www.gaia.com/video/morphic-fields-and-universal-mind-rupert-sheldrake [Accessed 13 Jul. 2020].

[8-6] Soil Association. History | Soil Association. [online] Available at: https://www.soilassociation.org/about-us/our-history/ [Accessed 23 Jul. 2020].

[8-7] Johnston, B. (1982). My Inventions. The Autobiography of Nikola Tesla. Williston, Vermont: Hart Brothers.

Cheney, Margaret. (1981). Tesla: Man Out of Time, Touchstone.

[8-8] Adler, D. (2016). Story of cities #37: how radical ideas turned Curitiba into Brazil's "green capital." [online] the Guardian. Available at: https://www.theguardian.com/cities/2016/may/06/story-of-cities-37-mayor-jaime-lerner-curitiba-brazil-green-capital-global-icon [Accessed 7 Jul. 2020].

[8-9] Dr Martin Luther King Jr. (n.d.). Where are we going. [online] Available at: https://www.drmartinlutherkingjr.com/wherewearegoing.htm [Accessed 24 Jul. 2020].

[8-10] Common Dreams. (n.d.). The 11 Most Anti-Capitalist Quotes from Martin Luther King Jr. [online] Available at: https://www.commondreams.org/views/2019/01/21/11-most-anti-capitalist-quotes-martin-luther-king-jr [Accessed 24 Jul. 2020].

[8-11] Mollison, B. and Holmgren, D. (1990). Permaculture one, by Bill Mollison. 5th Rev. Ed. (pbk). Tagari.

[8-12] Ethical.net. (2019). The 12 Principles of Permaculture: A Way Forward. [online] Available at: https://ethical.net/ethical/permaculture-principles/.

[8-13] Merriam-webster.com. (2019). Definition of BIODYNAMIC. [online] Available at: https://www.merriam-webster.com/dictionary/biodynamic.

[8-14] Biodynamics.com. (2019). Who Was Rudolf Steiner? | Biodynamic Association. [online] Available at: https://www.biodynamics.com/steiner.html [Accessed 27 Nov. 2020].

[8-15] Smuts, Jan Christiaan (2010). Holism and Evolution. La Vergne, In: Kessinger Publ.

[8-16] Gaia.com. (n.d.). Creating with the Field. Rewired [online] Available at: https://www.gaia.com/video/creating-field?fullplayer=feature [Accessed 24 Jul. 2020].

[8-17] Sheldrake.org. (n.d.). Morphic Resonance and Morphic Fields an Introduction. [online] Available at: https://www.sheldrake.org/research/morphic-resonance/introduction [Accessed 24 Jul. 2020].

[8-18] Sheldrake, R. (2011). The presence of the past : morphic resonance and the habits of nature. London: Icon Books.

[8-19] Bertold Ulsamer (2008). The art and practice of family constellations : leading family constellations as developed by Bert Hellinger. Heidelberg: Carl-Auer-Systeme-Verl.

[8-20] Bohm, D. (2008). Wholeness and the implicate order. London ; New York: Routledge.

[8-21] Ethical Consumer (2020). Beyond Consumerism: 'Five Weeks of Anarchy'. July/August 2020. P. 38

[8-22] Presencing Institute. (n.d.). U-Theory Process [online] Available at: https://www.presencing.org/aboutus/theory-u. CC License by the Presencing Institute - Otto Scharmer, https://www.presencing.org/resource/permission.

[8-23] Planning (2020). 20-minute neighbourhoods. [online] Planning. Available at: https://www.planning.vic.gov.au/policy-and-strategy/planning-for-melbourne/plan-melbourne/20-minute-neighbourhoods

CHAPTER 10

[10-1] History.com Editors (2018). Harry Truman. [online] HISTORY. Available at: https://www.history.com/topics/us-presidents/harry-truman

[10-2] Achter, P.J. (2018). McCarthyism | History & Facts. In: Encyclopædia Britannica. [online] Available at: https://www.britannica.com/topic/McCarthyism

[10-3] William R. Lee & Cornish, E. (1971). A SYSTEMS CONCEPTION OF PERSONALITY. [online] Available at: http://www.clarewgraves.com/source_content/WSP_cc_edit.html [Accessed 12 Aug. 2020].

[10-4] Huseyin, Rezzan (2017). 8 Things You Need to Know about the Graves Model (or Spiral Dynamics theory). [online] Art of Wellbeing with. Available at: http://www.artofwellbeing.com/2017/09/05/gravesmodel [Accessed 11 Sep. 2020].

[10-5] Graves, Clare W. (2001). ; A Workshop with Dr Clare W. Graves. ECLET (Emergent Cyclical Levels of Existence Theory), Audiobook Vol. 1.

[10-6] Cook, John (2008). The Role of the Individual in Organisational Cultures: a Gravesian Integrated Approach. MI 4810, USA: Sheffield Hallam University.

[10-7] Bunders, K. (n.d.). Origins ▯ Spiral Dynamics Integral. [online] Spiral Dynamics Integral. Available at: http://spiraldynamicsintegral.nl/en/origin/

[10-8] Graves, Clare W. (1981). Summary Statement: The Emergent, Cyclical, Double-Helix Model Of The Adult Human Biopsychosocial Systems. Boston, www.clarewgraves.com.

[10-9] Dawlabani, S.E. (2020). Intro to Spiral Dynamics in Large Scale Applications. YouTube. Available at: https://www.youtube.com/watch?v=7JW5xiZ7fjg&feature=share [Accessed 20 Aug. 2020].

[10-10] Krumm, Rainer & Parstorfer, Benedikt (2018). Clare W. Graves : his life and his work. Bloomington, In: iUniverse.

[10-11] Pathfinder @ Global Performance Improvement. (n.d.). Business Cases. [online] Available at: https://www.pathfinder.management/references/. [Accessed 10 Sep. 2020].

[10-12] www.linkedin.com. (n.d.). Entrepreneurs! Be aware of the path ahead. [online] Available at: https://www.linkedin.com/pulse/entrepreneurs-aware-path-ahead-rhys-marc-photis-miod/ [Accessed 10 Sep. 2020].

[10-13] Global Performance Improvement (n.d.). What is the Business Pathfinder? [online] Available at: https://www.pathfinder.management/what-is-it/ [Accessed 11 Sep. 2020].

[10-14] Pathfinder @ Global Performance Improvement (n.d.). 7S Systemic Thinking. [online] Available at: https://www.pathfinder.management/systemic-thinking/ [Accessed 11 Sep. 2020].

[10-15] Capitol.texas.gov. (n.d.). 74(R) SR 901 Enrolled version - Bill Text. [online] Available at: https://www.legis.state.tx.us/tlodocs/74R/billtext/html/SR00901F.htm [Accessed 10 Sep. 2020].

[10-16] Maalouf, E.S. (2014). Emerge! : the rise of functional democracy and the future of the Middle East. New York: Selectbooks, Inc.

[10-17] Integral Leadership Review. [online] Available at: http://integralleadershipreview.com/table-of-contents/?slug=august-2018 [Accessed 31 Oct. 2020].

[10-18] IntegralUnited. (n.d.). About. [online] Available at: https://www.integralunited.org/about/?cn-reloaded=1 [Accessed 1 Nov. 2020].

AMON  BO  CONAN  DOC  ELI  FLORENCE  G  HORTENSE  INTI

BRISHNA CHARLIE DEVINA EBONY MACHIAVELLI FEENA GIDEON HALA

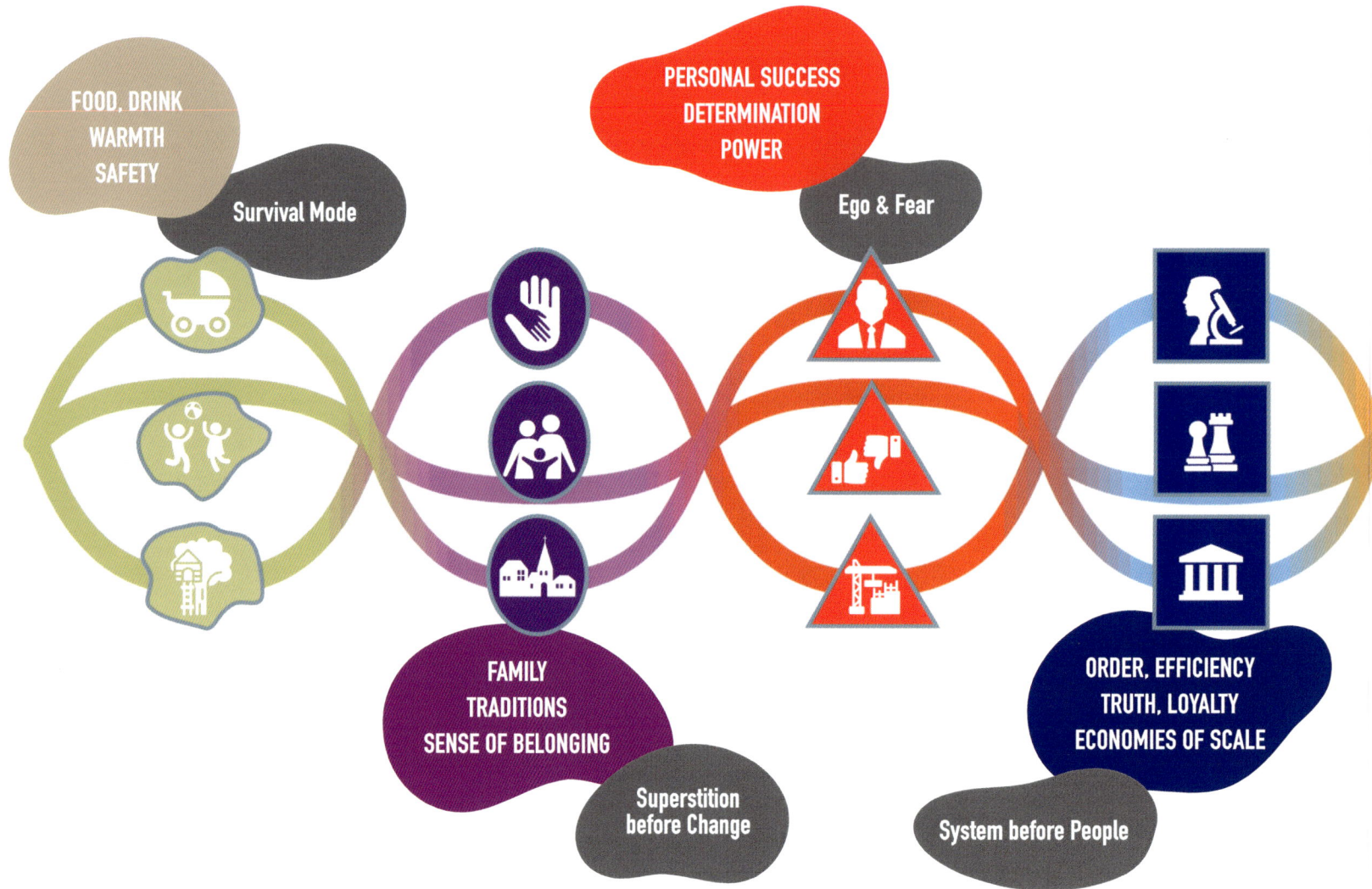

YOUR GUIDE

FOOD, DRINK WARMTH SAFETY

Survival Mode

PERSONAL SUCCESS DETERMINATION POWER

Ego & Fear

FAMILY TRADITIONS SENSE OF BELONGING

Superstition before Change

ORDER, EFFICIENCY TRUTH, LOYALTY ECONOMIES OF SCALE

System before People

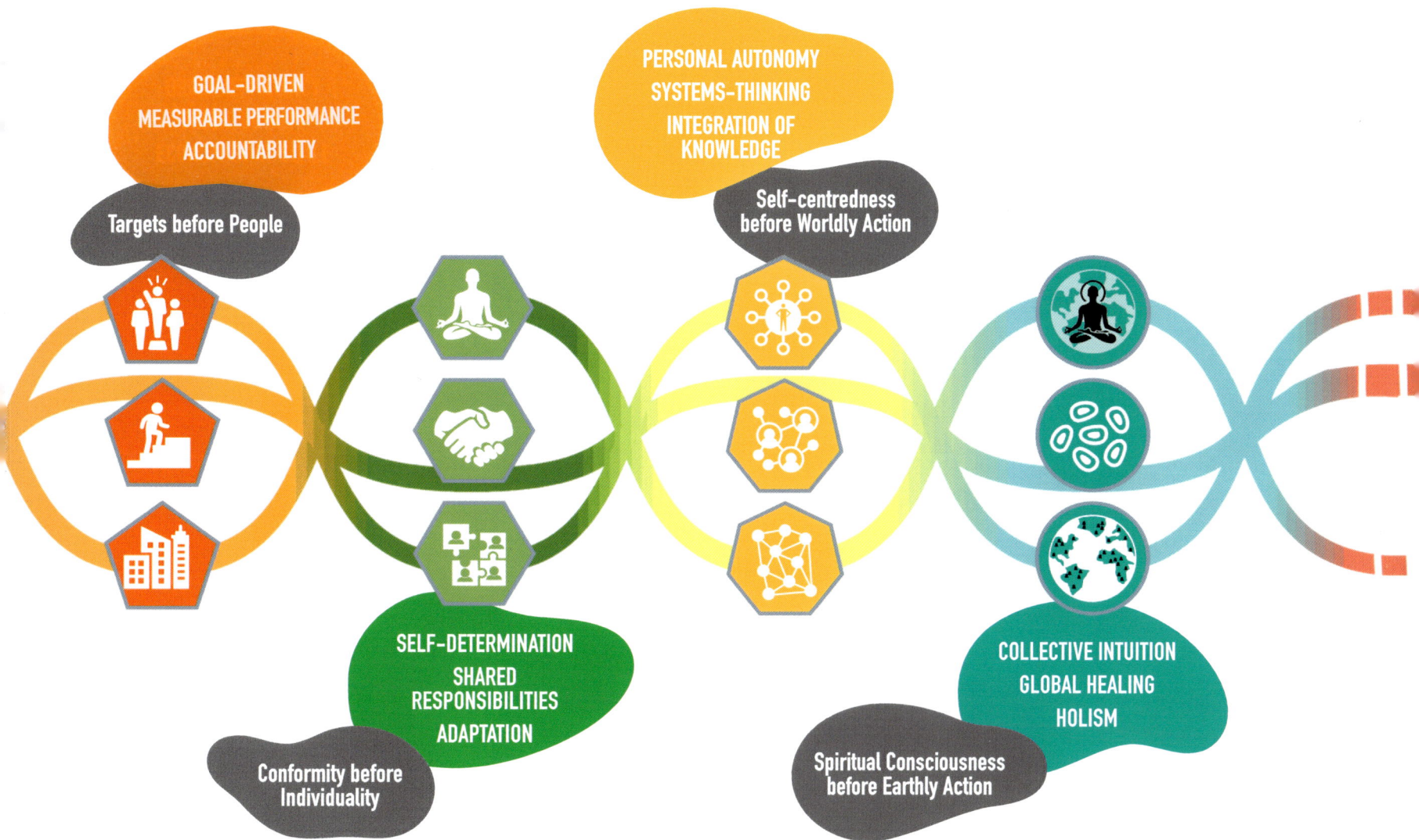

GOAL-DRIVEN
MEASURABLE PERFORMANCE
ACCOUNTABILITY

Targets before People

PERSONAL AUTONOMY
SYSTEMS-THINKING
INTEGRATION OF
KNOWLEDGE

Self-centredness
before Worldly Action

SELF-DETERMINATION
SHARED
RESPONSIBILITIES
ADAPTATION

Conformity before
Individuality

COLLECTIVE INTUITION
GLOBAL HEALING
HOLISM

Spiritual Consciousness
before Earthly Action

www.TheTurquoiseBrickRoad.com

CREATORS' PLEA

Writing about the different levels turned into a bit of a personal journey for us. We appreciate the mission-critical importance that the 8th layer brings to humankind and how vital it is to have more Hortenses in the world. We, too, want to contribute.

We would start off with regenerating an old farm or piece of land in a bid to create a space for biodiversity of the mind and land – a step towards healing the Earth. We are with Dr Vandana Shiva (scientist, founder of the Earth University and a biodiversity conservation farm) on this:

"It's time to reclaim wilderness as a state of being in harmony, a state of being in peace with nature, a state of being healthy."

Thus, we wish to make a straightforward plea.

We would like to get a few impact investors together to purchase an old farm or piece of land. After a period of time this venture should finance itself, be as self-sufficient as possible whilst also providing the investors with a natural place to come to, connect, regenerate and interact with one another.

All of us believe the time has come to organise and actively shape the health of our future.

Are you in?
If so, please reach out to impact@GPiPartner.com or on LinkedIn and we would be happy to connect and discuss this plan in detail.

The objectives come in a colourful range:

- Provide the right conditions for nature and the soil to regenerate themselves, which means diverse life can return to the land and environment around it
- Connect with the local community, bring traditions and indigenous plants and animals back to where they belong
- Create spaces for creative and innovative experimentation and thinking
- Align and comply with all relevant tax, legal, and health and safety standards
- Use modern technologies to utilise renewable energies and track all kinds of improvement in measurable terms
- Provide a space for social groups to connect and share; possibly work with organisations like the Positive Transformation Initiative to help people find their way back to nature and society
- Explore how the many lively dots are interrelated, how all life is part of a whole, and connect with similar initiatives across the world (e.g. Three Pools Farm in Wales, Knepp Castle Estate in Sussex, Tamera's Land in Portugal, and many others)
- Provide natural and creative spaces for 8th layer thinking and practices.

Colourful Training, Advising, Coaching, Facilitating & Blended Learning
www.GPiPartner.com

Pathfinder
Business Snap Shots, Culture Assessments & Performance Management
www.Pathfinder.Management